D0915880

Zarathustra's Children

Studies in German Literature, Linguistics, and Culture

Edited by James Hardin
(*South Carolina*)

RAYMOND FURNESS

ZARATHUSTRA'S CHILDREN

A STUDY OF A LOST GENERATION OF GERMAN WRITERS

CAMDEN HOUSE

First published 2000
by Camden House

Camden House is an imprint of Boydell & Brewer Inc.
PO Box 41026, Rochester, NY 14604–4126 USA
and of Boydell & Brewer Limited
PO Box 9, Woodbridge, Suffolk IP12 3DF, UK

ISBN: 1–57113–057–8

Library of Congress Cataloging-in-Publication Data

Furness, Raymond.
  Zarathustra's children: a study of a lost generation of German writers /
  Raymond S. Furness.
      p.   cm. – (Studies in German literature, linguistics, and culture)
    Includes bibliographical references and index.
    ISBN 1–57113–057–8 (alk. paper)
      1. German literature—19th century—History and criticism. 2. German
  literature—20th century—History and criticism. 3. Nietzsche, Friedrich
  Wilhelm, 1844–1900—Influence. I. Title. II. Studies in German literature,
  linguistics, and culture (Unnumbered)

PT345 .F87 2000
830.9'008—dc21
                                                                99-059756

A catalogue record for this title is available from the British Library.

This publication is printed on acid-free paper.
Printed in the United States of America.

For Rupert, Cordelia and Rosalind

Contents

Acknowledgements

THIS BOOK is very much an odyssey through uncharted waters and as such does not rely on earlier explorations except, of course, in the discussion of Nietzsche. I am deeply indebted here (how could I not be?) to many an insight gained from reading the acknowledged experts and to many a discussion with St. Andrews colleagues, especially Nick Martin and Malcolm Humble, whose patience I sorely tried. Friends in Germany, Tom Kerber above all, gave invaluable support in the early stages of the manuscript and uncovered much fascinating material. I am grateful to the Carnegie Trust and the German Academic Exchange Service for generous financial help which enabled me to spend valuable months in the Deutsches Literaturarchiv in Marbach, and also to the University of St. Andrews for periods of research leave which enabled me to hold the daily clamour at bay. I am grateful also to Bouvier Verlag, to Verlag Hinder und Deelmann, and to Kösel Verlag for permission to quote from Klages, from Derleth, and from Mombert and Däubler respectively. The Deutsches Literaturarchiv must also be thanked for granting me permission to reproduce the photographs used in this book. I must thank Sylvia Loughridge for preparing the manuscript; the deepest debt of all, however, I owe to my wife for quietly sharing me for a disgracefully long time with eight dead men.

R. S. F.
September 1999

Introduction

> And should I lower myself to the absurd position of having
> to *interpret* Zarathustra (and his animals)? I am sure that
> chairs and professorships at universities will be established
> in future for this purpose. But the present is certainly not
> the right time to understand Zarathustra, and I would
> indeed be very surprised if I were to meet five or six people
> who had *eyes* for what I am aiming at. . .
>
> — Nietzsche

> And there is always a longing
> For the untrammelled, limitless. . .
>
> — Hölderlin

IT WAS MICHAEL HAMBURGER who, some thirty-five years ago, first
drew my attention to what he called "that post-Nietzschean archipelago of German literature which no one mind can hope to map, let
alone inhabit,"[1] those writers such as Mombert, Däubler and Pannwitz
who have "entered literary history almost without having been read";
in a later book Hamburger again referred to these figures, together
with Morgenstern as writer of philosophical verse, adding that "literary
criticism has not yet begun to sift the copious works of this lost, post-
Nietzschean generation," works which "may never become accessible
to more than the tiniest minority groups."[2] My own *Literary History of
Germany 1890–1945* attempted a preliminary investigation for English
readers, but the task was far too vast to be executed satisfactorily within
a necessarily restricted compass. But here was a challenge, an area on
the map of twentieth-century German literature that had never been
fully explored. An archipelago? A country far from the madding crowd?
Mombert himself uses imagery redolent of *Also sprach Zarathustra*
(Thus Spake Zarathustra) to describe the isolation in which he was living, and not only he — in a letter to Rudolf Pannwitz he would use
images of height to convey this feeling of remoteness: "You know this
as well as I do — both as poet and thinker you are a high peak, very
difficult for men to climb, often obscured by clouds and mist, icy, with
fearful precipices and constantly exposed to avalanches, only accessible
to those with a good head for heights."[3] And not only Michael Hamburger; Roy Pascal also refers to Mombert, Däubler, and the Charon
circle around Rudolf Pannwitz and Otto zur Linde in terms of cosmic

insight and semi-mystical yearnings and uses similar terminology to portray their failure to communicate with a wider readership. "Their symbolism was too private, their systems too arbitrary and pretentious to be transferable to the experience of many others, and all such poets fell into the yawning abyss between poetry and philosophy that after *Zarathustra* engulfed so many."[4] *Nordlicht* and Orion, Charon and Sfaira, cosmos, sunworship, *Lebensrausch* and a quickening of transcendental longing in a world, ostensibly, without transcendence — it seemed that a Baedeker were needed to describe this unfamiliar territory, to make the terrain more familiar, the landscape less forbidding.

Post-Nietzschean, post-Zarathustra . . . It would have been surprising if Hamburger and Pascal had not mentioned Nietzsche and his most famous creation. For Nietzsche is acknowledged to be part of the modern experience. Erich Heller, writing in 1965, argued eloquently that, "as for modern German literature and thought, it is hardly an exaggeration to say that they would not be what they are if Nietzsche had never lived," that not only German, but European and North American intellectual preoccupations were "all part of a story told by Nietzsche."[5] His ubiquity is such that a confrontation with his writing is mandatory, and his contact with his literary heirs is so direct and intrusive that influence and transformation become a seamless process.[6] His works "influenced the entire 'cultural climate' of this century"[7]; his central status "will hardly be disputed."[8] Steven Aschheim has written of "Nietzsche's almost uncanny ability to define — and embody — the furthest reaches of the general post-Enlightenment predicament; to encapsulate many of its enduring spiritual and intellectual tensions, contradictions, hopes and possibilities."[9] In moments of manic euphoria Nietzsche knew of his own significance: he was "not human, but dynamite,"[10] and his name would forever be associated with "something monstrous, a crisis the like of which has never been seen on earth" (6, 365). In quieter moments he knew that it was his ambition, his torture and his joy to circumnavigate the radius of the modern soul, to sit in each of its corners (12, 440). The death of God, the greatest event in human history and the cause of extreme danger must needs bring with it the spectre of nihilism, "this most sinister of guests, waiting outside the door" (12, 125); the consequences of the death of meaning must be faced and transcended. To make men see the immense significance of the destruction of Christian morality and truth and to appreciate the equally enormous task of *creating* values that were free of decadent self-exculpation was his goal, to bring down the whole edifice of traditional Western evaluation in order that man should seek new values and affirm life and its eternal recurrence in a heroic act of self-determination.

Nietzsche, then, encapsulates the twentieth-century experience of crisis, of nihilism and adjustment to a world bereft of transcendental certainties. And one did not simply read Nietzsche; one "experienced" him. Aschheim has described the uniquely intense manner in which Nietzsche seemed to touch on those issues that contemporaries regarded as "key experiential dimensions of their individual and collective identity": he was "the prism through which (such) existential issues could be addressed."[11] It is also correct to insist that there was not one, but many Nietzschean impulses. In *Jenseits von Gut und Böse* (Beyond Good and Evil) Nietzsche insisted that every great philosophy was "a form of confession on the part of its originator, a series of involuntary and subconscious *mémoires*" (5, 19); his mouthpiece Zarathustra proclaimed that "Of all that is written I love only that which a man has written with his blood" (4, 48). Nietzsche's voice is intensely personal and the ego behind that voice is multifaceted, projecting itself in a variety of roles. In the 1886 "Attempt at a Self-Criticism" appended to *Die Geburt der Tragödie* (The Birth of Tragedy) he is "a new soul" (1, 15); in *Ecce Homo* he is "a psychologist without equal" (6, 305); in *Beyond Good and Evil* he is "an old philologist" (5, 37). Is he not also a poet? (1, 15); an "immoralist"? (5, 162); a "disciple of the philosopher Dionysus" (5, 250)? "Free spirit" (3, 137), a "good European" (5, 180) and the "Antichrist" (6, 302) are further manifestations, to which others might be added.[12] The prismatic nature of Nietzsche's thought, his rejection of systems and congeniality to so many contradictory tendencies means that his work is difficult to reduce to one particular essence; if there is one authoritative meaning it is to be found in the praise of creativity, implying a rejection of anything that is inimical to life, exulting in its ruthlessness and splendour.

T. J. Reed has spoken of the need "to document the presence of any strand of Nietzsche's thought which we believe went into a poet's work"[13]: he is discussing the latter's influence on Thomas Mann, Rilke, Kafka and Gottfried Benn. The strand which this book has separated and unravelled is Nietzsche as purveyor and instigator of some mythopoeic vision and as advocate of life, whose "yellow tangled tresses" Zarathustra will extol at a climactic moment in the book (4, 285). More than any other artist in the nineteenth century — apart, perhaps, from Richard Wagner — Nietzsche was aware of the fructifying power of myth: myth he once defined as "the concentrated image of the world" (1, 145), for myths are figures and formulas which bring together the most important value of an outlook or creed. They are life-enhancing in that they are the quintessential illustration of life's tragic glory, and within their graphic assertions are displayed man's triumph and agony. The mythical enactment of the human predicament is displayed against a cosmic background: Zarathustra's staff with the emblematic sun and sun-serpent on its handle assumes, as does Wotan's spear, an ultimate symbolic force. The imagistic power of Nietzsche's writing is striking indeed, and will be particularly prominent in *Thus Spake Zarathustra*, the book which it is unfashionable to praise but which is of cardinal importance for that myth-making tendency in German literature with which we are here concerned. And I shall not be ashamed to talk of influence here, ignoring the assertion that the concept of "influence" from one work to another can have no meaning when "meaning" is seen merely as a strictly internal function of a text. James Hawes is correct in his analogy from the original, planetary provenance of the word "influence" to argue that, although it is not always easy to determine exactly the influence of the moon on the earth or vice versa, an astronomer would be unlikely to suggest that we content ourselves with a notion of some unquantifiable "interrotational-ity."[14] Influence usually becomes a relatively simple and immediate response in which a later writer imitates or elaborates on something characteristic or original in the work of an earlier writer; with Nietzsche, as we have noted, the impact and the ensuing transformation by his literary heirs was intense and pervasive.

To what extent could a conscious attempt be made to emulate the style and message of *Thus Spake Zarathustra?* The attitude of artists and critics after 1945 was hostile, understandably so after this work was pronounced a holy national monument in the Third Reich and placed, together with *Mein Kampf* and Rosenberg's *Mythus des Zwanzigsten Jahrhunderts* (Myth of the Twentieth Century) in the Tannenberg Memorial, and many of Nietzsche's more striking — and controversial — utterances were wrenched out of context to provide the Nazis with their slogans. The appropriation of Nietzsche by the Nazis is not our concern here, but the question uncomfortably presents itself: when Nietzsche had become the incarnation of some timeless Nordic experience, a metaphysical presence transcending historical limitation, then what of *Zarathustra?* In 1947 Thomas Mann gave an important lecture on "Nietzsche's Philosophy in the Light of our Experience" at a meeting of the PEN Club in Zurich at which this work is, predictably, cut down to size and Nietzsche's extravagant claims for its unique greatness rejected as symptoms of mental aberration.

> This faceless, formless monstrous *Flügelmann* with the rosy crown of laughter on his unrecognisable head, his "Be hard!" and his dancer's legs is not an artistic creation but something rhetorical, an excited play with words, a tortured voice and a despairing prophecy, a spectre of

helpless *grandezza*, sometimes touching, but most of all embarrassing, a spectre tottering on the edge of the risible.[15]

Some twenty years later Erich Heller would regret the excesses of Nietzsche's style, the hammering and dynamiting, and chose instead to remind us of Nietzsche's rejoicing in the quiet lucidity of Claude Lorrain and seeking the company of Goethe's conversations with Eckermann and the composure of Stifter: eternity, eagle and serpent had "sadly aged."[16] Martin Heidegger stresses that *Zarathustra*, although constituting the centre of Nietzsche's philosophy, was nonetheless "outside the centre, being 'eccentric' to it."[17] In the 1970s J. P. Stern asks "Can the book be read without embarrassment?"[18] and David Luke, following Thomas Mann, speaks of "the ghastly facetiousness" of the text, its "embarrassing would-be humour" having something pathological about it, the "life-affirming superstructure [something] strained and hysterical."[19] Hollingdale bluntly states that "It is not even Nietzsche's 'best book'"[20] and H. G. Gadamer insists that "The style of this text is not for everyone's taste, at any rate not for my taste or the taste of my generation."[21] Richard Schacht will prefer to ignore *Zarathustra* altogether.[22] But recently a less dismissive approach has become evident in that the work's complex narrative structure is being examined, as is its striking imagery, a poetic style appropriate for expressing a vision of the world in the language of intuitive, not discursive, reason.[23] "Nietzsche was attempting a bold invention in *writing* and the result is complex and prismatic";[24] it is a philosophical work couched in poetry, Semitic (or Persian) rather than Hellenic, biblical rather than Greek. "The language of Luther and the poetic form of the Bible as the basis of a new German *poetry* — this is *my* invention!" (11, 60). To argue that Nietzsche's poetic prose is an awkward hybrid is to overlook Nietzsche's own insistence that "the great masters of prose have always been poets too [. . .] Good prose is always written face to face with poetry" (3, 447). To insist that prose and poetry are two separate modes of expressions is false, and philosophical thoughts should be placed "ceremoniously in the vehicle of rhythm, usually" — Nietzsche adds — "because they are unable to go on foot" (2, 164).

It is the intention of this book to see Nietzsche in a tradition of German *Dichterphilosophen*, poet-philosophers: to separate the activity of poetry from that of thought, Novalis knew, was "a sign of illness."[25] The empiricist, the sceptic, the man who expresses his admiration for Heine's "divine malice" will not concern us here, rather the visionary who called upon the "astronomers of the ideal" to seek new worlds, new vistas, "purple-glowing constellations and galaxies of beauty!" (3,

322). Stellar and solar imagery will loom large in *Zarathustra* as will the image of the ocean as an infinite experience of the soul — "Board ships, you philosophers!" (3, 530). There is no mere rhetoric here but a revelation of mysterious images and symbols which has the force of music. "Perhaps the whole of *Zarathustra* should be reckoned as music," Nietzsche suggested (6, 335); this "new soul," as we know, should have sung! It was Wagner who was the purveyor par excellence of powerful mystical impulses, of music dramas which were an enormously fecund source of redolent symbols, a pulsating fabric of inexhaustible richness and complexity that contributed more than any other artistic expression to the return of myth which characterizes the modern experience, an awareness of the numinous significance of fire and water, gold, chalice and spear as well as a host of related images. And Nietzsche, despite the troubled rejection and castigation of his erstwhile mentor and his unconvincing praise for the music of Peter Gast and Bizet, shares with Wagner the ability to take images of sunrise, height, mountain, sea and fire and convey deep and archetypal resonances. Nietzsche's own musical talent was limited and derivative: it was for Richard Strauss and Frederick Delius to express Zarathustra and his Mass of Life in powerful equivalents. And it was Wagner's vision of the Total Artist as redeemer of the world that Nietzsche would be unable to expunge, Wagner as the new Homer promised by Schelling who, "speaking once again in the undivided language of mythology, but of a higher mythology which has incorporated the discoveries of modern philosophy, will sing the new epic of a reunified age."[26]

> Why, it is like a miracle! The old Romantics are being dragged out from our dusty libraries, a growing learned (and unlearned) literature has already taken them up and it is not without good reason that our most modern literature and art calls itself neoromantic. And all of us who truly *live* in the present, not just bodily but spiritually too, we all feel that old Romantic *frisson*, we hear those melodies sound again over the gap of a hundred years and more.[27]

Thus Karl Joel (1905) describes the burgeoning interest in Romanticism of the young and all those who had tired of naturalism's drabness and an all too mechanical interpretation of existence; Samuel Lublinski also uses the term "neoromantic," linking it specifically with Nietzsche "who had succeeded in achieving what a Novalis had sought in vain, in creating singlehanded a mythology, a symbolic world-view, a religion." Nietzsche is compared to Friedrich Schlegel in his quest for a new mythological vision; he is also "the greatest stylist of the German language," his writing characterized by longing, by flight from the world

and by a fusion of the exquisite and the imperious.[28] The Romantic
Nietzsche, the iconoclastic lover of eternity who pointed to the rainbow bridge leading away from banausic mediocrity toward the heights
of perfection necessarily spoke to the young. Much has been written on
Nietzsche's influence on the youth movement of the early twentieth-
century, the cult of friendship, of nature, of euphoric idealism, of sun
worship, temple and hieratic brotherhood; the links with Novalis and
the "blue flower," and the awareness of the mighty epiphany of Dionysus in early German Romanticism should also be noted. (Richard
Dehmel had also drawn sarcastic attention to the "redeemer-cult and
blue flower" of the age, also to its "Zarathustrian doting on the Superman"; his mocking tone is a dissenting one).[29] Wagner may have
been the chief beneficiary of German Romanticism, acting as bridge or
channel to convey the power of myth and legend. Nietzsche for his part
continues the tradition of Romantic *Lebensphilosophie* in his praise of
dance, of freedom, of the supreme power of art and energy to transform sterile ratiocination and revivify the world. Nietzsche also knew of
the Romantic urge to resolve the conflict between knowledge and life,
where logic is "taken up into a whirling dance";[30] this most sophisticated psychologist is not ashamed to use language that would not be
out of place in Romantic fiction to describe that whirlwind of inspiration, that upheaval of the spirit which overwhelmed him in 1883 and
which would herald the advent of *Zarathustra*.

> Has anyone, living at the end of the nineteenth century, a clear idea of
> what the poets of more powerful epochs called *inspiration*? Well, I
> shall describe it. Without the slightest vestige of superstition one
> would scarcely be able to avoid believing that one was an incarnation,
> a mouthpiece, a medium of superior powers. The concept of 'revela-
> tion' in the sense of something suddenly becoming visible, audible,
> something that with an unspeakable surety and deftness shatters one
> in the depths of one's being is the best description of the experience.
> One no longer hears nor seeks, one does not ask what it is who
> gives — like a lightning flash the knowledge blazes forth, predeter-
> mined by necessity, that I never had a choice [. . .] (6, 339–40).

Heller may prefer "less lightning and more hesitation, less necessity and
more discretion," but he also must admit of the passionate brilliance of
the language of *Ecce Homo* from which this passage is taken, "the very
title of which betrays the incipient delusion of grandeur and which
nonetheless [. . .] bears witness to his genius."[31]

Revelation, incarnation, the feeling of being simply a mouthpiece
for the utterances of vast forces — is the Antichrist speaking here, the
madman who announced the death of God in *Die fröhliche Wissenschaft*

(The Joyful Science)? What is extraordinary about Nietzsche is the intense religiosity combined with an intellectual radicalism of the highest order. The "philosopher with the hammer" was driven to test all so-called truths to determine which were life-enhancing and which were not; as disciple of the philosopher-god Dionysus and advocate of the will to power he sought to extirpate Christian morality as a decadent creed, driving men to self-mortification, "ressentiment" and the perverse doctrine of original sin. Yet Nietzsche feared the consequences of godlessness, the unhooking of the earth from its sun of which the madman spoke: the desire to exult in freedom and to extol an *Übermensch* can never quite conceal a profound theogonic proclivity. Nietzsche, in Aschheim's words, was part creator and part beneficiary of a general erosion of traditional belief and dissatisfaction with an established church, and the fact that those in search of religious faith often took their inspiration from — apparently — the most radical of all atheists was ironic indeed. Yet was he an atheist in the commonly accepted sense? "How many new gods are still possible! In me, in whom the religious — that is god-*creating* instinct becomes active from time to time and at inopportune moments — how varied, how different the divine manifests itself on each occasion!" (13, 535). "God the Father has been dethroned, likewise God as Judge and as Rewarder [. . .], theistic notions cannot satisfy, although the religious instinct is in the process of growing" (5, 72/3). Those who sought a religious Nietzsche "could find allusions throughout his work. The language and style of *Thus Spake Zarathustra* (by consensus one of the great lyrical achievements in the German tongue) breathed the biblical spirit."[32] The language and style, then, of *Zarathustra* could encourage many religious constructs; only after the death of religion could a feeling for the divine luxuriate again.

"O Zarathustra, thou art more pious than knowest with thy lack of faith! Some god in thee converted thee to thy godlessness [. . .]" (6, 325). The Old Pope detected in Zarathustra's honesty a desire for truth which is more pious than the tepid conformity of the believer. *Thus Spake Zarathustra* is frequently seen as an anti-Bible, but it is apparent that Nietzsche and the biblical writers are at one in adopting the mythic form as the only authoritative one for the most important affairs of human life. The use of metaphorical imagery and of parables in *Zarathustra* owes much to the example of Christ's teaching ("Without a parable spake he not unto them"), and it is characteristic of both Christ and Zarathustra that they rarely say what the most important values *are*, but what they are *like*: there is a great gulf between the indirect, non-apodictic knowledge yielded by analogy and the direct knowledge yielded by logic.[33] And metaphor-as-symbol will provide a rich reservoir for those writing after *Zarathustra*: sun, eagle, bridge, rainbow, serpent, arrow, lion, child, dragon, grave-digger, tarantula — the list is long indeed, with beacon, shield, constellation, and images of seafaring clustering around the work. The style of *Zarathustra* may at times be parodistic but far more frequently allusive, with Jesus, "this most interesting decadent" (6, 202) related to the protagonist of a work which preaches heroic vitalism and negates, or transvalues, the ethic of the Sermon on the Mount. Nietzsche and Christianity is a topic too complex and multifaceted to be discussed here: suffice it to note Zarathustra's awareness of Christ's nobility (4, 35) and statements from elsewhere on His status as "freier Geist" or free spirit (6, 204) and His truthfulness (13, 106). "At bottom there is only one Christian, and he died on the cross": these words from *The Antichrist* (6, 211) have a ring about them with which many a believer, tired of institutionalised Christianity, would concur. Zarathustra as archetype? Zarathustra as in-corporating a "Jesus redivivus"?[34] The vision of "the Roman Caesar with the soul of Christ" (11, 289), proposed as an ideal in the notes to *Der Wille zur Macht* (The Will to Power), indicate that Nietzsche's in-terest was not solely parodistic, and "Nietzschean Christianity" not a mere oxymoron. Both Zarathustra and Jesus may be seen as historical, recurrent *types* with potential for self-transcendence, and the mythical resonances far outweigh mockery or ridicule.

It has been argued that "the book [*Zarathustra*] is focused on basic existential issues, not on questions of cosmology."[35] But these "ques-tions of cosmology," the mythopoeic and the visionary, will be dra-matically quickened by Nietzsche's work; he is, as has been suggested, heir to much Romantic thinking, renouncing analytic knowledge and using the boldest metaphors to further an intuitive vision of the world. Zarathustra-Dionysus inspired, uplifted and challenged the imagination of a generation, striking away the moribund and urging creativity and an energy which was eternal delight. Zarathustra as "gold star,"[36] as Persian prophet with the features of Leonardo da Vinci,[37] as dancer, as announcer of the eternal recurrence of all things, white-haired, finally, with his flock of doves — this figure haunted those seeking to express truths which, although not religious in any conventional sense, con-tained a mythical resonance. Zarathustra is a "Ja-sager," violently re-jecting notions of man's ineluctable fallenness, of otherworldliness which denies the beauty of life, of morbid self-flagellation; if Christ were to emulate Zarathustra, then His love must be of this earth and not any other.

Some short examples may be given here of Nietzsche-inspired Christology and of the powerful impact of the doctrine of eternal recurrence: they are unfamiliar but enlightening nonetheless. In 1894 Julius Hart, one of the writers of the Friedrichshagen Circle, published a dramatic fragment in O. J. Bierbaum's *Moderner Musenalmanach* entitled *Die Visionen in der Wüste* (The Visions in the Wilderness). A desolate rocky landscape is portrayed, lit by the last rays of the setting sun, with Jesus addressing the radiant disk and immersed in erotic feelings, longing to become one with it and reigning as a new sun-god: "O sun, thou and I [. . .] Stand still, o sun, I burn in love and longing — I am flame, flickering rapturous fire. . ."[38] As a black cloud crosses the sun Jesus lies, shuddering, on the earth; a flash of lightning leaps from the cloud and is transformed into a luminous snake which settles on Jesus and becomes a naked woman. His agony departs as the snake-woman (Lilith) caresses him. ("My head lies still upon thy young breasts / As upon red anemones [. . .]") His anguish is transformed into joy as a radiant light fills the air; Jesus enters paradise, and Lilith is seen kneeling before him. This vision of heaven is obviously a pagan one with Jesus knowing of sun and Eros; the young expressionist Reinhard Sorge will betray similar preoccupations. His short play *Der Jüngling* (The Youth) of 1910 has the rocky landscape, the wanderer from afar who descends from high mountains into a dark valley with a message of liberation, of restless striving and eternal longing. In *Der Antichrist* (1911), a "dramatic poem," Sorge extols both Christ and Nietzsche, before both of whom he bends his knee: both "dreamed of paradise," both "were crucified." A "Master" speaks to a disciple who loved Him but who fell from Him when He insisted that "My kingdom is not of this world." The disciple — Nietzsche-Zarathustra — proclaims that "*My, my* kingdom is of this world. . ."; the Master insists on "Eternal Life," the disciple on "Eternal Recurrence." The Master is betrayed, but the disciple insists on incarceration with Him in His tomb.[39] The doctrine of the eternal recurrence also occurs in Gustav Sack's fragmentary *Paralyse* (1913) where "a Dichter-Philosoph à la Nietzsche," struck down by "dementia paralytica," exultantly sings of the sunset in high mountains; as "Lord of the Earth" he rejoices in a vision of the eternal recurrence before a huntsman, taking pity on him, kills him with an axe. "The topic is hard and cruel — if only I were able to complete it!"[40] Christ and the sun, Christ and Nietzsche-Zarathustra in a tomb, a Nietzsche-invalid, stricken and yet loving life and longing for eternity — these three utterances prepare the ground for much that is to come.

"Er ist wirklich — unser Christus!" (He is truly — our Christ!):[41] Kubin's startling description of Nietzsche, coupled with the adjacent reference to "Zarathustra's rapturous, intoxicating draught" emphasises yet again Nietzsche's religio-mythical significance. Kubin also speaks of Nietzsche as "an underground magnet," and this image is a telling one. For when Erich Heller speaks of such major literary figures as Rilke, George, Kafka, Thomas Mann, Ernst Jünger, Musil and Benn, and such thinkers as Heidegger and Jaspers, he acknowledges that he is naming Friedrich Nietzsche.

> He is to them all — whether or not they know and acknowledge it (and most of them do) — what St Thomas Aquinas was to Dante: the categorical interpreter of a world which they contemplate poetically or philosophically without ever radically upsetting its Nietzschean structure.[42]

This present book, as has been stated, will not interpret the German literary canon yet again but instead examine those extraordinary, lesser-known figures who fascinate by the varying degrees in which they succumb to the invisible magnet's pull. The seven authors — Rudolf Pannwitz, Alfred Mombert, Ludwig Klages, Alfred Schuler, Ludwig Derleth, Theodor Däubler and (perhaps surprisingly) Christian Morgenstern — have been allocated a chapter each; the seven chapters may be read as separate meditations on writers on whom so little has been written hitherto in English or, indeed, in any language. It is tempting to use Nietzsche's image of gigantic figures "calling to each other through the barren spaces of time whilst, undisturbed by the spiteful babbling of the noisy dwarfs crawling below, the lofty spiritual intercourse continues" (1, 808). I have called them "Zarathustra's children" — in some the family likeness will be far more pronounced than in others and, as offspring, the seven show varying degrees of critical independence from their father. And the mother? It is only "eternity," Zarathustra repeatedly tells us, (4, 287–291) who was worthy of him — this was the only woman from whom he wanted children. Let us hope that the reputations of these seven sons are worthy of her.

Notes

[1] Michael Hamburger, *From Prophecy to Exorcism. The Premisses of Modern German Literature* (London: Longmans, 1965), 57.

[2] Michael Hamburger, *A Proliferation of Prophets. Essays on German Writers from Nietzsche to Brecht* (Manchester: Carcanet, 1983), 56.

[3] Alfred Mombert, *Briefe 1893–1942*, ed. by B. J. Morse (Heidelberg/Darmstadt: Verlag Lambert Schneider, 1961), 73 (hereafter *A. M. Briefe*).

[4] Roy Pascal, *From Naturalism to Expressionism. German Literature and Society 1880–1918* (London: Weidenfeld and Nicolson, 1973), 178–179.

[5] Erich Heller, *The Importance of Nietzsche. Ten Essays* (Chicago: U of Chicago P, 1988), 2.

[6] John Burt Foster, *Heirs to Dionysus. A Nietzschean Current in Literary Modernism* (Princeton: Princeton UP, 1981), particularly the chapter on "Influence and Transformation."

[7] R. J. Hollingdale, *Nietzsche. The Man and his Philosophy* (London and Boston: Routledge and Kegan Paul, 1973), 195.

[8] Patrick Bridgwater, *Nietzsche in Anglosaxony* (Leicester: Leicester UP), 9.

[9] Steven E. Aschheim, *The Nietzsche Legacy in Germany 1890–1990* (Berkeley, Los Angeles, London: U of California P, 1992), 313.

[10] The Nietzsche edition used here is the *Kritische Studienausgabe* in 15 vols., ed. Giorgio Colli and Mazzino Montinari (Munich: Deutscher Taschenbuch Verlag and Berlin/New York: Walter de Gruyter, 1988). Hereafter in the texts in brackets. The quotations from Nietzsche, as from all other authors, I have translated into English.

[11] Aschheim, *Nietzsche Legacy*, 185.

[12] I am grateful to Kathleen Higgins, *Nietzsche's "Zarathustra"* (Philadelphia: Temple UP, 1987) for this enumeration.

[13] In *Nietzsche: Imagery and Thought. A Collection of Essays*, ed. by Malcolm Pasley (London: Methuen, 1978), 185.

[14] James Hawes, *Nietzsche and the End of Freedom. The Neoromantic Dilemma in Kafka, the Brothers Mann, Rilke and Musil 1904–1914* (Frankfurt a. M.: Peter Lang), 18. A clear account of influence, here of Nietzsche on Thomas Mann, is found in T. J. Reed, *Thomas Mann. The Uses of Tradition* (Oxford: Oxford UP, 1974), 16.

[15] Thomas Mann, *Gesammelte Werke in 13 Bänden* (Frankfurt a. M.: Fischer, 1990), vol. 9, 683.

[16] Heller, *Importance of Nietzsche*, 16 and 71.

[17] Martin Heidegger, *Nietzsche* (vol. 2), trans. by David Farrell Krell (San Francisco: Harper and Row, 1984), 35–36.

[18] J. P. Stern, *A Study of Nietzsche* (Cambridge: Cambridge UP, 1979), 157.

[19] In Pasley, *Nietzsche: Imagery and Thought*, op.cit., 120.

[20] Hollingdale, op.cit., 73; Hollingdale continues "though certainly it is his most famous."

[21] In *The Great Year of Zarathustra (1881–1981)*, ed. by David Goicoecha (New York: Lanham, 1983), 341.

[22] Richard Schacht, *Nietzsche* (London: Routledge and Kegan Paul, 1983), xiii–xiv.

[23] See James O'Flaherty, *The Quarrel of Reason with Itself* (Columbia, SC: Camden House, 1988) for a perceptive chapter on "The Intuitive Mode of Reason in *Thus spake Zarathustra*."

[24] Higgins, *Zarathustra*, xvi.

[25] Novalis, *Schriften*, ed. by Richard Samuel (Stuttgart: Kohlhammer, 1960), vol. 3, 644.

[26] M. H. Abrams, *Natural Supernaturalism. Tradition and Revolution in Romantic Literature* (New York: Oxford UP, 1971), 224.

[27] Quoted in Hawes, *End of Freedom*, 23.

[28] "Nietzsche und die Neue Romantik" in *Literarische Manifeste der Jahrhundertwende*, ed. by Erich and Dieter Bänsch (Stuttgart: Metzler, 1970), 274–275.

[29] Richard Dehmel, *Ausgewählte Briefe 1902–1920* (Berlin: Fischer). (Letter of 14 June 1905 to Florens Christian Rang).

[30] Peter Pütz, *Friedrich Nietzsche* (Stuttgart: Metzler, 1967), 48–49.

[31] Heller, *Importance of Nietzsche*, 71.

[32] Aschheim, *Nietzsche Legacy*, 202.

[33] O'Flaherty, *Quarrel of Reason*, 231.

[34] See Donald F. Nelson, "Nietzsche, Zarathustra and Jesus Redivivus: the Unholy Trinity," *Germanic Review* 47:1 (January 1973), 175–188.

[35] In Higgins, *Zarathustra*, 163.

[36] See the letter to Heinrich Köselitz (Peter Gast) of April 23, 1883 in Nietzsche *Briefwechsel* (Berlin: Walter de Gruyter, 1981), vol. 3, i, 366, where Nietzsche explains that he learned purely by chance what the name "Zarathustra" meant.

[37] Heller, 70. The picture is the Leonardo self-portrait done in red chalk, which is in Turin. Nietzsche saw a reproduction in Peter Gast's room in Venice in 1885; it is reproduced in Joachim Köhler, *Zarathustras Geheimnis. Friedrich Nietzsche und seine verschlüsselte Botschaft* (Reinbek bei Hamburg: Rowohlt, 1992).

[38] *Moderner Musenalmanach. Ein Sammelbuch deutscher Kunst*, ed. by O. J. Bierbaum (Munich: 1894), 81–82.

[39] Reinhard Johannes Sorge, *Werke in drei Bänden*, ed. by H. G. Rötzer (Nuremberg: Glock und Lutz, 1962), vol. 1, 328–350.

[40] Gustav Sack, *Paralyse. Der Refraktär* (Munich: Fink, 1971), 138. The fragment appears in a letter (February 14, 1913) to Paula Harbeck.

[41] Alfred Kubin, *Aus meinem Leben* (Munich: edition spangenberg im Ellermann Verlag, 1974), 52–53.

[42] Heller, *The Importance of Nietzsche*, 2.

Rudolf Pannwitz.
Courtesy of Schiller Nationalmuseum and
Deutsches Literaturarchiv, Marbach.

1 : Rudolf Pannwitz

> I can conjure up for you out of nothing a German culture
> in any field, if not all of them — and not only German.
> And I can do more than this. But you must listen to me,
> and obey me, for eternal words can die away in the empty
> air. . .
>
> —*Aufruf zum heiligen Kriege*

> I am as old as day and night together
> As fiery radiance, petrified forever,
> And as a crow which, for a thousand years,
> Sits on a stone which as a grave appears
> And as a book which makes us act and feel
> But no one understands the secret seal,
> And as a spring which has eternal birth,
> And as a man who speaks into the earth.
>
> —From *Urblick*

THE DIFFICULTIES BEGAN at table. Christiane von Hofmannsthal, the poet's daughter, recalled that her father did not like earnest topics to be discussed at dinner. "I remember a visit from Rudolf Pannwitz who kept talking about Nietzsche in a high-pitched voice until my father interrupted: 'Herr Pannwitz, can't you talk about something more down to earth?' 'No,' Pannwitz interjected in a loud voice, 'No, I cannot'."[1] A crasser contrast between host and guest is difficult to imagine, the former an Austrian, sophisticated and exhibiting the refinements of a metropolitan culture, the latter a provincial Prussian, grimly autodidactic, descendant of generations of teachers and farm workers; the host an established poet and dramatist, an apolitical aesthete who, briefly, felt the need to address social and culture issues during the war, the guest a self-proclaimed prophet, antisocial and fanatical; the host insisting upon good taste, urbanity and tact, the guest determined to preach in a shrill and bigoted manner. Hofmannsthal's initial enthusiasm for Pannwitz could not fail to give way to doubts, reservations and, ultimately, rejection: it may not be too fanciful to see his "Schema" *Preuße und Österreicher* (Prussian and Austrian) as being a veiled portrayal of the differences between himself and Pannwitz, the Prussian being self-righteous, presumptuous and schoolmasterly, the Austrian coy, vain and witty.[2] Another anecdote is provided by Helene von Nostitz-Wallwitz who remembered slipping on the ice at Rodaun, falling headfirst and being amazed to find that Pannwitz had not noticed and continued his monologue on the burning topics of the day.[3]

Who was he? He was born in Crossen an der Oder, some thirty miles southeast of Frankfurt an der Oder, in 1881; a precocious child, he never played, and had no companions. After studying in the Gymnasium in Steglitz he became a tutor in the house of the pedagogue Ludwig Gurlitt and in 1901 he matriculated at the University of Marburg, studying German language and literature, philology and archaeology. Two years later he moved to Berlin and continued his studies; he met Gertrud Kantorowicz, cousin of Ernst Kantorowicz and friend of Georg Simmel, and it was through her that he made the acquaintance of Sabine Lepsius and received invitations to attend poetry readings by Stefan George in the Lepsius household. Gertrud Kantorowicz published under the name of Gert Pauly and it was she who recommended Pannwitz's "Das totengedicht" (The Poem of the Dead) to George for publication in the *Blätter für die Kunst*. The impact of George was immediate and overpowering: henceforth Pannwitz would imitate George's orthography and punctuation, and he would hail that poet as the one who "tamed the chaos, and created rules,"[4] the one, that is, who overcame the febrile plethora of artistic schools and movements at the turn of the century and imposed order. In *Was ich Nietzsche und George danke* (What I owe Nietzsche and George), published posthumously by Castrum Peregrini in 1989, Pannwitz continued to praise George as liberator and guide, but if the impact of George was overpowering, that of Nietzsche was Revelation itself. *What I owe Nietzsche and George* tells of ravagement, a sense of epiphany and liberation. "George lived, with Nietzsche, and I with them, upon another planet, an even remoter star"[5]: such utterances convey a sense of awesome affinity. It was *Thus Spake Zarathustra* above all, and the concepts of amoral energy and eternal recurrence that struck with the force of lightning. Impoverished, and unable to buy the book, the young Pannwitz borrowed it and copied out whole sections; especially important for him was the section "Vom Wege des Schaffenden" (The path of the Creative One) with its heady, provocative images and exhortations:

Art thou a new power, a new Law? A first movement? A wheel rolling
out of itself? Canst thou force the stars to revolve around thee? [. . .]
Thou must burn in thine own fire — how canst thou become new if
thou hast not first become ash? Lonely one — thou goest the path of
lovers: thou lovest thyself and therefore thou scornest thyself as lovers
scorn. The lover creates, because he despises! What does he know of
love who has not had to despise that which he loves!"(4, 82).

The presence of Nietzsche will reverberate throughout this chapter, for
Pannwitz responded to Nietzsche's daring idealism with an intense
abandonment. "I never saw my friend, my only friend, nor did I speak
to him; I was born in the year when he was stuck by the Aeon [that is,
the world-shattering doctrine of eternal recurrence]. . . I was nine when
I became orphaned [that is, when Nietzsche collapsed into insanity]. . .
I never overcame my friend's sunless obliteration"[6] — rarely has such a
tribute been paid by one thinker-poet to another.

In 1904 Pannwitz and Otto zur Linde founded the journal *Charon*
(Pannwitz would remain as co-editor until 1906): Charon, the ferry-
man of Greek mythology who carried the dead souls across the river
Styx into the underworld without questioning their origins nor their
status becomes a symbol for the poetic act itself, an act of pure dedication. The laconic opening to the first number, "We seek nothing [. . .]
we are not mystics, but simply reproduce reality"[7] may well have been
an attempt to avoid hyperbole and pretension, but the "Charontiker"
soon turned to Nietzschean terminology in their demands for a new
society and a new Man. In 1906 Pannwitz published in the Charon-
Verlag his essay *Kultur, Kraft, Kunst* (Culture, Power, Art) which
contained an attack on the poet Richard Dehmel and suggestions for
corrections to Goethe's poetry, particularly "Der du von dem Himmel
bist" and "Füllest wieder Busch und Tal." "It is George and Otto zur
Linde," we read,

> in whom there is an ethos, a prophetic tone, and an attempt at least to
> achieve a wholeness, a world. Zur Linde is more extensive, but a natu-
> ralist, almost a proletariat; George is more powerful and wiser [. . .]
> Each is, on his own, a daunting remnant, but welded together they
> represent an ethos, the sole achievement since Nietzsche. The rest is
> bungling, trash or filth [teilwerk quark oder dreck].[8]

Further publications include the pedagogical essays *Der Volksschullehrer und die deutsche Sprache* (The Elementary School Teacher and
the German Language, 1907) and *Der Volksschullehrer und die deutsche
Kultur* (The Elementary School Teacher and German Culture, 1909):
both are an ecstatic plea for acceptance of life's manifold richness. (An-

other essay, *Das Werk der deutschen Erzieher* (The Task of the German Pedagogues, 1909) was criticized for its "overwrought half-truths" and excessive vulnerability vis à vis Nietzsche)[9] A fragmentary novel *Die Führer* (The Leaders) also dates from this time. In it the character Kerstens (that is Otto zur Linde) speaks of the work of Kühleborn (Pannwitz) in the following terms: "You praise life's emotions so highly because none of them touches you [. . .] You aestheticise everything in a drunken intoxication. Everything is whipped into the heights, and the phallus prevails! Your Nietzschean momentum worries me — I fear you may lose your balance. . ."[10] It seems that Pannwitz is here uncharacteristically trying to objectify his own Dionysian stance, his youthful indebtedness to Nietzsche; the novel was abandoned however. Tensions between Pannwitz and zur Linde (the latter was unable to accept George's imperious stance, and Pannwitz's egregious attitudinizing) became intolerable and Pannwitz, alienating himself increasingly from the Charon Circle gave up the editorship in 1906.

In 1911 Pannwitz received a scholarship from Duke Friedrich II of Sachsen Anhalt which enabled him to devote himself to scholarship and to writing. His financial state remained parlous, however, and the complexity of his domestic arrangements (a wife and one, later, two mistresses, various children), together with an itinerant life style (Thuringia, the South Tyrol, later Dalmatia) betoken an inner restlessness. In 1913 he made the acquaintance of Hans Carl, proprietor of the "Allgemeine Brauerei und Hopfenzeitung" in Nuremberg (a journal devoted to information on brewing and hops) and persuaded him to found a publishing house devoted exclusively to Pannwitz's own writing: the breakthrough to a potentially wider readership came that same year when Hans Carl published the *Dionysische Tragödien*. These tragedies are dedicated to "Friedrich Nietzsche, the Creator of our new Life" and represent, Pannwitz explained, "a tardy answer and an expression of gratitude for his [Nietzsche's] deed."[11] He had started writing them as early as 1904 and they may be seen as complementing or indeed anticipating the work of Paul Ernst, Carl Spitteler and the Hauptmann of *Griechischer Frühling* (Hellenic Spring, 1908) and *Der Bogen des Odysseus* (The Bow of Odysseus, 1914). Hofmannsthal's *Elektra* (1904) is perhaps closest to Pannwitz in its portrayal of sombre violence and surging chaos. Pannwitz strove to reconstruct the Dionysian form of antique drama and to give poetic expression to the ideas that Nietzsche had formulated philosophically. The play *Der Tod des Empedokles* (The Death of Empedocles) also owes much to Hölderlin whose work Nietzsche had extolled and which had become better known through the efforts of the George circle, Norbert von Hellingrath especially. For Hölderlin the central problem of *Empedokles*, in all the fragmentary versions, is the relationship between man and the whole, between the limits of individuality and the pantheistic awareness of union with God. Empedocles's guilt is excess, an excessive love for man and a boundless desire to identify himself with the divine. As *hubris* increases, Empedokles sees that arrogance can only be expiated by his death: it is through the cleansing fires of Etna that he must pass in order to atone before nature. His death is an ecstatic leap into the volcano, into the heart of creation, into that fire which Heraclitus believed was the creator and destroyer of all forms of being, that fire from which Dionysus rose as "Dionysus πυριγενής." Zarathustra, we should not forget, similarly finds death by a leap into a volcano in one draft, into the Dionysian world of flux, energy and relentless ebb and flow, eternally recurring in fire, that symbol of transformation. In Pannwitz's play Empedokles, alone in his tower on Etna, is visited by the shade of Pythagoras who curses him ("The curse of death upon thee / Vile, vicious Empedokles!")[12] for having divulged esoteric mysteries to the populace: intoxicated by wine ("by the sinful god Dionysus") Empedokles has "in a base song, and with a dancing boy / In public place divulged to jeering crowds / And even mocked the truth. . . ." The ecstatic utterances and preference for ejaculation ("God! it gleams and rages! O Father! Fire! Etna! Elements!")[13] place Pannwitz close to Expressionism here; the cult of Dionysian intoxication anticipates the frenzied utterances of many a practitioner of that movement.

The second play, *Philoktetes: Ein Mysterium* is an interesting variation on an old legend. Edmund Wilson read the story as a parable of writing ("The victim of a malodorous disease which renders him abhorrent to society and periodically degrades him and makes him helpless is also master of a superhuman art which everybody has to respect and which the normal man finds he needs"):[14] here we have a Nietzschean figure who gives his bow and arrows (his wisdom) to those who visit him. The outcast realises that it is his vision that is sought and that he, the stricken one, is master of all, for poison brings madness, madness wisdom, and wisdom power.

> Ah, they seek my poison — now they see
> 'Tis not with Herculean weapons that they win
> Nor with Vulcanic metal, self-created
> But with my poison! . . . Yes, I now exult
> That they should need me, a base stinking man! . . . Ah! Ah![15]

Further echoes of Nietzsche are to be found in *Der glückliche König Kroisos* (Happy King Croesus), entitled "A tragedy of fate." Croesus rejects worldly pelf and, losing his gold, becomes one with the golden glory of sunset:

> O noble one! In losing all my gold
> I have my gold, my golden happiness
> And bathed in the glowing sunset I rejoice
> I am the happiest, joyful till my death![16]

Exultation, intoxication, golden sun and benediction — an *art nouveau*, neoromantic cluster of images portrays the crocus blossoming from "sphere and hemisphere." The fourth play, *Die Befreiung des Oedipus* (The Liberation of Oedipus) is a "Dionysian tableau" with scenes of orgy ("Where is the goat? Where is the goat? Let torches burn! The maenads come! The frenzied woman tear the god! Ah, Iakche! evoe! Iakche! Iakche, evermore!");[17] the last, *Iphigenie mit dem Gott* is, however, an "Apolline play," portraying the deliverance of Orestes and Elektra from manic fury. There is restless energy in these plays, alternating with static peroration; there is no plausible characterization, the mythological figures being mere mouthpieces for grave utterance. Hofmannsthal's reaction to *Happy King Croesus* is enlightening:

> The language is incomparable in many places, the soul's flame bursting forth. Perhaps it bursts forth too persistently, so that we only have flames which devour each other, metaphysical functions simply, and too few human beings — they are meant to be human beings, are they not? (One somehow gets the impression: Hebbel, too much "hebbeling").[18]

In 1914 Pannwitz moved to the Ammersee in Upper Bavaria; being of frail constitution he was not called up for military service. He began here his work on *Die heiligen Gesänge der Hyperboräer* (The holy songs of the Hyperboreans), a vast work of some thirty thousand hexameters which would remain unpublished, a paean of praise for the "People of Light," descendants of the god Helios. They are seen as the chosen people ("We Hyperboreans are not like other peoples / We were, are, and remain the eternal ones. . ."),[19] yet there is a rejection of racism and war: Pannwitz could not tolerate the rampant jingoism of many of his fellow countrymen. ("The emissaries of hell now swarm across the earth, / False Hyperboreans, dispatched by a false Leader / Stirring up storms, and dreams that are steeped in blood. . .")[20]) The spirit of Hölderlin is again evident, also Nietzsche in the proclamation of joy, love of life and of the eternal recurrence:

> It is life that I love, and the thought that it is eternal
> Gives reassurance to me, in which I can lose myself wholly
> Yes, yes, it returns! It does not fade into the formless. . .[21]

It is impossible to do justice to this immense work here; we await a definitive edition. Suffice it to mention that it contains some thirty "books," grouped under such sections as "The Book of Books," "The Books of Power," "The Books of Mildness," "The Books of Fulfilment," "The Books of Foundation," "The Realm of the Hyperboreans" and "The Deeds of the Hyperboreans": a Zarathustra ethos prevails in such subdivisions as "The Book of War," "The Book of the Prophet," "The book of the Legend of the Superman," and "The Book of Love and Eternity." Another unfinished torso, equally vast, is *Der Dichter und die blaue Blume* (The Poet and the Blue Flower), an esoteric reworking of Novalis's *Heinrich von Ofterdingen* in which Klingsor appears as a German Dionysus: such action as there is takes place on the Mondsee in Austria where Pannwitz had repaired in 1915. It is not difficult to see the figure of Pannwitz himself in the figure of Heinrich; a journey down the Danube is described and various poets (Hofmannsthal as the "Herr von Wien") join the boat. The "Venusberg" section, some thirty thousand lines long, and approximately half of the (uncompleted) whole deals with the lunar realm as opposed to the realm of the sun: various sections ("Undine") deal with the figure of the temptress and also the Demiurge. The work may be seen as a tribute to the glories of German Romanticism against a background of brutality and strife, a Europe in which Germanness was becoming synonymous with barbarism. Pannwitz's plea is simple and sincere:

> Give songs, o azure flower,
> Forests, eternity,
> From German, deep enchantment
> And bells that sound piously . . .[22]

It has been claimed that Pannwitz considered himself first and foremost a poet, yet sacrificed his private and personal satisfaction to publish works he considered beneficial for his contemporaries, a "Gedankenwerk" dealing with the crises of the age. "He even put off his 'Dichtung' again and again in order to present that kind of 'Lebenshilfe' which the day demanded and which he was [. . .] so well qualified to offer."[23] Pannwitz's lyric poetry will be discussed at the end of this chapter and we shall here return to the "Gedankenwerk"; in 1917 Hans Carl published *Die Krisis der europäischen Kultur* (The Crisis of European Culture), that book which Hofmannsthal greeted with unstinting enthusiasm. It makes difficult reading, a hectoring book dense with uncapitalized and poorly punctuated prose where "capitals and periods are seen as semantic barriers obstructing the flow of the work."[24] Pannwitz, thirty-six, assumes the mantle of the sage to pronounce upon Europe's crisis and a possible way ahead: as Praeceptor Germaniae he sought for a fusion of myth, philosophy, poetry, history and politics, an eclectic vision which would redress the ills of the age and lay the foundation for a new Europe. *Die Krisis* takes a panoramic view of European history, claiming that "the European flower" originated in Greece, then emerged in Rome, then Italy, France, England and, finally, Germany; Germany's strength is seen in its being "more barbaric, fresher, more basic and more powerful" than countries with a longer cultural tradition. A strain of pure Nietzsche is heard in the following statement: "That which lives wishes to live more fully by growing more powerfully in itself; the genus 'Man' does not live if it does not live more fully, growing more powerful in itself — this is the Will!" (47).[25] With staggering hyperbole Pannwitz compares Nietzsche with Christ, with "the cosmos"; as the Jew Paul arrogated to himself the Christian message, twisting and altering it, so Nietzsche is reduced to becoming a prophet solely for Germanic "Übermenschentum." His fate is that of Christ who was crucified as was, through Him, the cosmos itself (43). The ideals for mankind are either "der reine buddho" (pure Buddhism) or Nietzsche: there can be no third way, and a religion of Nietzsche would represent the highest spiritual manifestation (48). The spirit is the creator, we read, and the creator the artist and the artist the Emperor; a superabundant ego, a superabundant goal and a superabundance of power and justice will bring about the transfiguration of the world. It was Napoleon's greatness that he acted with the force of spiritual vision, and Nietzsche's "Übermensch" likewise represents the highest spiritual aristocracy, its "last fruit and its sweetest grape" (51).

Pannwitz now attempts a definition of culture: "culture is the path of the creative spirit"(53). Nietzsche-Zarathustra demanded that art should be the "myth of the future"; the fusion of Dionysus and Apollo, adumbrated in *Die Geburt der Tragödie*, and the concept of *agon*, chiselled in finest marble, are held as the highest ideals, pointing to man as "the measure of all things" and "King of the earth" (53). Modern man, by contrast, is a fallen creature: the "sportsman-like, muscular, nationalistically-minded, militaristic and religious postmodern man of today is a mollusc with a crusty shell, a hybrid fusion of decadent and barbarian" (52). Following in Nietzsche's footsteps Pannwitz rejects the charge of superficiality levelled at French culture and extols "le roi soleil" and his court as the last great cultural renaissance in Europe (54).

Long sections follow on Voltaire, on the importance of a Celtic admixture and of the indebtedness of Europe to Persian and Arabic influ-
ences. Unlike Nietzsche, Pannwitz praises the Germanic culture of
Iceland and again extols the Celtic contribution: the Edda is praised as
the highest Nordic art, a mixture of myth and poetry (71). (It would
later be painful for Pannwitz to hear that the Eddas meant nothing to
Hofmannsthal, and even more distressing to learn that the Austrian had
never read *Thus Spake Zarathustra*).[26] The discussion now moves to
English literature; Shakespeare is deemed "the great Romantic and
naturalist" (92) and there is a sympathetic discussion of Milton, Byron,
Shelley, and Lawrence Sterne ("Tristram Shandy is one of the deepest,
and indeed freest, books that exist," 144). English culture is character-
ized by its middle way, half way between the wild formlessness of bar-
barism and the strict classicism of more sophisticated cultures (150);
British utilitarianism, cant and commercialism are excoriated, as is the
British desire to conquer the world through trade, (an inevitable
Americanisation, apparently, is the consequence). The attack upon
American vulgarity, triviality, and greed is bitter: an "Übermensch" is
needed to transcend the human, all-too-human aspects of modern life.
The book reaches an abrupt end; an appendix provides a pessimistic
coda, lamenting the impasse in which Europe finds itself. "Even
Nietzsche cannot have a direct effect — he is too strong for the weak
and even too strong for the strong" (180). The last utterances stress
the need for a trans-European dimension, something extra-European,
even oriental: here the diffuse and exasperating book comes to an end.

What is the general drift? It seems that neither national nor international concerns should be paramount, but something transnational, su-
pranational: Pannwitz also seems to belong to those like Hermann
Hesse and Hermann Graf Keyserling who sought to direct European
eyes to the values of oriental cultures. Nietzsche's "good Europeans"
are the ideal, those who have transcended petty nationalism. After the
end of the war (a war incurred, Pannwitz implies, by immature German
grandiloquence, British commercial interest, and French mendacity)
Britain would reject its anti-continental attitudes and become more
closely integrated into a European Union; Germany, re-educated and
free from irrational violence, was to act a leading role. Essential was the
opening to the East, with Austria and the nascent union of Bohemia,
Moravia and Slovakia preparing the way and acting as a bridge to Rus-
sia and beyond. The "crisis" however is ill-defined, but resulting in all
probability from pettiness, cupidity, a lack of high idealism, and a general moral bankruptcy. Hofmannsthal's enthusiastic response seems ex-
aggerated, but he likewise felt that an immense crisis was at hand, the

"domus Austria" about to collapse, and malignant forces threatening to engulf those European traditions he held most dear. It seemed that Pannwitz had touched a raw nerve and Hofmannsthal, albeit temporarily, was impressed by his charismatic arrogance. Pannwitz, we learn, was "equally great as poet, philosopher and historian,"[27] and Hofmannsthal goes as far as to claim that he, Hofmannsthal, had been seized by "an unstoppable tornado." The most startling admission is surely found in that same letter where Hofmannsthal declares that Pannwitz was "the greatest event in my life, even including the first meeting, in 1892, with Stefan George."[28] But this intellectual bondage was, as we know, a brief aberration, and Hofmannsthal distanced himself, finding Pannwitz's Zarathustra gestures bewildering and offensive; an "incident" at Schloß Neubeuern, caused by Pannwitz's uncouth and boorish behaviour toward the Countess Ottonie von Degenfeld-Schonburg, hastened the inevitable cooling.[29]

In 1919 Pannwitz sent Hofmannsthal his *Die deutsche Lehre* (The German Doctrine), a series of oracular utterances which were described by Döblin as "a complete débâcle": Hofmannsthal persisted, despite the estrangement, to praise the book, comparing its effect to "a storm which swept throughout the lowlands," "a spiritual conflagration."[30] Döblin's reaction is probably the more plausible: the work is unreadable in its pomposity, its arrogation of grave wisdom and priestly imperiousness. The work, some four hundred pages in length, proclaims as a motto that "The German will be the salt of the earth and a light unto the world";[31] the "Spirit, thy Master" begins his perorations for "The people shall grow verdant beneath the hands of a prophet: he melts with his people as with a bride" (5). The Germans are addressed thus:

> You Germans! Your fatherland was never a home [Heimat] to you, and thus could never have permanence. Learn to love that which is still home to you, instead of this Fatherland: then you will gain yourselves. . . (39)

> You men and women of the German people! The Spirit, thy Master speaks: think not of revolution but of the Great Midday, the Hour of all time. Let thy highest star be one with the locks of thy head! (49)

The prophet (Pannwitz) announces that he is the prophet of the Hyperboreans and proclaims their mission: that they should represent the "Dämongott" Dionysus before all peoples (62); that they should disseminate "Naturreligion," the religion "of the most passionate cycle" like vegetation throughout the earth (63); that they should become a holy people of "Arjas" (black or fair) and breed throughout the earth in a nobility of blood and spirit (63); that they should inspire each generation to seek the blue flower, being as "vitally young" as Goethe, as "youthful in love" as Jean Paul and as "rejuvenated by death" as Novalis (63). This race, the German-Hyperboreans, should build a "sun tower" as a token of expiation, of atonement for themselves and for all peoples; this should be hacked from the highest mountains and a pure, eternal flame should forever burn upon it as a sign that man should forever cherish the holy light (63). The Spirit, thy Master continues his utterances, proclaiming that he is no magician, no redeemer: it is not redemption, but fulfilment that he preaches (65), and his features and stance become increasingly those of Zarathustra, minatory, blessing, and urgent.

The section "To the German Warriors" explains that "Warriors should be blessed. Verily, it is not the warlike elements of this war [First World War] but that which was not warlike that was its most offensive and outrageous characteristic"(69): section ten of the first book of *Thus Spake Zarathustra* comes forcibly to mind. "To the Christians" explains that there is "not one god, but many: there was not one god, but one spirit" (75). "Concerning the Vultures" is dedicated to an apocalyptic vision, but "Strong is the martial spirit of our mother earth, and her powerful breast lifts the young mountains to the eternal light" (100). The mood is dark in "Of the abomination of peoples," and flight is recommended:

> Come, man, flee with me into the forests! Many trees grow there whose branches and twigs are bare, but the trunks are still powerful. The evergreens rejuvenate our hearts and minds. A beech tree stands here, neither the highest, nor the lowest: a spring leaps forth at its feet — look! the snow has yielded to green grass — look! The blue flower blossoms here! (117)

This fusion of Nietzsche and Novalis may appear bewildering, but Novalis was much read at this time: Georg Brandes's[32] six-volume history of nineteenth-century literature had greatly influenced Thomas Mann, for example, who recognised that Novalis had anticipated some of the ideas formulated in *Der Zauberberg* (The Magic Mountain, 1924). Novalis also occupies a curious place in Thomas Mann's *Von deutscher Republik* (On the German Republic, 1923) where his eroticism is unconvincingly linked with the intense physicality of Walt Whitman. Novalis featured in the millennial fantasies prevalent in Germany after collapse and defeat with many a dark saying on pain, eros, transcendence, art, and death; his presence haunts, as has been noticed, many pages of *Die Hyperboräer*. (The praise of pain, the concept of the "irreligious" nature of the artist, the awareness of the association of lust, religion and cruelty, the claim that every sickness is a musical problem and many other aphorisms of Novalis seem strangely Nietzschean: this would have come as no surprise to Pannwitz.)

The section "Man" informs us that "Man is petrified and trapped in his own will. . . He must forge pinions, pinions of the spirit and of the spirit's passions. He should be free of his own flesh, freed by the redemptive love for the Superman!" (126). "Overbreeding" laments the superfluous mass of humans, Nietzsche's "letzte Menschen" (127); man should attempt to create from a genuine present a genuine future, and transform himself into "Superman" (138). This figure emerges again in the section "The Great Doctor"; this doctor would be a saviour of the human body, a task-master of nature and the one who will prepare the way for the Superman (141). "The greatest teacher teaches Life; the greatest teacher exults: 'So be it! Let us create the Superman!'" (149). Further sections extol youth, power (not transient, but eternal) and a new nobility — the great are as a mountain range, peak after peak rising to the highest vision; they are manifestations of a creative force, these "menservants and maidservants of the Superman!" (179). The laconic reference to the Jews in *Thus Spake Zarathustra* (Book one, "Of a thousand and one goals") is here elaborated: the Jews are, as the Germans, an ancient race "which has never gazed into the sun [. . .]" a "people without land"; both Jews and Germans are exhorted to "seek the sun together, the sun of the Hyperboreans," where "there is no path nor way" (228–30). This section ends with an oblique reference to Nietzsche again: "Neither by land nor by water beyond the North, the realm of ice, of today — beyond the beyond — remote, away. . ." (230). Such, apparently, is the intensity of this self-identification with Nietzsche that Pannwitz must needs succumb to stammering agitation.

The section on the German artist proclaims that his vision is fixed upon the achievement of the impossible (a Faustian ring, here): this is why his work is stranded upon the border between "the creation of worlds" and "Pfuscherei" (bungling: 263). The German artist's path is long, dangerous, almost aimless, but it is the path of greatness. The German artist is also priest and prophet, and exhorts his people thus:

> My German people! Do not brood on vengeance and on a vengeful war [. . .] thy great and holy duty, as people of the blue flower, precludes such actions. Grow abundant with the growing light, fulfil the secular world-light, the world-year, become as a preacher, as prophet of the world flower, of the blue flower, grow and reign. (281)

The plethora of grave utterances increases in hyperbole: most wincingly embarrassing for the modern reader is the section "The sexes. Woman, Love, Marriage." Pannwitz claims that "The most sublime duty of woman is to entertain an easily fusible metabolism within her body" (292). Menstruation should be sanctified once more as it was in earlier times — this will produce a truer chastity in the worship of the hymen and of bourgeois marriage (293). During menstruation the sexes should be separated. Filth and foulness do not arise from the flesh, but from the spirit. "It is not the torrid vapours that pour from the wombs that are dreadful, but the cold thoughts that impregnate them" (297). "It is said that man is impure and woman pure — nay, the woman is impure, everything about her is foul. She cannot purify herself physically, neither can the bowels of the earth ever be cleansed. This is her infinity, her wholeness, fecundity, eternity" (307). But where, the prophet Pannwitz cries, are the goddesses, the nymphs?

> Where are the gardens of paradise and the houris? Where Aspasia and Maintenon? Neither Wala nor Valkyrie nor Melancholia, neither Cornelia nor Madonna nor Beatrice are here. From the golden temple of Aphrodite we have sunk to the dark mound of Venus, and finally to the open market place for free love [. . .]. (314)

The reaction of Pannwitz's wife and mistresses may well be imagined.

The work draws to its close. "The religion of man is a religion of nature, a religion of life, of the elements of the natural cycle, and of the divine" (353). The prophet looks back to Zoroaster the Persian, and blesses him — and himself. "Blessed be the great-grandson of my Parsee purity, blessed be Zarathustra, the hero beyond good and evil, the redeemer of the pure and holy cycle, the prophet to the Great Midday, the creator of the Superman, the teacher of the eternal recurrence of All Things, and the father of a son!" (385) — the son being Pannwitz himself. Tumult, hyperbole and bathos characterize the final pages: the German people are advised to work, to breed "Kleinvieh" (410), that is, rabbits and goats, and to heed the voice of the Spirit, now not a "master," but a friend — "Work now, work o German people of work, bring to fruition the precepts of *The German Doctrine*, that its final words may bring forth thy final deed!" (416). Thus ends what must be surely the most amazing of the strained and overwrought utterances to greet the fledgling Weimar Republic in its earliest days.

Pannwitz was grimly prolific at this time, publishing between 1919 and 1922 ten *Mythen,* or mythological epics, and some ten *Flugblätter,* pamphlets, dealing with the political situation in a highly idiosyncratic manner. Germany's hour of humiliation was to be transcended by exhortations and reminders of spiritual achievement: a clear, Nordic air prevails. *Baldur's Death* (1919) a "May Festival," is manifestly influenced by the Eddas and portrays a clash between the god of light, Baldur, and his dark brother Hödur, between radiance and brooding hatred. The "Poet" reminds the German people that they scarcely know any more who Baldur is, and yet he remains "a primeval dream of all blond dreams."[33] The German people are "geistschwer," "heavy with the spirit," yet they have not yet found their "image [. . .], world-song and world-game." Their fall resulted from "Unsauberkeit" and "Schmutz," or baseness and depravity, and it is only the memory of light which can bring them salvation. This pretentious and unconvincing reworking of the Nordic legend met, as we know, with little enthusiasm from Hofmannsthal ("I simply didn't like it"), nor from the reading public as a whole. *The Song of Elen* (1919) again invokes a prehistoric world of giants, heroes and gods with Elen as a Leminkainen figure and a "black stone" as a fount of runic knowledge; it is dedicated to the cultural historian Kurt Breysig (1866–1940) and a debt is acknowledged to Breysig's work on the origin of the concept of divinity. *Das Kind Aion* (The Child Aion, 1919) is a criticism of Europe before 1914, a continent addicted to vulgar commercialism and blatant materialism: it is couched in forced terza rimas and projects the image of the child playing with a golden ball as a picture of hope and redemption. Other "Mythen" (*The Elf, Eros and Psyche*) are tedious and undistinguished.

Of the ten pamphlets, the *Aufruf zum heiligen Kriege* (Call for a Holy War, 1919) and the *Einführung in Nietzsche* (Introduction to Nietzsche, 1920) are the most remarkable. The former verges on megalomania and is comparable only to Derleth's *Die Proklamationen*, although Pannwitz rejected Derleth's work, calling it a poor imitation of George's *Stern des Bundes* (Star of the Covenant) and repudiated the cult of templars and the eccentric admixture of "Claudel, Zarathustra, the orient and Prussianism."[34] Christ's grave utterance concerning the need for strife and the sword opens the work, to be followed by Pannwitz's pronouncement "I, who through the enunciation of *The German Doctrine* declare a holy war of the living against all those who wish neither to live not to die. . . ."[35] A war has been fought for five years, Pannwitz explains, yet there was no goal: it was not a holy war. All that was noble was destroyed, and all that is vulgar has triumphed. Another war must be waged, the greatest and most terrible, that of life, of faith, of the spirit. "In this most fearful hour of need, of gaping and terrifying abysses I, who thought and enunciated *The German Doctrine* will show you the true path, a path with many steps, so that all who are powerful in their youth might follow me. . . ."(2). "I seek neither self-sacrifice not heroic deeds, but loyalty, that each should remain true to that which is divine in him, and also his earthly existence" (2). In the midst of these perorations is inserted a quotation from George's *Stern des Bundes*:

> Ten thousand must be struck by holy madness
> Ten thousand felled by holy pestilence
> Ten thousand by the holy war. . . .

The conclusion is the staggering quotation which serves as a motto at the beginning this chapter: "I can conjure up for you out of nothing a German culture in any field, if not all of them — and not only German. And I can do more than this. But you must listen to me, and obey me, for eternal words can die away in the empty air" (19). Such arrogant hyperbole is matched only by Nietzsche's extraordinary claims in *Ecce Homo*, but may not be excused, as in Nietzsche's case, with the onset of clinical insanity.

The eighth pamphlet, the *Einführung in Nietzsche*, is more acceptable, despite its hyperbolic tendency. "The name Nietzsche is the highest conception the name of Germany can reach, the highest holiness of the German spirit, and the guilt and the bad conscience of all German people."[36] His true existence, Pannwitz asseverates, is not that of a writer, it is in every sense the career of a semi-divine hero. The closest approximation is to the greatest King of Babylon — Gilgamesh. Nietzsche, we learn, "has no likeness in Europe, and Europe has no means of measuring him" (2). His works "bear witness to the immortal deeds of the spirit, primeval creations from the logos of undiluted knowledge, prophetic wisdom of creative world-renewal and transfiguration of humanity, cosmic rebirth of the divine aeon" (3). He is not a prophet for the people, "but a prophet for the prophets" (4). Like every great man, Pannwitz insists, Nietzsche originated in a religious movement. "German Romanticism, in all its greatness, was such a movement, and Nietzsche fulfilled and conquered it" (4). "Nietzsche was the first in Europe to recognise that the spiritual world was a mythology" (5); he is related to Christ in "the storming of his loving heart against intractable dullness, with the eruption of his volcano which bursts all boundaries, with the ruthless suppression of mendacity in thought, word and answer" (14). It follows that his work "may only be understood as the semiotics of a suffering, creative saviour" (14–15). His "incomparable greatness" is his "stepping beyond spiritual knowledge towards creative deed" (17); he is "the most passionate, creative lover of values and hence hard, ascetic even, towards individuals" (18). Pannwitz's Nietzsche-image is manifestly hagiographical, emphasizing the mythopoeic qualities and seeing him as martyr and prophet, bearing the features of Max Klinger's bust, a German Nietzsche rather than the francophile, deriving his greatness from some cosmic energy.

Pannwitz's views on Nietzsche and Christianity are illuminating. "Nietzsche's battle against Christianity is at bottom a *Kulturkampf*, a battle between classical and Christian culture for the future of Europe, European mankind as a whole [. . .]" (29). The hatred of Nietzsche, as of Goethe, was not directed against Christ, but the Crucified. In his youth Nietzsche discovered two gods, Dionysus and Apollo. "They were the first European gods, and they will be the last. . ." Nietzsche's thunderbolt, "écrasez l'infâme!," taken from Voltaire, is "not directed against the person of Christ, but against Christian culture" (31). Pannwitz is close to Klages in the following statement: "The thunderbolt struck Christian values, values which were decadent, were oriental, Jewish, late-Romantic [. . .]. They were the ideals of the rabble, full of *ressentiment*, and their aims, overt and covert, were the destruction, the levelling out of all values" (31). Nietzsche, in contrast, created "a complete ethical vision, not only the noblest in Europe, but in the whole world" (33), rejecting Socialism, materialism and naturalism as vulgar manifestations of the masses. Pannwitz points out that the values of the rulers, of the conquerors, derived from the Parsees — truthfulness, freedom, bravery, holiness, respect, magnanimity, goodness — ideals which are of those of "a rich, blessed divine breed, and nothing to do with democracy" (33–34). Again, Nietzsche and Christ are extolled as "azure, sunlit childlike spirits of fire" (36): both were outsiders and idealists, but Nietzsche "had to suffer immeasurably more than Christ, created infinitely more and reached over into a far more unthinkable future [. . .]" (37). Pannwitz insists yet again that Nietzsche "was not fighting Christ, but his shadow, the suffering act of crucifixion, the crucified cosmos" (37). The pamphlet ends on an exultant note: Nietzsche's work is incomparable, he is "the only one who will wrestle through millennia. No thinker contains such contradictoriness, no one but he embraces all that is real and possible, and no one is so extravagant, so lavish [. . .]" (41). The final pronouncement runs as follows:

> And I say unto thee, o humble and creative youth of the next Nietzsche epoch, thou who rule today as the immortal dynasts of Nietzsche himself — I speak this watchword, this slogan unto thee, thou who dwell in the spirit, and serve the earth: not sacrifice, but exertion." (45)

Dedication is extolled, and idealism, service, and self-overcoming: this is the diffuse and utterly impractical programme which the erstwhile pedagogue and Praeceptor Germaniae *in spe* addressed to the young of his day, extolling Nietzsche as the brother of, and successor to, Christ himself.

Another work that appeared almost contemporaneously with Pannwitz's pamphlet and which again exhorts German youth to look on Nietzsche — and specifically Zarathustra — as a model is Hesse's *Zarathustras Wiederkehr* (The Return of Zarathustra). This short essay appeared anonymously in Switzerland in 1919; it was reprinted a year later, under Hesse's name, in Berlin. It was written in the last days of January 1919, and appeared anonymously at first because Hesse claimed that he did not want the younger generation, those whom he called "the expressionists," to be inhibited by the name of an established literary figure.[37] Hesse experienced a renewal of interest in, and a growth of admiration for, Nietzsche at this time, a realisation of Nietzsche's uncompromising refusal to pander to the grandiloquent sabre-rattling of his age which stood in sharp contrast to the failure of so many German intellectuals who supported the German cause in the First World War. Nietzsche as the "Untimely One," the lonely one, the last representative of the German spirit who castigated and deplored the vulgar philistinism and meretricious posturing of so many of his countrymen — this is the Nietzsche that Hesse praises, the Nietzsche above all of *Zarathustra*, and it is the love of the young for this writer and his work that Hesse calls "the dearest, the holiest that youth can experience" (11, 42).

The essay itself admonishes the young of the day to reject revanchist attitudes and lachrymose nostalgia; what is needed is an acceptance of destiny, the creation of a new personality and the readiness to forge a new spirit, a new manliness. Zarathustra, Hesse writes, has returned; those who have loved him, and who have returned from the trenches, defeated and humiliated, seek him out. They find him, smiling, listening to a public speaker and urge him to address them. They walk together, but the young are disappointed, expecting Zarathustra to be violently agitated and seeking to emulate the soap-box orators. He explains that he cannot harangue them, being neither speaker, priest, general nor king: he is a hermit, even a "Spaßmacher" (a jester). They are disillusioned, explaining that they have been through the war and expect something more from him, not this detachment. Shouting is heard, and the noise of firearms, and Zarathustra sees that the young wish to join in the fighting. He therefore speaks to them, not as a teacher, he insists, but as a "Mensch," a human being. "Zarathustra is the man whom you are seeking within yourselves, the upright one, the one who is not seduced" (10, 473). His first homily is "On Destiny," and in it the need is emphasised to accept the hammer blows of fate without flinching; dreams of vengeance are to be forgotten, as should Kaiser and Fatherland. The next section, "On Suffering and Action" praises pain as a purifying fire; the third, "On Loneliness," extols the one who cuts away the dross of existence and seeks essential authenticity; the fourth, surprisingly, is entitled "Spartakus" and expresses admiration for the energy and the vision of the Spartacists who are seen as being infinitely preferable to the sullen bourgeois. The section "The Fatherland and its Enemies" prescribes the following task: "Our aim is to recognise our destiny, to make our suffering our own, to transform its bitterness into sweetness and to grow rich in our adversity" (10, 487). The section "On Germany" asks the question: why are the Germans so hated? Zarathustra deplores their arrogant assertion of superiority and sees that "Germanic virtue" is a sham: "With the help of your Kaiser and of Richard Wagner you have made an operatic mockery of 'Germanic virtue' until nobody in the world believed in it but yourselves [. . .]. You constantly spoke of God, but it was the purse that was always in your hands" (10, 491–2). The criticism is stern, but there is also hope: "Yet I believe in you, I believe in something in you Germans for which I have carried an ancient and profound feeling of love [. . .]. You are the most pious people on earth [. . .]. May you learn to seek the God within!" (10, 493). A final section states that true action, true manliness is found not in books, not in oratory, but on high mountains, and the path leads through suffering and loneliness. Departing from his listeners, Zarathustra urges them not to worship him, not to emulate him, and makes his final pronouncement: "Your future, and your difficult, dangerous path is this — ripen, and find the God within" (10, 496).

What are the points of similarity? Pannwitz's tone is harsher, more hectoring; Hesse is more emollient, more restrained. Both writers, however, see the earnestness of the task in hand, and both turn to Nietzsche as mentor and vates. For Pannwitz there is something almost Christ-like in Nietzsche's struggle, in the quest for idealism and the achievement of the highest values: Hesse makes no reference to Him here. Both stress effort (Anspannung); both see the need to strike out on the path of loneliness. Hesse seems closer to specific historical events — the humiliation of Germany, the turmoil and the Messianic hopes for renewal (he is aware of the Spartakus movement); Pannwitz is more cosmic, contemplating azure, sun-lit spirits of fire. He did not indulge in humanitarian work in Switzerland as Hesse did (the relief of internees, the editorship of *Die Interniertenzeitung*) but it should not be overlooked that he was briefly involved in discussions with Eduard

Beneš and others on the place of Czechoslovakia within the new map of Europe and sought, in the long essay *Deutschland und Europa* (1918) to envisage a Europe free of petty rivalries. But the idea of Germany's self-realisation under the tutelage of Zarathustra and the praise of a mystical race of Hyperboreans shifts Pannwitz's thought once more into a mystical realm, a world difficult of access and visited by few.

What distinguishes Pannwitz above all from Hermann Hesse is the almost fanatical quest for some vast, all-embracing vision, a compulsive search for oneness and a determination to respond to the totality of things. Udo Rukser places him alongside Simmel and Dilthey in his insistence on stressing the positive interaction of mind and life, a dialectical tension between life as limiting form and life as unlimited flux;[38] August Wiedmann compares him with "those highly eccentric figures" such as Count Keyserling and Rudolf Kassner who attempted to harmonise soul and spirit, thought and being, Eastern and Western notions of the cosmic.[39] Pannwitz's elusive, difficult goal may be seen as the complete re-evaluation of man, art, science and culture envisaged as the expression of an evolving cosmos obeying the laws of eternal recurrence, with Nietzsche-Zarathustra as the supreme prophet. A "holistic dominant" (Wiedmann) becomes more and more apparent in his work, a "cosmopathy" expressing man's deepest spiritual inclinations. The Dalmatian recluse sought nothing less than "the working out of an organic, developing world-view, not a system, but form everywhere." The pedagogue in Pannwitz sought to pronounce that which the autodidact had absorbed — in every field. "That which I had borne within me was formed into mystical, cosmic poetry which I fused with my primeval, elemental world-view [. . .]"[40] A "Symphilosophie" in the spirit of Novalis is the goal, a "Weltstoffbezwingung," a ring of wisdom hammered and refined in the Nietzschean fire. A major statement, over four hundred pages long, appeared in 1926 under the title *Kosmos Atheos*; it was meant as part of a vaster work to be entitled *Die Freiheit des Menschen* (The Freedom of Man). Pannwitz would later explain that atheism was not his premise but rather a philosophy of nature and of consciousness without theological preoccupations. It was when reading Dante's *Divine Comedy*, he explained, that he was overwhelmed by the knowledge that it represented "the crystal form of the lost cosmos"[41] and by the realisation that existence without a "cosmos" was not possible. Pannwitz's stance is religious in that religion, for him, was the worship of cosmic wholeness; transcendental yearnings were of no interest as transcendence represented a form of impotence, a lack of veneration for all that existed. *Kosmos Atheos* is not easily digestible, concerned as it is is with the "Renaissance of vocal music from the spirit and as a creation of Kosmos Atheos," with "a morphological phenomenology, founded on a critique of consciousness and of the basic meaning of mathematics," and with " the Word as a Cosmos in the art work of vocalism." Pannwitz's interest in music had been quickened by an affair with the violinist and singer Margarete Hoffmann; he had also met and greatly admired the young Viennese musician Hugo Kauder who had sent him three compositions for voice and piano using texts from Nietzsche, Otto zur Linde, and Stefan George (he would later set various poems by Pannwitz to music). In *Kosmos Atheos* Pannwitz writes as follows:

> With Hugo Kauder music found its way back to poetry, poetry which had been lost. With reverence and fervour an individual who came from the spiritual world of Mahler and who had set Nietzsche, George, zur Linde, and Pannwitz to music listened with a world-open ear (mit einem welthorchenden ohre) to the deepest secrets of a poem [. . .].[42]

Kauder was able, Pannwitz continues, "to change the drift into musical decay, that atonality which developed from the pantonality of a Mahler, into a constructive tone-row." Long meditations follow on Pythagoras, geometry, the morphology of plants; a Goethean attempt is made to embrace all human knowledge, to express cosmic verities through philosophy, music, mathematics, poetry, biology and art. It is not possible to discuss Pannwitz's own musical compositions here (he had created a five-tone harmony based upon laws known to the pre-Socratic philosophers and in ancient China); the sketches and drawings *Dalmatinische Einsamkeiten* have, somewhat charitably, been described as "recalling the simplicity of outline of the drawings of the Sung dynasty."[43] The impression left by *Kosmos Atheos* is of a restless, monomaniac spirit, seeking to pronounce, demonstrate, amaze and exhort. It is difficult not to think of that "Original" in *Faust II* whose arrogant solipsism Faust robustly rebuked.

In 1929 there appeared the collection of aphorisms and maxims *Trilogie des Lebens* (Trilogy of Life). A turgid pseudo-philosophy gives way to a series of grave utterances: again, a Zarathustrian world is invoked. "The spirit is near, as near as my heart, surprising as a new day! Awake! The morning dawns!"[44] "Existence is godlike! The path is true veneration of all divinity. Thou art that which is created in thee" (24). "Cowardice of poets! Dare, lonely hero! Conjure! Let choirs scream forth! Build temples! [. . .] I am man, the most splendid man, the one who suffered all things" (24–25). One section is entitled "The Utterances of the God Dionysus," another "Zarathustra's Other Temptation," and in this latter we read: "My will is allpowerful, and wild as magic (56) [. . .] The eternal recurrence of all things and the Superman whose great body conceals the soul of the saviour — these are the All! The Over-All!" (58). "The old God is dead and the New Man not yet born — how shall we teach the children, the young? The book of the spirit is finished; the book of things has not yet been written" (62). Zarathustra is a phoenix, reborn in "the fiery burnt offerings of the sun" (76); he laments the evening darkness: "Alas, it is now evening! It is the evening of many evenings, the dark evening of many, many days!" (94). "O Zarathustra, star of stars! Evening star! Sing, o sing a song of evening!" (95) It is in this section that Pannwitz interpolates his personal lament, the sense of loss at his "friend's" collapse, Nietzsche's sunless obliteration; the threnody, however, is short-lived and the section "Morning" greets the sunrise, the quest, the journey into the realms of light: "Morning! Helmsman! Thundering towards the island of the gods!" (113). Further sections include "Nature" (O artist and mother of artists! We are incomparable when imitating thee, for we are thy sons, and thou art not externally, but internally our mother [130].), "The Omniscient Ones" (We omniscient ones are the disk of the sun and the bridge to the Superman [132].), "The Body" (Zarathustra rose from the sea and spake: "This is the body, the body of Man" [135]), "Helena" (I Helena say unto thee, o Zarathustra, that I am equal to thy greatest form, innocent and lovely [148]), "The Dance," "The Satyr," "The Daemon," "Zarathustra's Realm" and "The Goddess of Love." The work finishes with an ecstatic cry: "Arise, ye who are deaf and blind! Arise, ye who are dead! I say unto thee: The World-bell tolls! Rejoice! Rejoice! All shall be well! The Aeon of the earth is born!" (290). This is Zarathustra's Great Midday, the Feast of Feasts, the drunken celebration of triumph, of "Ja-sagen," and Pannwitz is the most exultant acolyte. "And the morning dawned, and a world appeared again in the radiance of its sun, manifest in the magic of its life" (132) — an Adriatic radiance and one which Mombert, as we shall see, hailed and saluted as the dwelling-place of a congenial mind, sunk in the contemplation of a rose and brooding on the "Glut-Gesetze," the passionate laws of the cosmos.[45]

It is interesting at this point to consider the relationship between Pannwitz and Mombert and, later, between Pannwitz and Däubler. Pannwitz had known Mombert's work since 1904 (Mombert, however, had refused to contribute to the Charon); he sent Mombert the *Dionysische Tragödien* in 1913, but it was *Die Krisis der europäischen Kultur* and *Die deutsche Lehre* which elicited a warm response, and a lively correspondence ensued. In 1922 Pannwitz wrote a glowing review of Mombert's *Aeon* drama in *Das Inselschiff* and explained that Mombert was the first great mythic writer (Mythiker) since time immemorial, and that *Aeon* was not a created cosmos but a creative man within a cosmos, a man feeling himself create the cosmos, an ecstatic reaction of the psyche to the cosmogonic process.[46] The *Aeon* drama was "a scream of longing out of chaos, out of love for chaos" (103). The action of such works was "a spiritual-physical trajectory from an 'un-world' though creativity to a world: the peripeteia — finis historiae, aeternitatis" (108). Pannwitz speaks of "a new German spirit of antiquity blossoming from Mombert's work, a sensuous, pan-sensuous rapture," and quotes lines from *Aeon* which portray a rose bush emanating from the poet's skull and sending its tendrils across the rolling earth (109). The two men met for the first time in 1927 in Bayrisch-Zell and later in Dalmatia; on Pannwitz's fiftieth birthday (1931) a Festschrift appeared to which Mombert contributed, singling out Pannwitz as one of the few who were undertaking a comparable cosmic journey. "On one of the manifold paths of the great Cosmos, during my passage through the star called Earth, it was a joy for me to have met his mystical figure — it was the assuagement of my spiritual loneliness by the radiance of a kindred spirit".[47] Pannwitz in turn published an article on Mombert in *Die literarische Welt* to commemorate the latter's sixtieth birthday (1932); Mombert's seventieth was also marked by a letter from Charlotte Pannwitz, writing from Koločep, and Mombert drafted letters to Pannwitz a few weeks before his death in Winterthur. It was to Pannwitz that Mombert had sent his succinct, apodictic credo: "When all that is created, all the cosmic entities pass, have passed, there remains the Creative Spirit — this, the dream and the measure of all things. Dare to represent this!";[48] it was also to Pannwitz that Mombert addressed that letter of loneliness and isolation, acknowledging him as "a difficult peak to climb," a writer lost in "swirling cloud and mist, ice-bound, with plunging precipices, accessible only to the very few." And what of Däubler? The writers were less close: the sonnet Pannwitz composed on Däubler's death speaks of other goals, but also of the gratitude felt for Däubler's great dream of the sun which bathes in lambent rays both North and Nile (and Däubler's massive head is greeted, circumscribed by the sparkling rainbow).[49] Däubler greatly admired *Der Tod Baldurs* but had little interest in the philosophical writings; Pannwitz struggled through *Das Nordlicht* (The Light of the North), cursing its bulk and claiming to regret having to read it, but also admitting its significance to Hofmannsthal.[50] The two men met for the first time on the Mondsee in 1921; two years later Pannwitz reviewed *Das Nordlicht* in *Das Inselschiff*, now calling it "an apocalypse born backwards and forwards, a revelation [. . .] a World-Myth."[51] More substantial is an article written in 1956 where Pannwitz reviewed the *Dichtungen und Schriften* of Däubler which had appeared that year: Däubler is described as having his origins in expressionism, but reaching far beyond this movement. The discussion is a sympathetic one and Däubler is extolled for insisting upon radiant energies and spiritual transfiguration. He is seen, finally, as standing closer to Apollo than to Dionysus, a poet who insisted that Christ was a manifestation of the sun-god, suffused by that spiritual light which illuminates all things.[52]

Pannwitz, as polymath, sought to embrace and experience all manifestations of human history and knowledge. He measured himself constantly against the great — Nietzsche, Dante, Goethe, George and Hölderlin; his work, he insisted, was centaurion, fusing mind and body, philosophy and poetry (the essay *Was ich Nietzsche und George danke* describes an experience in the forests of Thuringia where the image of the centaur Chiron suddenly arose before him). The essay *Logos Eidos Bios* (1930) sought to reduce philosophical concepts to images, and to face abstractions with sensuous immediacy of understanding. Recognition of his prolific writing and high intellectual endeavours came in the appointment to the Prussian Academy of Arts in 1932; he left, however, in the Spring of 1933, unable to pledge his support for Hitler. Deprived of what little income he earned in Germany he led an increasingly precarious existence, reworking earlier material, translating and meditating upon the darkening political situation in Europe. He went to Switzerland in 1939 and stayed until the Spring of 1940; the return to Koločep was fraught with difficulties. During the war, with fighting in Yugoslavia, bombardment, Italian and German occupation, Pannwitz continued to write, on the human predicament, on destiny, on Nietzsche and the necessary transformation of man. He finally returned to Switzerland after 1945 and lived there till his death. The centaur Chiron, we remember, was healer and tutor to the heroes Jason and Achilles. Pannwitz likewise sought to diagnose and to seek a healing solution to the ills of post-Second World War Europe. The final essays eschew the cosmic vision, seeking to analyse the sources of nihilism in the atomic age; the insistence is always upon the greatest cultural manifestations of the past and their abiding relevance to modern man. *The Crisis of European Culture* was republished in 1947, and the following year saw the treatise *Politics and the World Age*; this and the essay *Peace* (1950) are mature reflections on culture, democracy, social and economic factors. Nietzsche's concept of a "good European" is preserved to the last, a figure of nobility who can, Pannwitz believes, serve as a model for the future.[53]

This chapter will now conclude with a brief discussion of Pannwitz's lyric poetry. In 1926 Hans Carl published the selection *Urblick* (Primeval Vision), and in 1963 a more comprehensive anthology appeared, *Wasser wird sich ballen* (Water Will Mould Itself). For many, Pannwitz's poetry is "Gedankenlyrik" (philosophical poetry) in the manner of Hebbel; others see his verse as being "a rare combination of plasticity and musicality." Three poets are manifestly of interest here: Nietzsche, George, and Hölderlin. Like Nietzsche, Pannwitz cultivated lyric poetry alongside philosophical speculation, and we know that both Nietzsche and George were revelation itself. Nietzsche's achievement as a lyric poet is assured, his predilection for impressionistic and highly concentrated utterances, also longer odes, or hymns, as well as his cultivation of epigrams are characteristic. Frequently in Nietzsche a lonely individual is portrayed, and a mood is crystallised in elemental images; in the longer utterances, the *Dionysos-Dithyramben*, for example, the style is staccato and disconnected, where "joyful savagery" is juxtaposed with a shrill jocularity.[54] Landscapes are landscapes of the soul, where desert, rock and sun hint at some fearful illumination to come. Nietzsche's admiration for Heine, the latter's "divine malice" is frequently in evidence; it is entirely lacking in Pannwitz, who is closer to George and shares with him the classical idea of formal beauty, a sense of solemn consecration, and element of incantation and a rigorous self-discipline. Hölderlin's presence is found in the frequent use of Alcaic metre and the description of landscapes shot through with some spiritual presence. Pannwitz is essentially eclectic and the poetry is cerebral; there is little sensuous sound-painting but an obsessive pattern of ideas and images derived from an elemental landscape (sun, rock, star, water, lightning, mountain, island, stone, gold) suffused with literary and religious topoi (soul, light, chaos, ring, blueness, rainbow). The poetry is cosmic rather than philosophical: it views human nature *sub specie aeternitatis*, ignoring the social, the domestic and the purely human dimension. The following discussion must be highly selective but will attempt to point out the poetry's characteristic features; some utterances are lapidary and grave, some are couched as odes, while others use strictly classical verse forms.

An early poem, "Das totengedicht" (The Poem of the Dead) has already been mentioned: it was published in the *Blätter für die Kunst* and greatly admired by George, who called it "music for unhappy souls." It is a long, haunting poem written in trochaic pentameters which tells of a mandrake existence, poised between normality and abnormality, remote from the community of the living. (Much later Pannwitz would describe it as "a unique and solitary wondrous flower, born under the star of Arnim's *Isabella von Ägypten*.")[55] It was a common enthusiasm for German Romanticism that drew Pannwitz and Otto zur Linde together at this time, but Pannwitz distanced himself from the flirtation with irrationalism after the meeting with George and his circle. The collection *Primeval Vision* (1926) is prefaced by the grave utterance "Over the roaring primeval waters / Circled the word, its omphalos sealed"[56]: the poetic act springs immediately into the world as Pallas Athene sprang from the head of Zeus, Hölderlin's "Reinentsprung-enes" whose origins are a mystery. "Fremde" (Strangers) stresses the incomprehensible nature of human existence, where poetry is ignited by "an alien light in an alien world" (81). *Urblick* also contains that short poem which is used as a motto at the beginning of this chapter: the poet is associated with age and petrified gleaming flames, with a lonely crow in a millennial wilderness, with arcane incantation, ceaseless water and a vatic communication with chthonic powers (68). The glory of the cosmos, particularly of the radiant star Sirius, is extolled in the pithy interchange between Death and the "Sterbling," an insignificant mortal man:

"Art thou ready?"
"I must see the star Sirius again."
"So thou wishest to live?"
"I know as little of life as the others."
"And Sirius?"
"I saw it as a child, with fervour and with shuddering ecstasy. I suffered, then, and created."
"Didst though forget it?"
"Yes, I forgot Sirius."
"I shall now lead thee to the feast of death."
"Ah, I am not ready."
"Do what thou must."
"I must see the star Sirius again."(79)

The dross of quotidian existence may extinguish man's longings for transcendence, but the "Sterbling," before extinction, longs to see the glittering stellar fire once more. One is forcibly reminded of Ernst Barlach's *Der arme Vetter* (The Poor Cousin, 1918): the man-made lantern may appear to give a brighter light than the splendour of Sirius, but spiritual illumination triumphs to bring about a mystical excarnation.

The second major anthology, *Wasser wird sich ballen* (Water will mould itself) appeared some thirty years later, in 1963: the title refers to the description in Goethe's late poem *Paria* of the miraculous moulding of water into a glistening ball by the chaste, pure wife of the high priest. Here purity of vision is closely linked with creativity, and a cluster of images (ball, sphere, ring) hint at that "aus sich rollendes Rad," the "wheel rolling out of itself" that Zarathustra had associated with innocence and eternity. (Otto zur Linde had also elevated the sphere to mystical proportions in his *Die Kugel. Eine Philosophie in Versen* which appeared in 1909, with a second edition in 1923). The poems in *Wasser wird sich ballen* tend to be longer, less grave; several poems address Zarathustra, Nietzsche, Stefan George, Mombert and Däubler, and we find the earlier themes (loneliness, eternity). The anthology begins with "The Poem of the Dead"; this is succeeded by "Die Einsamkeit" (Loneliness) which praises this condition using images of height, lightning, radiance and gold. Further poems extol the watchman; echoes of Goethe (Lynkeus) are noticeable. The "Song of the Miner" takes up the Romantic theme of descent into subrational darkness and the experience of luminous treasure and truth; of interest is also the utterance "I am the azure flower, and I beg / You should not touch, nor ask, nor beg of me [. . .]"[57] The highest vision is beyond interrogation, and poetry and love are an ultimate revelation. A spiritual aristocracy is adumbrated in "Those who have the gift of radiant eyes," the Biblical "To him that hath shall be given"; those blessed with the joy of luminous transcendence see strength and beauty everywhere and, with bounteous love, they bless and affirm (243). The undifferentiated mass, Pannwitz implies, lives a brutal and meaningless existence, and it is only the few who have the gift of creative energy.

There are two important poems in this collection which directly relate to Nietzsche, one is a "Hymn of Praise" entitled "To Zarathustra" and the other a long ode with "Nietzsche" as its lapidary title. "To Zarathustra" is written in classical form and greets Zarathustra rising from the glowing sunrise:

> As the light lifts thee, Zarathustra! The sun is azure and the air is
>   azure and azure
> In radiance — the miracle of the dome surrounds us
> The shuddering heaven and horizon
> High, earthly! But the holy song
> Resounds against the diamantine waves, and thy voice
> Shatters against the reef [. . .]

(38)

Zarathustra is portrayed as artist, as sculptor, rising in the "midday mirror of islands," emerging with serpent, eagle and laughing lion; he "blossoms above us, storm of the cosmos . . . primeval sun, filling the womb of earth and fructifying it" (39). The world of Greece and Rome has passed, but Pannwitz greets the Hyperboreans: they are the heirs of Zarathustra, living in golden innocence. The poem ends with a reference to the cranes of Ibycus and to vengeance, acknowledging the gift of poetry from the latter, but seizing the "arrow from the god," from Zarathustra himself who comes to destroy the moribund and the meretricious. It is as a disciple that Pannwitz speaks, a god-intoxicated acolyte: the reference to Bacchus/Dionysus hints again at frenzy and life-affirmation. The poem "Nietzsche" speaks as "life-tearing ploughshare" and "roaring bull," announcing "a new world, a new soul, a new meaning, a new man" (329). He scatters the seeds of his sickness and transforms them into skylarks, his "thousand deaths" becoming Easter and resurrection; he takes man to a high place and shows him the glories of earth; the burden of god's death, of a new freedom is imposed. The destroyer is the creator: Nietzsche's agony and exaltation are extolled in a rapt incantation, and the god Zarathustra is portrayed as the deity whose kiss is the kiss of life.

> I bless the cosmos
> I bless mankind
> I bless all essences
> I bless all things
> I bless words and values
> I bless deeds and destinies
> I bless evil and good
> I bless bodies and souls
> I bless sorrows and all joys.
>
> (332)

The poem ends on a note of fervent exultation, praising Man above all, to whom all seas flow, all mountains rear, all dawns rise, burning in an ecstasy of love.

The poem to Stefan George is more restrained and is written in classical Alcaic metre:

> Late it was, very late did I find, highest and closest! The voice
> With which to speak to thee. Silent my song praised the dead.
> Often our paths crossed, and yet
> I then believed that I was of merit [. . .]
>
> (40)

George found him and saved him, Pannwitz, disciple of "the loneliest one." This poem reiterates what Pannwitz has written elsewhere; as

Nietzsche created visionary ecstasy, so George created "norms," and the poem ends in gratitude, thanking the older poet for the fruitful *word*, the plastic *sense*, exultant *life* and the joy of *form*. A second poem (333) is similarly hagiographical, seeing George as master, mentor, and bringer of light, a poet whose iron control conceals a passionate devotion. The ninth of the *Illyrian Elegies* speaks again of George's greatness and Pannwitz's gratitude; Hugo von Hofmannsthal is also mentioned, as is Wolfskehl, Otto zur Linde, Albert Verwey and Otokar Březina (152)[58] and it comes as no surprise to find Mombert and Däubler in the pantheon. The poem "An Mombert zwischen Ragusa and Venezia" (To Mombert between Dubrovnik and Venice) is a further act of homage.

In his review of *Das Nordlicht* Pannwitz commented that Däubler belonged to a generation that was almost extinct: did he feel this about himself and Mombert? The grandiose plans, the utopian visions, the homilies and hyperborean effusions fell on deaf ears. The autodidact who could "conjure up out of nothing a German culture in any field" eked out his penurious existence in domestic confusion at Koločep and was troubled, on the mainland, by distant artillery and the rumbling of lorries at night, driving from Greece and Albania. A late poem, "Die Dichter" (The Poets), speculates that the poetic age is past, that age "which stood in highest efflorescence when I was young" (348).

> Long I waited, long I hoped
> For a generation to succeed me, but none
> Came who were genuine [. . .] I remained true to poets I loved,
> I have forgotten naught of their music, yet
> I am alone, lamenting autumn,
> I, a swan, alone, poor swan song!
>
> (349)

The elderly poet, after the war, acted as spokesman, as we know, and lecturer on the post war age, the atomic age, yet there was little resonance for "Weltalter," "Aeon," or "Kairos." The unfinished work, forbidding in its nimiety, awaits publication and interpretation. I have uncharitably compared him with the Baccalaureus in *Faust II,* that "Original" who arrogates to himself omniscience: a gentler picture would be of a lonely sage, speaking "into the earth" in devout contemplation. The final picture is one of the octogenarian who, "before leaving this life in lamentation," addresses the cosmos and seeks to know when he would see it again. The reply is comforting: "Here, before this flower, which stands on this path, at this hour, this precious second" (356).[59] It will be such moments of pious gratitude that will remain in the mind of at least one reader far longer than the rodomontade and the pretentiousness.

Notes

[1] *Hugo von Hoffmannsthal — Rudolf Pannwitz Briefwechsel 1907–1926*, ed. by Gerhard Schuster (Fischer: Frankfurt a. M., 1993), 733.

[2] Hugo von Hoffmannsthal, "Preuße und Österreicher. Ein Schema," *Prosa* vol. 3, ed. by Herbert Steiner (Fischer: Frankfurt a. M., 1952) 407–408. It was published in the *Vossische Zeitung* as "Der Preuße und der Österreicher," 1917.

[3] *Hofmannsthal — Pannwitz Briefwechsel*, ed. cit., 783.

[4] Rudolf Pannwitz, *Wasser wird sich ballen. Gesammelte Gedichte* (Water will Mould Itself. Collected Poems), (Stuttgart: Klett, 1963), 359.

[5] Rudolf Pannwitz, *Was ich Nietzsche und George danke* (What I Owe Nietzsche and George), (Amsterdam: Castrum Peregrini, Jg. 38, 1989) Heft 189–190, 94.

[6] Rudolf Pannwitz, *Trilogie des Lebens* (Munich-Feldafing: Hans Carl Verlag, 1929), 96.

[7] *Literarische Manifeste der Jahrhundertwende, 1890–1910*, op.cit., 476.

[8] Quoted in Alfred Guth, *Rudolf Pannwitz. Un Européen, penseur et poète allemand en quête de totalité* (Paris: Librairie Klincksieck, 1975), 46.

[9] Guth, 92. (The review was in *Die Tat*, Leipzig, December 1910).

[10] Guth, 96.

[11] Rudolph Pannwitz, *Dionysische Tragödien* (Nuremberg: Hans Carl Verlag, 1913). This is the dedicatory motto.

[12] Rudolf Pannwitz, *Dionysische Tragödien*, 16.

[13] *Dionysische Tragödien*, 63.

[14] Edmund Wilson, *The Wound and the Bow. Seven Studies in Literature* (London: W. H. Allen, 1952), 263

[15] *Dionysische Tragödien*, 83–84.

[16] *Dionysische Tragödien*, 192.

[17] *Dionysische Tragödien*, 249.

[18] *Hugo von Hofmannsthal — Rudolf Pannwitz Briefwechsel*, op. cit., 129. The reference to 'Hebbel und verhebbelt' is a pun referring to Hebbel's predilection for abstruse configurations.

[19] Guth, 332.

[20] Guth, 340.

[21] Guth, 362

[22] Guth, 419.

[23] Lutz Weltmann, "Eminent Europeans: An Approach to the work of Rudolf Pannwitz," *German Life and Letters* 9 (1956), 307.

[24] August Wiedmann, *The German Quest for Primal Origins in Art, Culture and Politics 1900–1933* (Lewiston/Queenston/Lampeter: Edwin Mellen Press, 1995), 31.

[25] Rudolf Pannwitz, *Die Krisis der Europäischen Kultur* (Nuremberg: Hans Carl Verlag, 1917), 30. (Hereafter page reference in the text.)

[26] *Hugo von Hofmannsthal — Rudolf Pannwitz Briefwechsel*, op. cit., 22.

[27] *Briefwechsel*, 649.

[28] *Briefwechsel*.

[29] *Briefwechsel*, 226.

[30] *Briefwechsel*, 420, 649. Alfred Mombert also received a copy and wrote an enthusiastic reply (8 November 1920).

[31] Rudolf Pannwitz, *Die deutsche Lehre* (Nuremberg: Hans Carl Verlag, 1919), 1. (Hereafter page reference in the text.)

[32] Georg Brandes, *Die romantische Schule in Deutschland*, in *Die Hauptströmungen der Litteratur des neunzehnten Jahrhunderts* (Berlin Charlottenburg: 1900), 21–22.

[33] Rudolf Pannwitz, *Baldurs Tod. Ein Maifestspiel* (Nuremberg: Hans Carl Verlag, 1919), 21–22.

[34] *Briefwechsel*, 470.

[35] Rudolf Pannwitz, *Aufruf zum heiligen Kriege*, (*Flugblatt* 6) (Munich-Feldafing, 1920), 1. (Hereafter page references in the text.)

[36] Rudolf Pannwitz, *Einführung in Nietzsche* (*Flugblatt* 8), (Munich-Feldafing, 1920), 1. (Hereafter page references in the text.)

[37] Hermann Hesse, *Gesammelte Werke* (Frankfurt a. M.: Suhrkamp), vol. 11, 39–40. (Hereafter page references in the text.)

[38] Udo Rukser, *Über den Denker Rudolf Pannwitz* (Meisenheim am Glan: Anton Hain Verlag, 1970), 2.

[39] Wiedmann, 31.

[40] Rudolf Pannwitz, *Umriß meines Lebens und Lebenswerkes* (1968), 147.

[41] *Umriß*, 150, 312.

[42] Rudolf Pannwitz, *Kosmos Atheos* (Munich-Feldafing: Hans Carl, 1926), 166.

[43] Weltmann, 312.

[44] Rudolf Pannwitz, *Trilogie des Lebens* (Munich-Feldafing: Hans Carl, 1929), 132. (Hereafter page references in the text.)

[45] *A. M. Briefe* contains twenty-two letters to Pannwitz.

[46] In *Das Inselschiff* 3, (Leipzig, 1922), 104–109.

[47] *Rudolf Pannwitz Fünfzig Jahre* (Munich-Feldafing: Hans Carl, no date (1931)), 49.

[48] *A.M. Briefe*, op. cit., 47.

[49] Rudolf Pannwitz, *Wasser wird sich ballen*, 153.

[50] *Briefwechsel*, 422.

[51] "Theodor Däublers Hauptwerk," *Das Inselschiff* 4, (Leipzig 1923), 52–59.

[52] "Zu Däubler: Dichtungen und Schriften," *Merkur* (1956), 1117.

[53] For an account of Pannwitz's late essays see Weltmann.

[54] W. D. Williams, "Nietzsche and Lyric Poetry," *Reality and Creative Vision in German Lyric Poetry*, ed. by August Closs (London: Butterworth, 1963), 85–89.

[55] Rudolf Pannwitz, *Was ich Nietzsche und George danke*, 71.

[56] Rudolf Pannwitz, *Urblick* (Munich-Feldafing: Hans Carl, 1926). (Hereafter as page references in the text.)

[57] Rudolf Pannwitz, *Wasser wird sich ballen*, op. cit., 236. (Hereafter as page references in the text.)

[58] There are striking parallels between the German and Czech writers: Březina (1886–1929) was also originally a pedagogue and lived as a recluse, seeking to evolve a complete philosophical and artistic system. His books sought to present an interlocking interpretation of existence, moving form despair to salvation.

[59] For a perceptive study of Pannwitz's examination of Nietzsche's concept of the Eternal Recurrence see Hans-Joachim Koch, "Die Nietzsche-Rezeption durch Rudolf Pannwitz," *Nietzsche Studien* 26 (1997), 441–467.

Alfred Mombert.
Courtesy of Schiller Nationalmuseum
and Deutsches Literaturarchiv, Marbach.

2 : Alfred Mombert

> Many find themselves in a common danger when
> confronted by great spiritual entities. They keep their
> distance from them and cover them with a blanket of
> ignorance, throughout the whole of their lives, as
> phosphorus is kept under water so that there is no danger
> of fire. And yet to be submerged in Mombert's visions
> would do no reader any harm. . .
>
> — Hans Carossa

"I HAVE NO TIME to worry about 'the times'. It is my task to create lasting harmonies."[1] This apodictic statement by Mombert reflects the earnestness of his quest, the refusal to be distracted by arbitrary historical manifestations from his task of praise and creativity. "I arrived at the Rhine via Orion and the Pleiades" (2, 609) is another self-description, one not of whimsy, but a serious comment on that cosmic viewpoint which he came to see as his particular position. He was born in Karlsruhe in 1872; after his legal studies and his doctorate he practised as a lawyer in Heidelberg until 1906. Thereafter he devoted himself entirely to writing and to religious and philosophical study. He was a close friend of the poet Richard Dehmel, who thought highly of his poetry, as did the writer Stanislaus Przybyszewski. His first collection of lyric poetry, *Tag und Nacht*, appeared in 1894, to be followed by *Der Glühende* (The Fervent One, 1896), *Die Schöpfung* (Creation,1897), *Der Denker* (The Thinker 1901), *Die Blüte des Chaos* (The Blossom of Chaos, 1905) and *Der Sonne Geist* (Spirit of the Sun, 1905). Between 1907 and 1911 Mombert composed the *Aeon* trilogy, a symphonic drama of the human spirit which portrayed harmony, disharmony and return to serenity after alienation and disruption. Mombert spent the First World War as a officer in Poland; he published *Der Held der Erde* (Hero of the Earth) in 1919 and *Atäir* in 1925. Another psychological drama, *Aigla* appeared in 1929. In 1928 Mombert became a member of the Prussian Academy of Arts: being of Jewish extraction, he was removed in 1933. He ignored the increasing barbarism that surrounded him and worked on the completion of his last epic,

Sfaira der Alte (Sfaira the Ancient); he was seized in 1940 and transported, with his sister, as we shall see, to the concentration camp at Gurs in the south of France (Carl Einstein had also been detained there). It was in this camp that the second part of *Sfaira* was completed. Mombert was released in 1941 after much tribulation by the intervention of Hans Reinhart. who brought him to Winterthur: here Mombert died, aged seventy, in 1942. A German-Jewish writer then, who strove to ignore the banal and the ugly, seeing in the flash of light in a tourmaline crystal ultimate truth itself, and who insisted on the following programme: "When all that is created, when all the cosmic entities pass and are gone, then it is the creative spirit in these entities that remains. This, the vision and the measure of all things. Have courage, and portray this!" (2, 617)

Mombert's early poetry must be seen against the background of that particular artistic tendency to which the terms neoromanticism, symbolism or Jugendstil are uneasily applied; it differs from these in that it seeks a transcendence of the more trivial topoi of impressionism and the frivolity of certain authors associated with Jugendstil and reflects a fervent monistic nature worship, a sense of elemental wonder found in the poetry of Richard Dehmel. Jost Hermand has traced the movement away from artistic narcissism toward a type of sentient cosmic mysticism which characterized much of the poetry of the *Jahrhundertwende*.[2] It was Arno Holz who prepared the way in his *Phantasus* collection of 1898–99, the ornamental elements giving way to a desire to see human life from a cosmic standpoint, where the naturalist-impressionist aspects are subsumed under some wider, universal gaze: the poet may walk down the Friedrichstrasse on a dark winter's morning, but is transported in his mind to a green meadow with castles and white nymphs, or he speculates upon his previous existence as an iris, seven billion years before his physical birth. His erstwhile colleague and collaborator Johannes Schlaf would likewise reject the tenets of naturalism and, in *Frühling* (Spring, 1896) speculate upon monistic pantheism and dissolution and call upon the sun in an ecstasy of joy. The floral, decorative elements of Jugendstil give way in the poetry of these years to a more solemn, hieratic quality where life is frequently extolled as a dark mystery. The poetry of Richard Dehmel is exemplary here, one of Mombert's closest colleagues; in *Zwei Menschen* (Two People, 1901) the portrayal of the sexual act moves towards transfiguration as the lovers are transformed into mythical, religious figures — Isis, Osiris, Luke the Evangelist and even personified light itself. A pan-erotic, cosmic principle suffuses the world of silver birches, swans, and dark lakes and adds a more dramatic, portentous quality. We have argued elsewhere that the imagistic character of Nietzsche's writing is striking and it is particularly prominent in *Zarathustra* where the imagery is so replete, so associative in its interaction that a narrative structure takes second place. The "greatest linguistic genius since Goethe"[3] injected a dynamic and rhapsodic fervour into the impressionist poetry of neoromanticism; Heller's claim that Nietzsche's fame as author of *Zarathustra* "rested massively as if on a throne designed by some *art-nouveau* or *Jugendstil* artist"[4] needs modification. The dramatic force of Nietzsche's writing transfigured the moon-drenched landscapes of symbolism into something more vital; both the drabness of naturalism and the *symboliste* effeteness were to be swept away by images of lightning, fire, storm and hammer. A more heightened, cosmic dimension entered the topoi of Jugendstil; this is noticeable in the poetry and prose of Max Dauthendey and Stanislaus Przybyszewski, two fervent admirers of Mombert. And Mombert will likewise move away from preciosity towards the blossom of chaos and the projection of a vast reveller into the cosmos, an emblem of joy and Dionysian energy.

The collection *Tag und Nacht*, published when Mombert was twenty-two years old, contains much that is redolent of the impressionism of the age, a Rilkean world of hushed and rapt nature appreciation, some poems dealing with the plight of the poor and others which are highly stylised, yet an individual tone also breaks through. "Die Stadt" (The Town: 1, 24) depicts the squalor of the town, the dark streets, consumptive workers, the stench of factories and "filth, filth, filth" — yet there is a rapturous transfiguration beneath the radiance of the sun which breaks through the miasma, illuminating the gold of the cathedral dome, the carriages and the white stallions. The poem "Abend" (Evening: 1, 31), with the fervent conversation between man and woman, owes much to Dehmel in its "Verklärte Nacht" atmosphere; "Schwüle" (sultriness: 1, 46) is reminiscent of the poetry of the Swiss writer Conrad Ferdinand Meyer and betrays much *précieux* refinement in the portrayal of the dark lake, the slim youth and the rose petals. What *is* distinctive is Mombert's remarkable ability to create dramatic pictures of a concentrated intensity: "Mondaufgang" (Moonrise: 1, 48–9) with its description of the rising moon and the murder of the man who scorned the rapt fervour of those who were watching it, creates an atmosphere of menace and strange beauty; "Die Nacht" (The Night: 1, 53) is a succinct and impressive portrayal of the mad king upon his balcony, demanding proof that the sun would rise again, whilst the grinning crowd cowers beneath. *Day and Night* has much that is derivative but also a few poems of genuine originality, an intensity which hints at that which is to come. Mombert sent the poems in

September 1894, to Detlev von Liliencron, a poet revered by Rilke as well as by Dehmel; he explained to Liliencron that the poems were "warmly emotional" rather than "critically structured," but that nevertheless he wished to burden Liliencron with this "juvenilia" (*A. M. Briefe* 10).

The second collection, *Der Glühende*, is dedicated to Richard Dehmel: *Day and Night* had been "Gedichte einer Jugend" (poems of youth), whereas *Der Glühende* is "ein Gedicht-Werk" (a poetic work). It is an anthology that greatly impressed Stanislaus Przybyszewski who, in the following year, dedicated his own *Auf den Wegen der Seele* (On the Paths of the Soul) to "the magus, the 'Fervent One' Alfred Mombert" and who also published in his Polish journal *Zyćie* a glowing appreciation of Mombert and his work. "For some years now I have been following the career of this astonishing soul, lost in the dreams of primeval, eternal Being, listening and harkening to the songs that are not of this earth" (*A. M. Briefe* 211). Martin Buber likewise demonstrated the high esteem in which he held Mombert by later dedicating (1908) his *Ekstatische Konfessionen* to him and by quoting him in *Daniel*.[5] In *Der Glühende* the poetic "Ich" steps forth into a more tumultuous world than hitherto, a world shot through with pain, ecstasy, torture and fearful joy, a world strangely compounded of *Phantasus* and the *Dionysos-Dithyramben*; we are now on the threshold of expressionism. "Diese wilde Glut" — this wild, fervour, Mombert explains, was permitted to have its fling ("austoben"), after which the poet was cured (*A. M. Briefe* 2). The whole cycle was to be read as a whole, the eighty-eight poems illustrating a strange, psychic journey; the landscape is metaphysical, not depicting nature in a representational manner, but bringing together various impressions received by the poet's mind to create a new world, governed by his own subjective mood. Concessions made to contemporary reality (railways, labourers, slums) are few: the reader moves through a world compounded of *Zarathustra*, Max Klinger, and Böcklin.

The cycle begins with the death of a prophet, and the imperious command to step forth into life. Images of beauty, blood, and pain predominate as the poetic "Ich," beyond good and evil, prays to the Father figure and exults in the slaughter of innocents (1, 69). He is carried downstream towards a silver waterfall, rejoicing in life's rhapsodic plenitude and the fearful danger of cliff and cataract. The tone of these poems, mostly unrhymed snatches of an ode-like structure, is aggressive, ecstatic; the portrayal of the writhing women upon the rocks, the plethora of violent verbs ("zuckt! bäumt! windet sich! empor!") and the image of painful light derives from the *Dionysos-Dithyramben* (1,

73); the iconography of desert, light, cliff, and torrent betrays the Nietzschean presence. After a break in the text the mood shifts; a gulf is drawn between the vulgar attitude of the mob and the aloof poet, remote in azure loneliness or in the company of a "Weib." In one grotesque utterance the poet is seized and charged with the theft of — a potato. His persona resumes its stature and arrogates to itself the right to judge and condemn: he brings no solace, but rejoices in visions of "Schöpferkraft" (creative power), "Stolz" (pride) and "rasende Sehnsucht" (raving longing: 1, 80).

After conveying moods of defiance, exhortation and an awareness of threat the poems now form a cluster portraying loneliness and melancholy. Mombert's ability to create, with a few deft touches, a tangible situation which possesses a baleful, symbolic extension is found above all in the poem beginning "Ich saß auf rotem Pfühl im Prunkgemach" (I sat on a red pillow in a splendid room: 1, 80): the poet, in a trance, gazes at the woman who attempts — in vain — to clean the grimy windows. Mombert explained in a letter that the poem expressed the sickening awareness of failure by one who had sought to unravel life's mysteries: only the "most fearful melancholy remained." "I wrote this poem in an evil — yet splendid — moment" (*A. M. Briefe* 2). But rational explanations, the same letter continues, are unsatisfactory. "Do not seek for thoughts when reading my poetry, nor insert any — I advise you to surrender yourself utterly to the torrents and the feelings which it inspires, as you would to a piece of music." Melancholy, then, and thoughts of decline — the fervent one, "der Glühende," knows of such moments, of the "marble sadness of existence" and portrays them in a series of poems couched in a modern setting: the train rushing into the tunnel with the passenger, with trembling finger, seeking to find how long it was, and seeing the word "endless" (1, 93); the retreat into the corner of the room, as dark figures climb up outside to barricade the windows (1, 94). Yet violent energy also flickers and breaks through, as verbs expressing extreme vehemence ("zerblitzt," "zerschmettert") and neologisms ("prachtumbrandet," "gewitterschwelgend") re-emerge.

Wildness and melancholy give way in turn to a gentler tone, with images of snow, forest, and "Heimatgefühl"; the poet is lost in rapt contemplation and self-absorption. The short utterance "Schlafend trägt man mich / in mein Heimatland" (Sleeping I am carried / into my homeland: 1, 102) so moved Przybyszewski that he took its third line, "Ferne komm ich her" (I come from afar) as the title for his memoirs. (When Max Dauthendey's remains were brought home from the Dutch East Indies in 1930 it would be these lines which were sung to commemorate the occasion, with music by Armin Kalb.) Przy-byszewski responded to the Nietzschean stance of *Der Glühende*, the soul wracked in some fearful torment or exulting within an archetypal landscape, but the quieter moments are equally important, the joy de-spite pain, and the desire to praise: "Mein Haupt zu heben aus den Kis-sen. / Mein Haupt zu heben in die Herrlichkeit. / Mein Haupt zu heben in den Gesang" (1, 103). (To lift my head up from the pillows / To lift my head up into glory / To lift my head into song.) The Jugendstil element is also present, the swirling clouds, blossom and fruit, as is the dash of chinoiserie — the fishing scene, the gentle friend-ship and that world of limpid loveliness portrayed in Hans Bethge's translations of 1907 (and Mahler's *Song of the Earth*). And this remark-able collection ends not with defiance, or despair, but a hushed aware-ness at the grave of the poet's father of some eternal spirit, "das Ewige," that suffuses and sustains all phenomena.

In *Die Schöpfung* (1897) a creative process is extolled, and the mystery of existence is portrayed: a landscape at once familiar and also remote is created by a series of striking images. In this landscape fig-ures, voices, and eidola express and announce an awareness of awe, joy and sublimity. A German-Oriental axis prevails, reminiscent of Hölder-lin's concept of the "vaterländische Umkehr," the journey into remote realms before the return to the familiar locus; there are frequent refer-ences to sun, palms, sofas, and tents, and the praise of "Rumi" the thirteenth century Persian mystic and founder of the order of the Mev-levi dervishes whose mystic gyrations were the outward representation of the circling movement of the spheres. Closer to home, the poetry of Goethe's *Westöstlicher Divan* (the Hafis poetry) may also have provided an impetus. The two references (1, 152 and 158) to the remote Chil-ean island of Solas y Gomez (some sixteen hundred miles west of the Chilean seaboard, which Chamisso had visited in 1816 and described in his poem of that name) brings Hölderlin again to mind, the poet's unique reference to Tinian, the island in the West Pacific that seemed to him the furthest point his endangered imagination could reach. For Mombert, as we know, the journey would be longer, to Orion and be-yond, as the later poetry will show. *Die Schöpfung* tells of forest, moon and snow, of desert, sun and palm, of man, and woman, of origins and destinies. The poet's father and mother move through this landscape, vulnerable and yet noble: it was in their memory that Mombert sank two gold rings into the sea (on February 22 1914) off the island of Za-kynthos in the Ionian Sea ("a patre, a matre") as his notebooks tell us (*A. M. Briefe* 194).

The best known poem of this collection is "'Stürz' ein, o Seele, und erwache im Chaos!'" (Collapse o soul, and awake in chaos!: 1, 130), a poem frequently quoted in anthologies of expressionist poetry. The imagery is again Nietzschean: Zarathustra's awareness that "one must have chaos within oneself to give birth to a dancing star" (4, 19) emphasises the need for amoral energy, for a daring vitality which is at the heart of all creation. The soul must "collapse," and "awaken in chaos": rigid structures must give way to fecund disorder. The rhapsodic, cosmic sweep of much of Mombert's poetry, together with Walt Whitman's pantheistic fervour and Nietzsche's vitalism fed many of the sources of early expressionism. (It is also of interest that Herwarth Walden, who became editor of the vitally important journal *Der Sturm* in 1910, organised a reading of Mombert's poetry on 19 January 1906 in Berlin, and that Alban Berg felt drawn to set to music three of the poems from *Der Glühende*: the first of these, the famous "sleeping / I am carried. . ." was also inserted by Franz Marc and Wassily Kandinsky into their *Blauer Reiter* volume in 1912.) The ecstatic tone in Mombert also anticipates the hymn-like poetry of Werfel and, indeed, the excesses of Becher and other lesser lights: "Du Glut und Pracht! Du meine Schöpfermacht! Du Meer! Du Sonne! Adlerschrei!" (Rapture or Splendour, you! You my creative power! You sea! You sun! An eagle's cry!: 1, 191) and similar utterances prepares the way for the "O Mensch!" hyperbole of twenty years later. Mombert is attempting to express how the vital tension between complementary opposites pulses throughout eternity and also through the eternal recurrence of all things; the four great "wounds" that bleed through creation are defined as "Sonne, Feuer, Weib und Meer" (Sun, Fire, Woman and Sea: 1, 200). The tone is one of high seriousness, interrupted by whimsy (the addresses to the reader in the early part of the collection, and the preference for the year 1997, not 1897, for the date of publishing); Mombert's humour is also apparent in his suggestion to Dehmel (much to his publisher's disapproval) that a description of the Lord urinating upon the objectionable anti-Semite Professor Adolf Bartels might also be included (3, 116). Jost Hermand, in the article referred to earlier, writes of Mombert's "lyrical vehemence," his fantastic flood of images and self-intoxication meant to convey the impression of some Dionysian element. The images, Hermand explains, possess a sensuous immediacy that fuses with cosmic archetypes; the poet, immersed in his own poetic realm, arrogates to himself an imperious position, becoming a "Soul-Emperor" about whom stars and planets revolve. "Thou shalt arise soon / a powerful hero / thou shalt arise and, radiant as the sun / rise high above the earth" (1, 126) — the lyrical ego is paramount, untrammelled by physical limitations. A "katabasis" or nocturnal journey is portrayed, a submergence into some chthonic realm which is juxtaposed with images of height and ice. Eagle and snake will also be found with increasing frequency in a poetic landscape redolent of *Zarathustra* and the poems "From high mountains" and "On the Glacier," a Rapallo and Sils Maria world which fuses with cosmos and galaxy.

The cycle *Der Denker* (1901) is dedicated to the constellation of Orion and consists of the meditations of twelve Thinkers; although this work is called a "Gedicht Werk" the personification of different elemental entities reflects Mombert's tendency to think in pseudo-dramatic terms. The cycle is reflective and serene in tone, exploring a landscape which is becoming familiar to us, of waters, planets, gardens and marble temples, a landscape inhabited by archetypal shapes and forms. The tone is frequently measured and stately: the poet's gaze, refracted through the twelve prisms, seeks an ultimate harmony. The soaring eagle represents that proud spiritual vision which Mombert knew was his to seek and find. A luminous landscape such as Hölderlin had expressed in his great hymns (and the reference to Etna in the song of the Sixth Thinker brings Empedocles to mind) became Mombert's goal, a spiritual experience more sublime even than that of Hölderlin who had succumbed to an incandescent decay. To enter this world, to move through such rarefied atmosphere was no easy task, as Mombert well understood. A letter written to Hans Reinhart (4 December 1902) seeks to clarify the situation. Reinhart had thanked Mombert for *Der Denker* and had sought to understand it, explaining that it had sprung, as had every work of art, from a human heart suffused by sorrow. Mombert's reply was blunt: such a description, he wrote, was not at all applicable to his work. "Firstly," he explained, "I have for a long time now given up writing from the *heart*, and now only write from the *spirit*. As the 'spirit' is something very rare these days, my poems are regarded by most people as 'incomprehensible, mad' even. And further, there is no 'deep sorrow' suffusing my poetry but the cosmos, with all its *suffering and joy*." Mombert goes on to reject the view that each great work of art is "necessarily a tragedy," claiming that "If you pay close attention you will find that I no longer have a trace of tragedy within me. My importance resides in the fact that I have created a state of soul *beyond* tragedy [. . .] Man is only tragic when he is an isolated individual: as soon as he embraces the cosmos the (lamentable) element of tragedy disappears. This is the spiritual meaning of the *Thinker* and, I believe, of all great spirits in the future" (*A. M. Briefe* 16). A letter of 8 November 1903 thanks Reinhart warmly for an essay which Reinhart had written on the poet but again stresses the need for "a little more respect" for the word *Geist* (spirit): "the Spirit is for me the *cor cordium* and has nothing to do with 'reason' or 'intelligence'. *Spirit* is the hovering bird [. . .]" Again, there are descriptions of falling ("I sank, overwhelmed by images of chaos, chaotic miracles." 1, 236), of movement, across water ("I sat in a boat, I drifted / on waters never charted," 1, 292) of grottoes of the soul where serpents writhe (1, 371): the dialectic tension between height and depth, between masculine brightness (high peaks and icy cliffs) and maternal darkness (fecund clefts, the bottom of the sea) is found most clearly here. The ego is carried along dark swirling waters but ultimately reaches that spiritual identification with Orion and Pleiades, standing beyond the turbulence of time in a diamantine infrangibility.

The year 1905 saw the publication of *Der Sonne Geist* and *Die Blüte des Chaos*: the former collection, with its choruses of comets and revolving stars, its spirit voices and celestial harmonies derives from the opening and end of Goethe's *Faust II* and impinges on the heliocentric world which Däubler will make his own. The two men met only once, in Venice, after Däubler had returned from Greece in 1931. *Die Blüte des Chaos* is a less rarefied collection, beginning with a portrayal of a Vanity Fair, that "blossom of chaos" which is the world; emblematic figures again utter gnomic statements, but the poems are more varied, extolling Fantasia (O Fantasia! Naked Goddess!) and create figures from Mombert's private mythology (Swedja and Urasima). The eagle, the naked youth, the crystal steps are quintessentially Mombert (1, 360); pictures of an Arcadian landscape are disturbed by the image of the blinding of the horses. But transcendent joy prevails, and the collection ends with the homely image of a feather from the "star bird's" pinion descending, one May night, on to a sleeping market place in Germany. The "blossom of chaos" refers to the world in its infinite variety, this world which, as Mombert explains in a letter to the writer Karl Hans Strobl, will "throw itself into my arms like a bride." This letter, written in 1905 (*A. M. Briefe* 20–21) is important in that it gives an (albeit sketchy) account of Mombert's poetic practice: the desire to grasp and hold ideas, feelings, pictures, the need to hold "I" and "world" in an almost erotic tension, the openness to music and to philosophy and the praise of those eras when in his view poetry, religion and philosophy were "one." This letter, incidentally, stresses the "symphonic" nature of Mombert's poetic offerings, with individual poems representing only one sound in the musical cosmos. Only by writing in this manner can "the life of the soul, the movement of the spirit and the higher harmony" be reproduced. "I am considered to be a lyric poet," Mombert explains, but "I am a *Sinfoniker*" and, he continues, "an epic writer." He was also astonished how little metaphysics, how little music has entered the bloodstream of modern man — how little Beethoven! It is this composer, he writes, to whom he felt most closely related; he deplored the fact that Beethoven was only "experienced" when "Beethoven evenings" were on offer. A further letter (*A. M. Briefe* 33–34) expresses the fervent hope that one day a musician would continue to express what Mombert had attempted to convey in words: "My sorrow is that I was not granted the ability to write the 'music' itself."

Mombert felt the pressing need to view all human experience *sub specie aeternitatis*, to link crystal, rock and stone with star and meteor, to see the vital forces within the psyche acting with and pulsing against the vaster forces without. And the process of self-transcendence, or initiation, or ennoblement has a dynamic about it which should be expressed, he believed, in dramatic form. The trilogy *Aeon*, written between 1907 and 1911, is a soul-drama or, indeed, psychodrama which is difficult of access: it portrays the emergence of Sfaira, best understood as a creative spiritual act, out of the soul's struggle for self-awareness. It is tempting to draw comparisons with Rudolf Steiner here, whose plays *Die Pforte der Einweihung* (The Gate of Initiation), *Die Prüfung der Seele* (The Testing of the Soul) and *Der Hüter der Schwelle* (The Guardian of the Threshold) date from the same period and were performed in Munich between 1907 and 1912. But the epiphanies that Mombert sought are very different from Steiner's, and Steiner's occult science, his spiritual-scientific cosmogony meant little to him. A letter to Hans Reinhart (13 December 1927) spoke disparagingly of Steiner (*A. M. Briefe* 81) regretting the "flow of all the little brooks and streamlets into the vast Steiner ocean," and questioning the cost and effort involved in rebuilding the Goetheanum after the first, built entirely of wood according to a clay model designed by Steiner and based upon his principles of gravitation and levitation, was burned to the ground on New Year's Eve 1922. Mombert's *Aeon* derives from other sources, Carl Spitteler's vast epic *Olympischer Frühling* (1900), perhaps, whose nineteen thousand lines of six-foot rhyming verse portray the emergence of a Siegfried figure (Herakles) to redeem the world from "compulsion forced upon us;" from Goethe's *Faust II* (Max Reinhardt had staged the complete work in the Deutsches Theater, Berlin, in 1905); from Shelley, whose grave, the grave of "my friend Shelley," Mombert described in a letter to the artist Karl Hofer in 1906 (*A. M. Briefe* 22). Shelley's rhetorical abstractions have their counterpart in Mombert's work: *Prometheus Unbound*, with its Asia and

Panthea (the two daughters of Ocean) and Demogorgon (a volcanic force dwelling in the underworld) prefigures the entities of *Aeon*. The cosmic coda of *Prometheus Unbound*, sung by a chorus of Hours, Spirits and Moons, is another anticipation. What strikes the reader, however, are the remarkable parallels with the work of William Blake, particularly the private mythologies which both writers create. Where Mombert speaks of Tilotama and Urasima, Blake has his Enitharmon and Urizen: the "four Zoas" of Blake (Los, Tharmas, Luvah and Urizen) would not be out of place in *Aeon*. Blake's drawing *Nelson guiding Leviathan* would be an appropriate illustration to the section of the first part of the *Aeon* trilogy where Nelson, "the fervent one," is portrayed in the cosmic ocean's turmoil (2, 87). The English poet who dined with the prophets Isaiah and Ezekiel and who did not see the sun as a round disk of fire but as a company of the Heavenly Host has much that is familiar to the student of Mombert, as is borne out by the following aphorisms: "He who sees the infinite in all things sees God; he who sees the ratio only sees himself only" and "Vision or Imagination is a Representative of what Eternally Exists, Really and Unchangeably. Fable or Allegory is Form'd by the daughters of Memory, Imagination is surrounded by the daughters of Inspiration."[6]

In *Aeon* Mombert creates a coherent, if esoteric, cosmogony. An eternal dialogue is posited between "chaos," that is the infinite possibilities within the universe, and the established forms of the cosmos themselves. Human history is seen not merely as a mechanical sequence of events but a vital interaction between the creative forces within the world and man's imagination. Aeon himself is a poet-figure who "makes no active contribution to the evolution of the world, but develops the process whereby man's achievements become transferred to the realm of immortality."[7] Language is vitally important here, and the trilogy begins with Aeon "awakening to language." Human consciousness is portrayed, and an orderly relationship between self and world is established. Aeon must unite "World" and "Spirit" (a Hegelian synthesis, this: in a letter to Martin Buber (*A. M. Briefe* 23) Mombert described Hegel's utterances in the *Phänomenologie des Geistes* as being more ecstatic than those of the Sufi); he must drink from a goblet that contains the essence of the world, for this symbolic act will bring awareness to the *World-Soul*. World history impinges in the figure of Nelson, Blake's "Tharmas" who "took the winnowing fan; the winnowing wind furious / Above, veered round by violent whirlwind, driven west and south, / Tossed the nations like chaff into the seas of Tharmas."[8] The figure of "der Starrer" emerges, representing "the shadow," or the darker side of "der menschliche Geist," being introspective and unproductive. He is a necessary companion, however; Aeon drinks and embarks upon the final stage of his humanity, the achievement of pure consciousness. He now suffers isolation — even Fantasia, the creative manipulation of secular images leaves him. Aeon's role is creative also, in that his awareness and expression of what he sees shapes the world into a new and enduring form: it is *limited*, however, as not all of his ideas and visions can be translated into practical terms.

The second part of the trilogy stresses flux and change: no state of harmony between man and cosmos can prevail since new changes necessitate an eternal striving for balance. The figure of Tiona represents the world's beauty of form: the love between her and Aeon is disrupted by the appearance of "Urfrühe" or chaos, Aeon's former love. Urfrühe is the primal source of all things, like the Mothers in *Faust II*, or Wagner's Erda (Tiona is described as her daughter). It is not sufficient for Aeon to add a spiritual dimension to existing beauty and form; he must create from the primal source. He has, however, the freedom to mediate between existing perfection and the new possibilities offered by "chaos." He loves both, the earlier Ich-Du relationship is now abandoned as the turmoil of conflicting cosmic forces overwhelms him. His spiritual freedom becomes a burden to him, and he longs to escape from the responsibilities of "Geist" to the dark womb of Nature. The burden of self-consciousness is a perennial theme, found most poignantly in Hölderlin, whose Empedokles seeks to escape from solipsism and isolation by the leap into the fires of Etna. (Had the drama been completed, however, Hölderlin's Sicilian sage may well have overcome the predicament of being torn between the desire for intense subjectivity on the one hand and the urge towards self-obliteration on the other.) Aeon finally accepts that he must subordinate his feelings as an individual to his role within the universe as a whole: "Ich Aeon . . ./ Zwischen Welt und Chaos / Schwankend . . ." (Aeon, I, trembling between world and chaos. . .) A higher reality is sought for, a harmony achieved through the dynamic tension between these two poles (2, 149).

The third part of the trilogy shows Aeon as the creator of history: the present age is envisaged as the final stage of world history which, for Mombert, begins with Semiramis, princess-daughter of the fish-goddess Ataryatis, who reputedly reigned over Syria for forty-two years. As Astarte — the biblical Ashtoreth — she represents the female principle; in Mombert's spiritual epic, or word-symphony, the relationship between her and Aeon is reminiscent of that between Faust and Helena, and the figure of Sfaira will have much of Euphorion within it, although not the latter's incandescent destiny. *Faust II* is again hinted at in that Aeon is accompanied by various spirits representative of the history of man — a Phoenician, an Arab, a Norman, a Greek and Semiramis herself. These are all prisoners of history in that they characterize one particular era: he, however is the "Geist der Freiheit," the spirit of freedom. The Norman and the Phoenician spirits feel that time has obliterated man's achievements; the Arab and the Greek have a more positive stance — the former referring to man's free will and his ability to unravel mysteries, the latter extolling that happiness generated by his own harmonious relationship with the rest of the world. Aeon, as part of the natural process, must also die, and the human race will come to an end. But the blond youth Sfaira arises from his body, the spirit of the new age, that is, man's life on earth may come to a close, and his memory may pass into saga, but the creative spirit that produced him lives on. Sfaira leaves the earth for the star Canopus, one of the Southern polar stars, taking with him memories of human existence which thus survives even though actual human life has ceased. "It is the creative spirit that remains — the vision, and the measure of all things. . ." This spirit lives on in Sfaira after the death of Aeon: man helps to create reality because what exists is coloured and altered through his perception. The artist depicts this creative spirit *and* embodies it: we have, in *Aeon*, a poetic, idealistic interpretation of man's relationship to the cosmic forces and the expression of the knowledge that the whole universe is imbued with a spiritual force or soul. This vast cosmogony Mombert presented to the world, or, rather to those few fellow countrymen willing to make the arduous journey into gnomic mysteries.

Aeon, as we have seen, drinks from the chalice containing the essence of the world; he represents "der himmlische Zecher." the celestial drinker akin to Zarathustra who blesses, affirms and praises. In 1909 Mombert published an anthology of his verse, in four sections, under this title, to be supplemented by a fifth section in 1922 (the third and final version will be discussed later). A "Zecher" or reveller also appears in the "Gedicht-Werk" *The Hero of the Earth* of 1914, a collection to which an appendix was added in 1916, and a foreword some two years later. It is informed above all by the spirit of Hölderlin: both the Norbert von Hellingrath and the Zinckernagel editions began to appear in 1913, and Hölderlin's mythopoeic awe when confronted by the Alps, the Rhine or the Danube, his spiritual odysseys and patriotic fervour were very important to Mombert at this time. The "Orion-Sänger" — the poet, Mombert, who sings of Orion — sits (or rather nestles) in ivy on the banks of the Rhine, much as the poetic "Ich" in *Der Rhein*, sitting in "dunkeln Efeu" (in dark ivy), broods on that German river, its energy and its cosmic destiny. In Hölderlin it is a "Genius" which

seizes him and takes him on that journey to "Asien": both poets portrayed that continent, cradle of civilization, in sensuous, dramatic terminology. Mombert preferred the figure of Tamburlaine to that of
Napoleon (whom he had originally intended for mythical portrayal) as
a representative of vast energy: Mombert's imaginative journey encom-
passes Central Asia and the Himalayas, the exotic cities of Tamburlaine
and the fecundity of India. The poetic act evokes and creates: it is an
act of rhapsodic incantation. There is lament at the decline of the symbolic power of ancient myths — "Saïs is dead / Jerusalem dead and
forgotten / The boy Hylas is dead / The constellation of Perseus is
sunken, shattered, dead" (1, 475) but Mombert evokes, and, by evocation, preserves: "Time harps in my heart-hollow" ["In meiner Herz-
Höhle harft die Zeit," 1, 433], and from a dark turmoil of pictures
emerges no allegory, no coherent nomenclature, but a "saying" in
Rilke's sense, a "Sagen" which is transmuted into a "Ja-sagen" by the
poetic act. Semiramis is again invoked, and a cosmic dance (in which
Dehmel and Mombert both take part) is portrayed. And Sfaira, that
creative, spiritual act, is again present. It is he — and the poet, through
whom he speaks, is the "Hero of the Earth" proud and exultant in his
creative powers: "I am that which was, is, and shall be" (1, 482). "Upwards! upwards! Into the aetherial cradle of snow!" (1, 424) — this is
where his gaze is directed: an eagle-like intoxication of height prevails.
"I climb ever higher — I tower upwards [. . .] My thoughts gleam
above the clouds" (1, 493). Ice, ether, granite cliffs are extolled to exemplify a sublime and radiant glory — but other, less sublime, heroes,
were waiting to step upon the European stage. That war which Carl
Hauptmann had uncannily portrayed in his play *Der Krieg* (War) of
1913, with its Archangels, Monstrous Figures, Great Power Beasts and
European Reckoner was now unleashed. Mombert, aged forty four, was
called up in 1916 and served in the occupied Polish territories. In the
summer of that year he appended a short "Nachspiel" to *The Hero of
the Earth*, a dramatic dialogue where the Thinker, in his tower, is visited by demons (or daemons) bringing news of turmoil and uproar, of
subterranean fires, mounds of corpses, destroyed cities and red "tulips"
of blood. Mombert's undoubted patriotism is evident in the portrayal
of Germania or Deutschland, a country of such formidable strength
that others flee: "O thou Germany : I love thee!" (1, 498). Germany's
military prowess is admired by the Third Demon; the Fourth Demon
extols her cultural glory (there is a reference to Mozart's grave). Germany must pass through pain and destruction for a new world to be
born; Mombert's gaze, as we know, is not fixed upon the mundane,
but upon spiritual entities. His portrayal of the war is akin to that of

George, members of whose circle encouraged a vision of Germany's superior destiny, her role as guardian of high idealism. It is bitterly ironic that Mombert's patriotism should be to no avail some twenty-five years later when, as a Jew, he would be forced, incredulous and bewildered, to leave behind his rooms in Heidelberg, his library and his collection of crystals, and join the forced removal to the internment camp. In 1918, that "Ur-Jahr" of world history, he added a vision of a radiant world emerging from the carnage, a world of baptism and blessing and "Then my German, my eternal heart will sing in this book" (1, 406). As an officer in occupied Warsaw, Mombert succeeded in hearing Beethoven's Ninth Symphony on two occasions, and Schiller's *Ode to Joy* would confirm his faith in the ultimate triumph of goodness, a faith that he never lost, though sorely tested (*A. M. Briefe* 41).

It is possible to see Mombert's work as being a gigantic monologue: indeed, Mombert himself was aware of the difficulties confronting the potential reader, but he realised also, as the letter to Rudolf Pannwitz has shown that he was not the only "outsider" in German literature. That letter also describes the increasing loneliness in which Mombert was living in Heidelberg, a loneliness possibly even greater than Nietzsche's. "I have not the slightest contact with the University. It is only very rarely that the odd student dares visit me; professors never" (*A. M. Briefe* 73). In 1925 *Atair* appeared, another "Gedicht-Werk"; the title is derived from the star Altair (or Atair), a first magnitude star in the constellation Aquila in the Northern Hemisphere. The collection is a memoriam for Heinz Luz Dehmel, Richard Dehmel's son, who was killed in the fighting in 1917. (Dehmel himself, although exempted from enlistment due to injuries received at school after a fall from a horizontal bar, joined the army in 1914 although he was over fifty at the time: his experiences were described in *Zwischen Volk and Menschheit* (Between Nation and Humanity) which was published one year before his death in 1920.) Heinz Dehmel becomes mythologised as the "young German hero" (1, 512) and there are many lovely passages which express his idealism and courage. George's noble threnodies in *Das neue Reich* (The New Realm) have a similar provenance, particularly the lament for the death of Norbert von Hellingrath, but Mombert's view, as always, is *cosmic*: the constellations and individual stars (Atair and Arcturus) are glorified, and Heinz Dehmel's memory is transfigured. And the earth is hailed as an eternal source of joy: the poet's gaze moves from the constellation Antares to the sweep of the comets, the waves of the Pacific, the storms of Cape Horn, the "Traum-Musik" of Asia, the roses of Persia, the violets growing on

Mount Etna, the albatrosses over Kerguelen, the shore of Borneo, the larks on the banks of the Rhine. A darker counterpoint is found in the references to gas mask and flame-thrower, but Sfaira's horse leaps over them in an act of joyful defiance. The sombre turmoil of human history can never, for Mombert, stain the pristine radiance of vision, of the spirit's creative ecstasy: a cosmos peopled by Urasima, Fantasia and, here, Priscadea transcends the dross of human violence. Mombert's poetic creation is unique, comparable, perhaps, only to the work of David Jones who began writing his *In Parenthesis* in 1927 (*Ataïr* appeared in 1925), an epic work of mixed poetry and prose where the sufferings of Private John Ball are related to the long history of war and embedded in Welsh legend and the work of Malory. But Mombert's vision is more august, more remote and more *inhuman*: Nietzschean "Ja sagen" fuses with a mystical sense of eternal cosmic forces, where the glory of the morning star transfigures and redeems all human suffering.

Mombert's tendency to see the interaction of cosmic forces from a dramatic standpoint has been commented on: he was drawn to create a dramatic, as well as a lyrical-epic, *œuvre*, although it is difficult to imagine a theatrical representation of his visions. His work is an *epic* arrangement of lyrical poetry, an epic of unimaginable dimension. A discussion of Mombert as dramatist would link him to certain expressionist playwrights who sought, as the "Poet" did in Reinhard Sorge's play *Der Bettler* (The Beggar, 1912) to speak through symbols of eternity, rejecting art as mimesis and extolling some quasi-religious awareness. One thinks also of Sorge's early drama *Odysseus* and his own "vision" *Zarathustra*, both written in 1911, the latter naturally instinct with the Nietzschean presence. Sorge also admired greatly Mombert's *Der himmlische Zecher* and expressed disappointment on not having it to hand. (*Werke*, 1, 27) Notions such as Nietzschean self-overcoming and a spiritual regeneration inform many of the plays of expressionism. Kaiser's *Hölle Weg Erde* (Hell Way Earth, 1919) culminates in a luminous effulgence which transfigures humanity. Paul Kornfeld's *Himmel und Hölle* (Heaven and Hell) of the same year portrays wilderness and redemption. Barlach, in *Der tote Tag* (The Dead Day, 1912) speaks of man's higher derivation and, in *Der arme Vetter*, originally called *Die Osterleute* (The People of Easter), of a nebulous excarnation. Hasenclever's *Jenseits* (Beyond, 1920) attempts a mystical portrayal of life and death. If expressionism is defined as a revolt of the spirit against reality, with transcendence, redemption, transfiguration, and resurrection as frequent and important themes, then Mombert may be seen as having similar preoccupations. But the portrayal of the soul under stress, racked and burning in some fearful incandescence is alien to him, and much of expressionism's bathos and extravagance would have seemed to him meaningless, if not absurd. We have also commented on his rejection of Rudolf Steiner, albeit that Steiner's soul dramas prefigure certain aspects of Mombert's work. The world of Aeon and Aigla is uniquely Mombert's own, hieratic, sublime, not marmoreal, but suffused with an awareness of radiant energy.

In 1929 and 1931 Mombert published two dramas, *Aiglas Herabkunft* (Aigla's Descent) and *Aiglas Tempel* (Aigla's Temple: 3, 266). In a notebook he jotted the following comments: "Hölderlin spoke a lot, and often, of 'the gods.' But we must let them appear for themselves, speak for themselves! This is very important!" A letter to Hans Franke (15 April 1929) explains:

> You know full well that I think, immediately, in figures [Gestalten]. If I have been successful in chiselling a new, throning goddess by poetic means, then I will be happy. We do not live in the age of Phidias — but perhaps there is a yearning for this (despite the superficialities of this spectacle of civilization) . . .

The *Aigla* plays will be the nearest Mombert ever approached to drama in any recognisable form, with tableaux, choruses, a Sänger (Sagemund — with much of Mombert in him) and a landscape compounded of Böcklin, late Goethe, Hölderlin and, strangely, Richard Wagner. The prologue portrays the poetic act of creation and the emergence of archetypal figures (Mombert's reading of the sacred books of the Parsees, ascribed to Zoroaster, is apparent in the description of darkness and light). The two brothers Himanntir and Thaumas have much of Prometheus and Epimetheus within them; Spitteler's epic *Prometheus und Epimetheus* (1880–1) would have been familiar to Mombert with its elevated, semi-Biblical rhythmical prose (similar to *Thus Spake Zarathustra* and predating it) and its portrayal of the two brothers, the one refusing the crown if the price meant conforming to a codified collective, the other meekly accepting, preferring the familiar and the procedural. The first play, *Aiglas Herabkunft* has as its theme the deification of Aigla, her epiphany and transformation from cosmic entity into goddess. She is associated with radiance, "Glanz": her name seems to indicate this (Ai-gla) (2, 272). It is perhaps of interest to note here the name "Vasanta," which Mombert bestowed upon a mysterious concert-pianist with whom he enjoyed a platonic relationship for fifteen years. Vasanta, apparently derives from the Sanskrit stem "vas," meaning "to gleam." Vasanta, the "radiant one" (there are also connotations of Spring) gave much to Mombert, crystals and shells from her sojourn in Iceland, exotic feathers and also more practical gifts; she also allowed him free access to her summer-house on Hiddensee. Aigla's presence is portrayed as a divine awareness in the world of men: the second play, *Aiglas Tempel*, is resonant with turmoil from human history, and the temple itself is troubled in its serenity by emissaries from without. Sagemund, the minstrel, sings of the glories of earth, despite the news brought by wanderer and warrior; Mombert's adamant refusal to admit of the triumph of negation and savagery, and his absolute conviction of the ultimate triumph of the human spirit, are indeed rare.

On January 10, 1928 Mombert was, implausibly, elected to the Poetry Section (Sektion für Dichtkunst) of the Prussian Academy of Arts: a photograph taken in 1929 shows him sitting with the canonical writers Thomas Mann, Ricarda Huch, Bernhard Kellermann, Hermann Stehr, Eduard Stucken, Walter von Molo and Heinrich Mann. The brief and inglorious existence of this section does not concern us here, fraught as it was by tensions and implacable hostilities from which Mombert remained aloof. On January 16, 1933 Mombert gave a poetry reading in the Academy which was also broadcast; Oskar Loerke described the reading as very slow, very tender and very quiet — "not easy to follow, but spellbinding . . . Mombert was, in a way, happy."[9] Two weeks later, on January 30, Hitler became Reichskanzler, and the days of the Section were numbered, tarred as it was, in Hitler's eyes, by the brush of its Weimar origins. The new *Reichsschrifttumskammer* spelled its end. Jews were "nicht tragbar" — not acceptable to the new order — and it was this expression which Mombert will use in a letter to the writer Rudolf Binding, who had showed concern for Mombert's position. Mombert explained, characteristically, that, "for a long time now I have been living in a spiritual region inaccessible to the onslaughts of darkness and demons" (*A. M. Briefe* 110–111): Binding need have no fear for him. He continues to speak of what is "tragbar" and reminds Binding that he once saw, in the Hofburg in Vienna, the jewelled insignia of the Habsburgs, above all the imperial crown itself, bearing in gold and marquetry the forms and names of three figures, three Jews: King David, King Solomon and the Prophet Isaiah. These were "borne," were carried, by the Austrian emperors, as the German people had carried the "non" Aryan bible within its soul for almost two thousand years. The tone of the letter is not one of bitterness but of hurt astonishment at the virulence of the anti-Semitism now apparent in Germany. Now more than ever it was necessary to cultivate the world of the spirit; on congratulating Oskar Loerke on his fiftieth birthday (*A. M. Briefe* 113) Mombert spoke of those "guests" who would sit at Loerke's table, the spirits of Hölderlin, Novalis, Shelley, of Hafis and the Persian poet Rumi. There would be no admission for the vulgar, for the brutish. A later letter, in 1940, quotes Hölderlin's translation of Pindar's eighth Pythic ode: "Men are but a shadow's dream — but when the radiance of the god-given is upon them, then gleaming light is here, and lovely life" (*A. M. Briefe* 141). And in the face of growing darkness and age Mombert insisted on his basic optimism, a knowledge that "all will be well," even if one corner of planet earth were tainted: "I am absolutely optimistic — indeed *criminally* so! — but only for the worlds in their entirety, not for the little corner of world in which we must dwell (nor for 'the fate of Europe')" (*A. M. Briefe* 142). Old Sfaira (this name he increasingly took as his own), the creative spiritual act, moved effortlessly among the galaxies whilst Germany moved into an even deeper madness.

In December 1920 Mombert had jotted down the following: "Poetry is only present when all mystery, all science and all religion have become a *world-game*. Everything is play. And then — we have SFAIRA" (3, 290). Sfaira, we know, emerged from the husk of Aeon and soared upwards: he symbolises a creative, spiritual act, and one which Mombert is here identifying with a divine act of play. This creative energy fills the universe with mythological emblems; Nature is not experienced as a self-contained entity but as something shot through with mysterious forces that give it a spiritual affinity with man. His cosmology has been called "a poetic, idealistic interpretation of man's relationship to the cosmic forces, and one which shares the basic Gnostic premise that the whole universe is imbued with a spiritual force, or soul, whose significance far exceeds that of material reality."[10] Adorno's comment on Wagner, that he did not quote myths merely as metaphors, that beneath his gaze everything becomes mythological,[11] is also true of Mombert and, indeed, to a higher degree, for Mombert did not "quote" — he created his own. Loerke noted that philosophy and poetry were one for Mombert;[12] only rarely did the two not fuse effortlessly, and an allegorical situation ensued which required translation, interpretation. The force of Mombert's poetry, as Christopher Middleton noted, lies in its imagery; vertiginous depths of statement expressed in powerful images of ice, fire, sun, mountain-top, desert, hero, sage, maiden and mother, which disclose distinct archetypal patterns.[13] Mombert is not rich in rhythmic invention, relying largely on a trochaic or dactylic beat, whatever the length of line. But the sustained oratory, and breadth of spatial imagery have scarcely an equal in German poetry, and his last statement, the "Mythos" *Sfaira der Alte*, is his greatest achievement.

The work first appeared in 1936: in 1942 a second part was printed at the expense of the Swiss poet and dramatist Hans Reinhart, not only patron now, but rescuer, and presented to Mombert two months before his death. The first part begins with a loving invocation of the German landscape, its forests, groves, nightingales and mountains; Sfaira rests and listens to ancient legends ("unendliche Sagen vom Werden der Welten") and a tree which reminds the reader of Yggdrasil or Wagner's world-ash (2, 353). The German countryside appears before him — a forest path in the Harz, a mountain lake, an old Franconian town (and ironic it is that the capital of Franconia, Nuremberg, would be the "Reichsparteistadt," soon to pass decrees reducing Jews to a status of inferiority), a park in Alemannia, the Hohenstaufen area of Swabia, a dripstone cave, an inn in the Erzgebirge, a lime-tree near the castle in Heidelberg, the rocks of the Fichtelgebirge; most moving is the "Voice of the Madonna in a Chapel in Württemberg," a quiet meditation in rhymed couplets (2, 368). The poetic gaze then takes in the Alps and greets Venice: "Gold glänzen die Dächer der Stadt Venedig" (2, 379). Here Mombert touches the world of Däubler, who had died in 1934 ("his life had been enviable," Mombert wrote to Reinhart (*A. M. Briefe* 114), "he had managed to live according to his own spiritual impulses — and in the most beautiful places on earth"). A journey by sea takes us to Calamotta (Koločep) off the coast of Ragusa (Dubrovnik) where Rudolf Pannwitz lived, hailed as "der deutsche Dichter-Denker" (2, 384), one who brooded on "the glowing laws of the cosmos," and also his home beneath the German oak-tree. Cosmos and Germany: in Pannwitz we see a second Mombert surely, one who steps from a "holy solemn" olive-tree into a world not of Hitler (although Pannwitz would be forced to flee the Adriatic during the war) but of Hölderlin (2, 386). Another island, the Ionian island of Zakynthos (Zante) is greeted from whose shore, as we know, Mombert sank two golden rings into the sea — and then Cythera, its "azure miracles, its opal splendours." It is the dolphin which accompanies Sfaira through the Greek archipelago; the land journey, through the Caucasus into Central Asia, will have an eagle — or two eagles, from Elbrus and Kazbek — as guides and heralds. The journey ends on the heights of the Himalayas, on "Berg Moira," where Sfaira plays upon an organ of ice his rapturous blessing. A "Zarathustra Redivivus?" Perhaps, but there is no imperious hyperbole in this vast spiritual epic; the elevated tone is that of Hölderlin, particularly the latter's "Die Wanderung," in the movement from "Fortunate Swabia, my mother" to the great shout "But I wish to see the Caucasus!," and "Der Adler" where "my father" [the eagle] flies to the "Indus," and there are undeniable echoes of Novalis's novel fragment *Heinrich von Ofterdingen* in the odyssey to the East, and the various incarnations (2, 439). Above the Himalayan peaks the spirit of poetry, of creative joy — Sfaira — moves with the archetypal forms of angel, demon, giant and Okorma. On earth, however, a different journey awaited the poet.

Before considering Mombert's arrest and his final poetic utterances a brief comment should be made on his anthology *Der himmlische Zecher*, a final selection of his own verse which Mombert was preparing in 1939 and which appeared posthumously in the Insel-Verlag in 1951 (he had prepared two earlier anthologies under the same title, one in 1909 and a second in 1922, as has been noted). This 1951 edition, some three hundred and thirty-five pages long, was an essential guide to Mombert's work before the definitive three volume *Dichtungen* edited by Elisabeth Herberg in 1963; the quintessential Mombert was presented, a selection by the poet himself, the majority of poems being taken from *Die Schöpfung, Der Denker, Der Glühende, Ataïr* and *Der Held der Erde*. The poems, or passages, were chosen to create a mythology which is projected into the cosmos and rendered through an atmosphere of 'Welttrunkenheit,' an intoxicated, ecstatic awareness of chaos and form-giving energy. And it is for the reader to grasp that there is no linear development but a continual state of metamorphosis on multiple levels. The distinction between outer and inner worlds, between universe and self disappears, and flux and Dionysian energy prevail.[14]

There are seven sections in the book; the heroic-creative principle takes place first in the earthly sphere, then follows an ever-increasing abstraction of setting and action until finally the total removal of reality culminates in the transformation into a mythical dream-realm. During this process the earthly hero or "ich" assumes the divine task of moulding the infinite, or "chaos," into form: on a universal level this act of creation out of chaos results in cosmos; the extended journey of the "ich" is intended solely as a symbol for the exploration of the endless possibilities of existence within the human spirit.

The "himmlischer Zecher," or "divine, celestial reveller" is created from a composite of heroes or "egos" in Mombert's poetry. In the first book the poet separates himself from all human ties and begins this journey of exploration: the poem from *Der Denker* (1, 282–3) illustrates this with a Böcklinesque portrayal of the poet, upright on a boat, moving dreamily across dark waters towards a figure who points towards the distance, towards "mein Reich," "my realm." In book two the hero exercises his poetic powers in ways which show he is emulating the actions of an "Urschöpfer," an emblem of archetypal creativity; many poems are taken from the collection *Die Schöpfung* and are already familiar to us. A "woman" is presented whose breast is "as blessed as the galaxy of glittering stars" (1, 131). The poet greets her, for it is he who, thousands of years previously, had "hammered that diadem which sparkles upon her brow." In the third book the claim is made that the only real freedom from chaos is to embrace it utterly: the hero-poet has grown old but experiences rebirth in the figure of a son or "Sfaira," the youthful dancer upon the waters whose "golden head-band glitters with a solar radiance" (1, 472). The theme of rejuvenation is continued with the hero longing to join Sfaira on his journey through the cosmos, and from this point in the cycle the hero's development moves into sidereal and purely mystical levels which are represented by Urasima's heavens. The last three books portray, in symbolic figures, the fusion of heaven and earth, the transition towards a final mystical flight and the ultimate identification of poet-hero with the "celestial reveller": man becomes one in rapturous abandonment with creativity itself. It was this celebration of union with all that Nietzsche baptised with the name "Dionysus," and the climax of Mombert's anthology is an image of an overflowing chalice and the garden of the world, eternal clarity and the dance of goddesses.

As was mentioned at the beginning of this chapter the entire Jewish population of Baden and the Palatinate was rounded up in October 1940 and conveyed in lorries and vans via Marseilles and Toulouse to the large internment camp at Gurs in the Basses Pyrénées, between Pau and Lourdes: Mombert and his sister, who was seventy-two years old, were included. Letters to Hans Reinhart (later to be smuggled out of Switzerland by the singer Else Domberger and passed on to Hans Carossa and others) tell of the indignities and the hardship: one uncharacteristically bitter outburst exclaims "Has anything like this ever happened to a German poet before?" (*A. M. Briefe* 144)[15] The camp, originally meant for internees from the Spanish Civil war, was primitive and the conditions became increasingly intolerable. Yet a view of the snow capped peaks of the Pyrenees brought inspiration to "der alte Sfaira," as did the knowledge that Reinhart would do all he could to enable the poet to enter Switzerland. "My earlier existence has sunk, but my fantasy world lives"; these words in a letter (November 27 1940) show that Mombert was determined to remain with gaze on high (the Goethean — or Mahlerian — "Blicket auf" was the injunction which he strove to obey, despite the darkness, the cold and the lack of satisfactory hygiene). A transfer to Idron, near Pau, early in 1941 brought relief (prisoners aged sixty five and over, and who were in a position to guarantee financial independence, were to be released and permitted to reside in unoccupied France); later that year Reinhart organised the move to Winterthur. And it was Reinhart, we know, who

2 : ALFRED MOMBERT • 71

presented Mombert with the second part of *Der alte Sfaira* as a token of esteem and of a conviction that the poet, a desperately sick man, should see the consummation of his life's work.

The oratory is as sustained as ever, and the tone of sublimity unabated. But the poet has been into the darkness: the section "In der Finsternis" is an expression of the fearful winter of 1940–1941, yet also a miraculous transfiguration of bestiality and degradation: "I now see my land / I now see my place — / I see the tents of darkness; / I see the diamond-gleam of the gates of the Underworld. . ." (2, 555). In squalor and ugliness the spirit gazes upwards towards Orion, the Pleiades and Cassiopeia: "Arisen with the depths / I thrust my sword-glance through the barrack-roof. . . My gaze through the narrow crack / You tender ones!" (2, 556) And yet the torturer approaches, the denigrator and destroyer, the Demon himself, the "despiser of the crystal law . . . the destructive demon of the world of images . . . the filth of chaos, the festering dragon from the morass of death" (2, 558) who fouls the Castalian source of joy. With imagery which anticipates that of Paul Celan, the poet, Sfaira himself, expresses the bitterness of the taste of death upon his lips; the torturer, with the metal noose slapping against his thigh, stand in arrogance before him.

> Night ash upon my lips — bitter — bitter . . .
> Who are you then? . . .
> But your eyes, if we can name such eyes
> these fearful pits of vice
> drop poison-pus
> and where it drips the earth's pure womb
> twitches in foul revulsion. . .
>
> > (2, 558–9)

In the face of insolent brutality the poet is helpless, yet the poetic act, the manipulation of expressive images, can transcend evil and create a luminous world of joy: *Der alte Sfaira* ends on a note of mystic rapture, a cosmic vision of light, azure and crystal. As Sfaira passes into death and transfiguration (or, rather, this particular incarnation) he once more turns to the loveliness of earth, untainted by the squalor and the baseness of human perversion, and the ultimate apotheosis of the poem, and indeed of Mombert's *œuvre*, with its "Geisterchor" and "Chor der Göttinnen" echoes the climax of *Faust II*; the nadir of German cultural history is also the moment when the poet feels his affinity with the highest manifestation of that culture. "Sei immer selig, deutsches Land" — "Be ever blessed, German land": this final statement emphasises his faith in the insuperable, creative powers of the universe.

Mombert died on April 8, 1942. He desired that his ashes should not be buried in "the heavy earth" but be taken, on a clear day, into the high Swiss mountains and allowed to float into the air. Swiss law did not permit this; his urn was placed in the base of his bust in Hans Reinhart's garden in Winterthur.

Notes

[1] Alfred Mombert, *Dichtungen in drei Bänden*, ed. by Elisabeth Herberg (Munich: Kösel, 1963), vol. 2, 617. (All references to Mombert's work are from this edition unless otherwise stated.)

[2] Jost Hermand, *Lyrik des Jugendstils* (Stuttgart: Reclam, 1969), 63–75. See also "Die Ur-Frühe. Zum Prozeß des mythischen 'Bilderns' bei Mombert," *Der Schein des schönen Lebens. Studien zur Jahrhundertwende* (Frankfurt a. M.: Athenäum Verlag, 1972).

[3] Gottfried Benn, *Werke* (Wiesbaden: Limes Verlag, 1962), vol. 4, 1046.

[4] Heller, *Importance of Nietzsche*, 70.

[5] Martin Buber, *Daniel. Gespräche von der Verwirklichung* (Leipzig: Insel, 1913), 83. The quotation "Gott und die Träume" is taken from the collection *Schöpfung* (Creation) and called "a song of early blessing"; it is a song which Daniel loves, but he also recommends danger and exhorts his young friend Reinhold to create on the edge of Being, on the edge of the Abyss.

[6] William Blake quoted in Anthony Blunt, *The Art of William Blake* (London: Oxford UP, 1959), 26.

[7] Christine Barker, "Mombert's Cosmology: The Aeon Trilogy," *German Life and Letters* 29 (1975–76), 303.

[8] Blake quoted in Blunt, 102.

[9] Oskar Loerke, *Tagebücher 1903–1939*, ed. by Hermann Kasack (Heidelberg/Darmstadt: Verlag Lambert Schneider, 1956), 260.

[10] Barker, 306.

[11] Theodor Adorno cited in Raymond Furness, *Wagner and Literature* (Manchester: Manchester UP, 1982), 97.

[12] Loerke, 71.

[13] Christopher Middleton, "Sfaira der Alte," *German Life and Letters* 13 (1959–60), 59. Middleton stresses the momentous rhythmical power of Mombert's poetry, the unique combination of emotional grandeur with mystical illumination "The poem is a kind of rhapsodic spiritual epic, a 'Zarathustra Redivivus' which reads also at points like *Heinrich von Ofterdingen*

[. . .]. At all events, these two parallels guide the reader little if he flags under the strain of Mombert's hyperbolic manner and feels baffled by abstruse meanings."

[14] I am indebted here to Marilyn Scott-James, "Constellar Images as the Structural Basis of 'Der himmlische Zecher,'" (Diss., U. of Oregon, 1975).

[15] A most moving comment on this question was made by Jean Améry (who had also been at Gurs) in *Jenseits von Schuld und Sühne. Bewältigungsversuche eines Überwältigten* (Munich: Szczesny Verlag, 1966) in the section "Wieviel Heimat braucht der Mensch?" Améry gently chides Mombert for not realizing that he had ceased to be a "German poet" the moment that he became "Alfred Israel Mombert, deportee from Karlsruhe." "Mombert was not a German poet in the barracks at Gurs — this is what the hand required which did not try to stop him from being deported. He died without a past and we can only hope that he was able to die in some degree of tranquillity without realizing it" (100). For Améry the experience of the expropriation of his own culture was the most tragic of all: his book has been translated as *At the Mind's Limits: Contemplations by a Survivor on Auschwitz and its Realities* (Bloomington: Indiana UP, 1980). The quotation above is taken from that translation.

Alfred Schuler.
Courtesy of Schiller Nationalmuseum and
Deutsches Literaturarchiv, Marbach.

3 : Alfred Schuler

> On the host of her vulva was burning the swastika, the
> token of fire. . .
> — Alfred Schuler

> Was it then real, this circle? When the torches
> Shone on the pallid faces, and the vapours
> Floated from vessels round the holy youth; your words
> Lifted us, flaming, into worlds of madness. . .
> — Stefan George

> It is my firm conviction that, since the death of Nietzsche,
> there has been no greater, no more esoteric event for
> mankind than Schuler's demise.
> — Ludwig Klages

ONE OF THE MOST AMAZING letters ever written by petitioner to monarch must surely be the following, written in 1898 on a parchment roll by Alfred Schuler and addressed to the empress Elisabeth of Austria:

> Condemned to death, inexorably, by the overwhelming substantiality
> of the present, dedicated to life as to the hearth and swastika of the
> coming world, I approach YOUR MAJESTY with the staff and bonds of a
> supplicant and stand before the MAJESTY OF YOUR SOUL, blinded and
> drawn by a radiance which gleams between pillars and many-coloured
> fragrances [. . .] Maimed in existence, excluded from resonance in
> word and image, without means of developing my talents I saw my ec-
> stasies shudder on walls, in foliage, in the delights and enticements of
> the living and my life, which sought the roots of existence, haunted by
> noose and murderer. Desperate for help my glance encircled all. Eve-
> rywhere the same. . . A crust of hatred around the earthly globe. The
> corpse of an ancient, dying swastika in the most extreme degradation.
> And where — seldom indeed — an eye in gold and ripeness cut away
> this crust, then I saw — again — most certain catastrophe. But a voice
> cried out: 'Porphyrogenetos, beseech the Empress for help . . . seek

help from the highest of your symbols. That which is unique belongs to the one who is unique. See, a flame gleaming in purple. A lamp burning above black waters. If SHE does not know you, then expire gently! My primary copper are you [. . .] You are the proof of my sun, as yet concealed which, child-like and seething, flames to new horizons [. . .] I now seek to lay the mystery of my urn at your feet: my Caaba. My most Inner Being. How much of the precious sap it still contains, or how much has been drunk by greedy vampires I do not know. . ."[1]

The effect that this peroration may have had will never be known: the Empress was murdered in September 1898 as she walked from her hotel to the steamer in Geneva, before the document was put into her hands.

"My Caaba, my copper" — the terminology is as bizarre as the contents of the Tabularium itself, a collection of highly charged, hieroglyphic pronouncements which the parchment roll was meant to accompany. This consisted of twenty one plates made of thin, very hard cardboard, twenty centimetres long and ten centimetres wide, covered with a gleaming cochineal red and gilded at the edges. The left hand border of each plate had four holes for the insertion of cords which were also gilded and threaded with polished gems. The first and last of the plates were covered with intricate tracery and rich ornamentation; the remaining nineteen contained those fragmentary, gnomic utterances which Schuler considered to be his most important. The plates were contained in a tightly fitting case coloured with a patina of copper; the front of the case was decorated by a richly ornamental golden band, about one centimetre across, and a golden circle, seven centimetres in diameter in which there stood a winged figure of Eros moving through the zodiac and holding in his right hand a blossoming pomegranate, in his left a lyre with the inscription ΚΟΣΜΟΓΟΝΟΣ ΠΑΝΤΑ ΠΟΙΕΙ (illustration in *Cosmogonische Augen* 479). The inscriptions were exclusively Schuler's own work; the ornamentation and figurative decoration were aided by a painter with whom he was acquainted. It took him some eighteen months (and the whole of what remained of his modest capital) to complete: it was, as we know, not delivered.

Who was he? A discussion of his work is not made easy by the fact that he published nothing in his lifetime apart from one review and one poem,[2] and by the luxuriant tangle of anecdotes which led to a general misrepresentation and obfuscation. Legends are legion: the plan to cure the insane Nietzsche by "korybantiasis" (the dancing of beautiful ephebes dressed in copper, *FuV* 60); the "Roman feast" (29 April 1899) at which Schuler declaimed his portentous visions with such rapture and conviction that Stefan George fled and sought solace with beer-drinkers, fearing for Schuler's sanity;[3] the defection of Alfred Schuler and Ludwig Klages from the George-Kreis and the declaration of war on Karl Wolfskehl sent in a letter with a black seal, a declaration which Schuler insisted be delivered to Wolfskehl by a soldier;[4] the fear expressed by Franziska Gräfin zu Reventlow of a physical attack by Schuler;[5] the refreshing irreverence of Roderich Huch (the violet rings which Schuler saw whilst masturbating);[6] the acerbic comments of Theodor Lessing.[7] Yet Rilke's sincere admiration for Schuler, together with Wolfskehl's generous comments in his New Zealand exile, should also not be forgotten in any attempt to reach an understanding of Schuler's recondite and opaque utterances. There is much that is daunting, even forbidding in Schuler's work, but its very uniqueness draws the interpreter to it.

Alfred Schuler moved from Mainz to Munich with his mother in 1887 and matriculated at the university, ostensibly to study history, art-history and archaeology under Professor Ludwig Traube, palaeographer and editor of late Roman lyric poetry and Professor Adolf Furtwängler, archaeologist in charge of various excavations in Greece (and father of the conductor Wilhelm Furtwängler). It soon became apparent that academic study was alien to Schuler. As a child Schuler had experienced, not unlike Heinrich Schliemann, an almost mystical rapture when confronted by artifacts of classical antiquity; fragments of pottery and coins covered with the patina of age obsessed him, and he responded with an almost erotic ravishment to objects dating from the Roman period. Theodor Lessing would later claim that

> there was nothing classical or religious for him which did *not* have some connection with Eros [. . .] His hedonistic-heathen philosophy, which abhorred anything which smacked of morality, stemmed from a homo-erotic attitude, something feminine and atavistic, which was only interested in masculine strength.[8]

Schuler's sexual proclivities are not our concern here: suffice it that the cult of the "passive" and the "maternal" owes much to Bachofen, whose influence was considerable. In 1893 Schuler made the acquaintance of Ludwig Klages and, through him, many of the Munich avant-garde, including the "pale salon-Jesuit Derleth" and his remarkable sister Anna Maria. It becomes difficult to separate the man from the lurid and frequently prurient anecdotes which thwart any attempt to discuss Schuler's ideas, but one of the most striking of his beliefs is his contempt for the modern world (for "progress") and his admiration for Imperial Rome, particularly its later emperors. There is much of Schuler in the figure of Chaim Breisacher in Thomas Mann's *Doktor Faustus* (in chapter twenty eight), although it has been argued[9] that Mann drew upon Oskar Goldberg here, author of *Die Wirklichkeit der Hebräer* (The Reality of the Hebrews, 1925); Breisacher exulted in the damnation of humanism, liberalism, and tolerance and sought the starkest, most authoritative absolute, despising Christianity and seeing alarming signs of degeneration in some of the early Hebrew prophets. In Schuler's case it is the post-Roman world which is castigated, and the intellectual tradition of nearly two thousand years is excoriated as "Gehirnstrolcherei," an untranslatable term but one which might be rendered as "cerebral vagaries." It was Life which Schuler would extol, not mere existence, but powerful, "shuddering," passionate life or "Blutleuchte," life radiant and suffused with erotic energy. And the ultimate symbol for this ecstatic, cosmic rapture will be the swastika, *fons et origo* of life-affirmation.

Nero as artist-emperor (Qualis artifex pereo!) and Ludwig II of Bavaria as his incarnation, the amoral cult of beauty fusing with the praise of Renaissance violence (Nietzsche's "Cesare Borgia als Papst": 6, 251) — this was the heady atmosphere which Schuler imbibed in Munich. The excesses of the late Roman emperors had fascinated the exponents of French decadence, but not only these: in Germany it is George's *Algabal* poems (Heliogabalus, but Nero's presence is undeniable), which are exemplary, as are Ludwig Quidde's essay *Caligula* (1894) and Oskar Pannizza's play *Nero* (1898); as early as 1866, however, Robert Hamerling, in his epic *Ahasuerus in Rom*, had exulted in pictures of splendour and cruelty. Both Nietzsche and Schuler were aware of Jacob Burckhardt's speculation (in *Die Kultur der Renaissance in Italien*, Leipzig 1898) of what Cesare Borgia might have achieved had he not been struck down by illness at a critical time and how he might, through poison, have decimated the College of Cardinals and secured the papacy for himself. This "healthiest of all tropical monsters" (5, 117), this "beast of prey, healthy and sound!" (11, 21) seemed to many to be a throw-back to a time before the triumph of Christianity, a time of Roman glory, of atavistic triumphalism.[10] Schuler absorbed much from Traube and Furtwängler but the strained and eccentric atmosphere of Schwabing encouraged and fostered an anti-intellectualism and a cult of irrational vitalism. Rome, "Blutleuchte" and Swastika — these three components are the strands that characterize Schuler's thought, although "thought" is a misnomer, for "telesmatic" (i.e. talismanic) pictures, emerging from the blood, eclipse ratiocination and communicate more deeply. For Schuler, as for Klages, the corruption of life began with Judaeo-Christianity and a "historical" (as opposed to a "cosmic") viewpoint, a will to rational truth which "de-actualizes" the world: this will be the central argument in Klages's *Der Geist als Widersacher der Seele* (The Mind as Adversary of the Soul, 1929–1932). And it is Klages who, in 1944, attempted a definition of Schuler's "Blutleuchte": it is "a continuous, deeply moving shudder . . . a dark strangeness which throbs and seethes in a secret dwelling, a wild, woeful exultation, mixed with the beauty of the storm. It is Eros and Child, golden unity of life and, as such, gazes into radiant visions. In it the mystery of maternal cosmos is made manifest."[11]

The obsession with Rome is apparent both in Schuler's fragments and in the series of lectures he gave under the title *Vom Wesen der Ewigen Stadt* (On the True Nature of the Eternal City); these were given in 1915 and repeated later. As soon as Schuler had matriculated at the university in Munich he sought out Henrik Ibsen, whose *Emperor and Galilean* had fascinated him, a work published in 1873 and only performed some twenty years later. Ibsen was in Munich in 1890, living in the Maximilianstrasse where Schuler visited him. On his way to Ibsen's rooms he composed the "Periodonikes" scene of a projected three volume Nero novel. *Emperor and Galilean* could not fail to make an impact on him, being a portrayal of a search for a religion which exulted in the joy of life and which refused to submit to the chill of Christian ethics;[12] the extraordinary opening, set in Constantinople, with Julian and his brother waiting for the mad Emperor's hand to fall on them as it had on their eleven murdered kinsmen, the march on Rome and Julian's murder by a Christian fell on fertile ground. It has only now been possible, thanks to Baal Müller's edition, to gain an insight into Schuler's fragmentary utterances, his hectic visions and heightened ecstasies, and this chapter will now try to elucidate them.

The *Cosmogoniae Fragmenta* (Fragments of a Cosmogony), is a mass of disordered material whose preface refers to a journey to Rome (1894) and a procession of masked figures, to dithyrambic convulsions and, strangely, to the music of *Carmen* which deeply moved the author (*CA* 72) as it had Friedrich Nietzsche some six years previously (Ludwig Derleth is also mentioned). A "Nietzsche-Trias" follows, a group of three aphorisms which seeks, with sensuous imagery to find a new sexuality, from an awareness of which "a miraculous palm tree" arises whose dates swell like "eine neue Sonne," (a new sun: *CA* 74); a voice laments the Christian concept of *agape* which cuts deeply into life's fecundity. These fragments were meant to be incorporated into the *Nero* novel and exult in images of violet and purple, of emerald columns and rose-entwined pillars, of perfume and incense (*CA* 75). A "Tabula Secunda" contains the following couplet: "What is Freedom in the Thrust of Becoming? Eros in Pan. / What is Eros in Decline and Death? Christian delusion" (CA 76). This is the basic and central dichotomy for Schuler, the "ultimus paganorum" (Wolfskehl); Christianity is seen as inimical to life, to sexuality, to joy, and the victory of the pale Galilean strikes at the very heart of life itself. Dithyrambic perorations proclaim the triumph of Eros in Imperial Rome, the triumph of that which is cosmic, of life exultant in alabaster temples, beneath umbrageous and fragrant trees, in the "amethyst-purple of dream-heavy poppy." "Let Eros alone be the light of thine eye" (CA 80) — this injunction climaxes in a vision of red moons circling in a "violet ecstasy," with green suns enveloped in a crimson, sparkling inebriation.

In the section "Trias Emesa Nazareth" Schuler evokes the spirit of Heliogabalus who was born in Emesa (now Homs in Syria), high priest of the sun god who, aged fourteen, became Emperor of Rome. George's *Algabal* poems, as has been noted, are the finest German contribution to the decadent cult of Heliogabalus, but George is but one of the poètes maudits who saw in the degenerate boy-Emperor the personification of wanton and sterile debauchery.[13] Louis Couperus's *De berg van licht* may be adduced as an example, as may Jean Lombard's *L'agonie*: this novel describes a Rome in the grip of barbaric and voluptuous cults where the Christians are struggling for survival against the rule of the fifteen-year old adolescent Emperor. Heliogabalus, mitred, bejewelled, long-haired, painted and effeminate, wishes to impose on Rome the worship of a phallic black stone, symbol of his tyrannical power. He proceeds around Rome with a motley entourage of naked women, eunuchs, priests, captives, subservient senators and various wild beasts. Heliogabalus leads the orgies, copulating publicly with both sexes; opponents are murdered and thrown into the *cloaca maxima*, where Heliogabalus and his mother would later find their deaths. For Schuler, however, he is a "Sonnenkind," a child of the sun, a figure in whom the "Blutleuchte," or blood-radiance is most powerful felt: he represents radiant, transfigured or "telesmatic" life, "open existence" (these terms will be explained more fully later); the "Nazarene" however, is denial, or "closed existence." Schuler knows that, geographically, the distance between Emesa and Nazareth is short indeed, but Roman and Jew are separated by an unbridgeable gulf (CA 81). A "Triptychon des Korybantischen Dithyrambos" exults in the wild dance of life, a praise for Life as its most naked, most intense — "I am the Light . . . I am the Eye . . . I am the pearl . . . I am the frenzy . . . I am Life" (CA 83) — here Nietzschean *Lebensbejahung* achieves its most triumphant expression.

Most fascinating is the section "Domus Aurea. Cella Ithyphalli. Reiter-trias." Here Nero's golden house is portrayed, with a room of the Erect Phallus. In the centre of the room was a mosaic pattern of a revolving swastika whose purple, twitching limbs revolved around a ruby centre in a golden apple: these limbs sprayed forth golden ears of corn. Again, a discussion of the importance of the swastika for Schuler follows later; what is also significant there is the fact that the praise of the phallus is transformed into the cult of the hermaphrodite in that a scrotum is described which is a container for oil, and the opening in the glans, from which a flame emerges, also has the form of female genitalia. Sexuality, however deviant or esoteric to the modern mind, was at the heart of pagan life, exemplified by whirling swastika, hermaphoditic oneness and dancing fire. Paralipomena to the *Cosmogonos* include a prayer for extinction, reabsorption into maternal darkness:

> O mother night
> Take now this last lamp [the poet] unto you
> into your gentle, black-wreathed holy hand.
> Its drunken wick has drunk, the fool, of too much oil.
> Its tongue longed longingly in too much death.
> To you, o mother, mother!
> Extinguish
> loosen. . . (*CA* 90)

Reference to Bachofen's *Das Mutterrecht* (Mother Right) follows later; suffice it here to comment on Schuler's increasing insistence on the maternal, on warmth and womb, source of fecundity and life: a section "My Mother" recounts that "My mother is triumphant night and my father the flaming diurnal star; I, however, am sweet dusk. . ." (*CA* 92). This is remote, indeed, from Zarathustra's solar imperiousness, but he, too, had longed for darkness, longed to be suckled, to receive and not to give (4, 136). The reference to "Horus-Istisch" (*CA* 93) and to Zeus elaborates the theme of fatherlessness; Horus, the son of Isis and Osiris, conceived after the death of his father avenges the latter's death after years of concealment (he is often portrayed as a falcon, or a child). Strange indeed that Nietzsche should claim, in *Ecce Homo* (1908) that "I still live as my mother, after my father had already died — to speak in riddles. . ." (6, 264). A final fragment attacks the desacralisation of the world by Luther and the Reformation, the extirpation of pagan ritual and a "Jewish rabies" that blights the earth (*CA* 93).

The *Neroniana* material relates to Schuler's plans for a work on Nero, a figure who fascinated him (and not only him) at this time. The plans for a Nero novel came to him, he writes (*CA* 101) after the meeting with Ibsen in 1890; the scattered notes contain a vituperative onslaught against Tolstoy, particularly *The Kreutzer Sonata* for its damnation of sexual love and advocation of *agape* — "the gospel of exhaustion" (*CA* 103). For Nietzsche, Tolstoy's cult of pity was a symptom of decadence (6, 174); Schuler deliberately contrasts it with "Cosmische Kraft" or cosmic power, "essential life," energy and fire (*CA* 103), with the quadrumvirate "Goethe-Nietzsche-Dionysos-Uebermensch" held as an ideal antidote. The *Fragmenta Neronis Domini* contains an ecstatic introit:

> He rears up
> Bull Dionysus
> Branded with golden sacrificial ribbons.
> Cosmos
> Stigma.
> Cosmos
> Brand.
> Ready for axe and axe blow.
> Bull rage
> Ready for heart blood
> To fill the chalice for the inebriate
> For drunk ones, for sunk ones
> Hot, steaming bowls of the heart's blood.
> For all that is trampled
> In fragments and ordure
> Light-eyes which dive into trembling garlands.
> For all that rend serpents in ravings of night.
> I close the ring of blood
> Around the child Aeon
> I open the mouth of ardour
> To the one unknowing.
> This flaming, seething
> rearing, dreaming
> lit with glittering sword flash
> Darkened by shields
> Corybantiasis
> Nero cosmogonos
>
> (*CA* 108)

A drunken tone of joy and suffering is expressed here, a Dionysian ecstasy with a god as bull whose gushing, steamy blood fills the sacrificial chalices as a wild dance is executed. Most remarkable is the section "Ex capite de cosmogonia" which runs thus: "Host in the shrine. Cosmos the pregnant life-cell. Tongue of fire the essence of life. Child-like peoples exult in the urn-shape. The urn is divine for them, a pregnant mother their primary idol. On the host of her vulva the swastika is burning, the sign of fire its revelation. Crucified wood and nails. Crucified fire. In the cult of the primeval cell is announced all that still come to pass. . ." (CA 109). Further utterances extol the "Cinquecento," that remarkable century in which a pagan life-affirmation arose again in art, an art of beauty and blood. It is a vision of "Lebensessenz," of "Blutleuchte" of radiant, gleaming blood, but the triumph of beauty and life was short-lived — a "monstrous black mass of slag, of scoria, of Nazarene brimstone" (CA 112) scorched the earth, and "murderous miasmas rose from choking canals." This was the conquest of Rome by Luther, for Luther destroyed the "cells of light," extinguished the joy of "Blutleuchte" and elevated the pale Galilean as the sole path to salvation. The attack against Luther is continued in "Nero triumphans": the "scandal of Wittenberg" ensured the rise of a world without sacraments, a world of materialism and utilitarianism. No longer are there festivals to commemorate "the marriage of the soul with the light"; vulgar conformism is the order of the day where Nietzsche's "last man" has triumphed — it is the age of the mob, the louse (CA 113). Noble features are no longer found, the prevailing physiognomy is that of the dog. In a moving section Schuler defends his own homosexuality: the homosexual world of feeling, as one of

> the most radiant centres of individualistic light-creation [Lichtbildungen] in the world of antiquity [. . .] disappeared immediately with the triumphs of Christianity from literature and art. That purple net which spun a transfiguration of the senses over objects and space is destroyed without mercy. (CA 114)

Christianity has no place for the Greek concept of *agon*, of noble struggle, a contest for the highest prize; *agape* prevents this. But Schuler also extols hardness and praises pain and violence:

> Birth bursts open the mother's womb. Birth for the mother is blood, is pain, an experience of death. The volcanic destroys when it erupts. This is the law of nature. Killing is the right of each fiery force. As it is the right of youth, the young, strong, blood-filled *sabella proles*, radiant in the steel and the gleam of weapons. (CA 113)

The praise of violence, of killing even, grates upon the modern sensibility. Even more startling is the elevation of the swastika as the ultimate symbol.

Whether it stood as Caius [Caius Caesar] with silver hands in an azure night and pulled the moon into the calvary of its embrace. Whether it sparkled as Otho in the white coral and linen on the shoulder buckles of common legionaries and triumphant in the leather-smell of collars or the handles of shields, leaping as a drunken spark into all hearts, to leap forth from all eyes, all lips as a radiant, shouting solar joy, whilst its vessel burst in sacrificial death [. . .]. (*CA* 118)

The swastika is seen as cosmic symbol, glittering in the night or stitched as imperial signature on the uniform of Roman soldiers. Schuler's wildly associative mode of writing now hails Nero, "the censer, who lit the purifying vapour, who arched the rings of love into the vilest corner, who draws the sweetness of honey from any common song, filling it with march-like visions of the future, letting it blush at its urgency." And *Swastika* ends with the following: "We hurl fire into the night and copper-rage till there is blood from town to village to hamlet. Till it seethes in town and village and hamlet. . . to the last poplar-darkened cottage over which the towering sunflowers dream in night and silver." "Copper-rage" reminds us of the "kuretes" or ephebes who, dressed in copper, were to cure the insane Nietzsche (an idea which, apparently, Langbehn also entertained: *CA* 31); it is obvious that an emblem of a swastika is used by Schuler in a highly idiosyncratic manner, as we shall later see. It is found once more in the last poem in the *Fragmenta Neronis Domini*, the haunting and elusive "Phallikos." The title refers to the ithyphallic Bacchic hymns which accompanied the procession of the phallus:

> In zenith of blueness we gaze now at purple.
> Tit of milch-woman.
> Omphalos, swelling.
> Within the scarlet mesh of the ribbons
> Swells now and fills now the golden phallus.
> Not man, not maid.
> Create, conceive is the same.
> The one who creates not, creates light.
> The one who conceives not, bears light.
> In the heart of the depths the One is now gleaming.
> From this
> Life rolls forth in golden spirals.
> Wider and wider the whirling swastika
> Wider and paler. Wider and colder.
> Soma and moonring freeze its flow.
> In zenith of newness we gaze now at purple.
> Tit of milch-woman.

Omphalos, swelling.
Within the scarlet mesh of the ribbons
Swells now and fills now the golden phallus.

(CA 119)

The omphalos is the navel of the earth, the site of Delphic oracle; in depiction it is fused with a phallus or uterine symbolism, hence supporting the significant notion of androgyny in Schuler. "Soma" is a Sanskrit word for the intoxicating extract from certain hallucinogenic plants; the moon is held to be the chalice of this intoxicant. The poem tells of whirling life, of swastika, swelling phallus and "milch-woman"; an epilogue describes "essential life," cosmic world cultures, hermaphroditic unity, and swastika as the zenith of human consciousness: the enemy is Juda. Juda is wretchedness, is "stinking goat-reek," is Sodom, onanism, the rejection of the Hellenic, of paederasty; it is pestilence, and the Reformation is a manifestation of Mosaic perfidy and the beginning of modernism, of mechanization and crass Americanization. It is syphilis, anarchy and "la bête humaine," stagnation and mendacity (CA 120).

There is much that is controversial here, much that, with hindsight, has a sinister resonance. Before these concepts may be discussed the remaining fragment should be examined, and some knowledge gleaned of the lecture cycle that Schuler gave in Munich during the war years. The next fragmentary grouping bears the neologistic title Cella Vulgivaga; the opening lines refer to Schuler's Nero obsession and also Ludwig Quidde's brochure on Nero. Quidde, an eminent historian and a politician with pacifist convictions, had published the writing in Die Gesellschaft (1894) and had tacitly criticized the policies of Kaiser Wilhelm II; Quidde's description of Nero had obviously Schuler's full support. The Cella Vulgivaga is especially cryptic with frequent references to dancing youths, spinning circles, swastikas, fly-wheels, masturbation and Poe's story The Pit and the Pendulum; there is a repetition of the swastika, token of fire, burning on the vulva of a priestess (CA 124) and to Nietzsche's cure (the dancing copper-dressed ephebes : CA 125). The most important utterance is the Odin Trias completed in 1899 and handed to Ludwig Klages inscribed in ornamental calligraphy. The title page contained a black square two and a half centimetres in length and breadth and held in a wide golden circle within which a swastika (upon a white base) rotates, and from the arms of which twelve golden stars emerge: the whole was held by another square with a golden inscription "Vitae, Lumini Intimo, Cellaeque" (to life, to the inner light, to the cell — CA 384). The Trias starts with Odin hanging on the tree in the "oil blue night," wounded by the spear, the "inner phallus"; he hears of the rune of love and descends, longing for physical beings, the "seething cell-hearth." The second passage describes Jesus on the cross, eaten by Moloch, the "cella judica." He does not find the rune, he is "unable to redeem the cross of the spinning swastika" (*CA* 129). He hangs on the cross, longing for love, but Moloch frustrates him. The final section portrays the poet's soul hanging, as Odin, in the tree in an oil-blue night. Shuddering, it finds the rune of love. The cross is given "feet," that is, it becomes a "Hakenkreuz" (or fylfot), a swastika, and the "cells" or living essences are liberated from materiality and dross. Schuler thought highly of this almost impenetrable utterance: Judaicised Christianity could not redeem the world, and more ancient, more potent symbols were to be worshipped.

The remaining fragments are less substantial; Müller speaks of the cultivation of an aphoristic style which attempts to emulate Nietzsche (*CA* 384). Schuler laments Nietzsche's loneliness and compares it with that of Elisabeth of Austria (*CA* 131); two aphorisms refer to *The Magic Flute* and attack freemasonry, the mason representing the "Proto-Bock des Mosaismus" (*CA* 133). "We serve a Queen of Night" — this statement will lead to a vehement attack against the world of the fathers that would not be out of place in an expressionist manifesto.

> Where you find patriarchs you should seize their white beards and drown their worthy wrinkled visages in urine — and, best of all, start with your own fathers. The hand of him who crushes their calcified grasp will never wither. For then our law prevails, the mother with the thousand breasts, the Christian whore of Babylon. (*CA* 133)

This is the world of the Magna Mater, where Bachofen eclipses Nietzsche and the moon triumphs over the sun, the moon which Zarathustra felt might give birth to a sun, but did not (4, 156). Nietzsche is quoted verbatim (*CA* 134): "What did the parson's son confess? 'Even the bravest of us rarely has the courage to face that which he actually *knows*'" (the quotation comes from *Götzendämmerung* (The Twilight of the Idols: 6, 59). Schuler proposes a quotation from Nero (as reported by Suetonius) instead: "There has not yet been a Caesar who in fact realised what he is actually allowed to do" (*CA* 134). Nero represents the supreme artist, beyond morality and exulting in his power, and Nietzsche's vision of Cesare Borgia as Pope, as has been noted, is a variation of this concept of Roman power and aesthetic imperiousness incorporated in one ruthless figure. Schuler also deplored the "Los von Rom" movement of his day for in the Catholic church he still detected ancient mysteries, the cult of Mother and Child, the symbolism of star and crescent moon (*CA* 140). The attack on Jahwe-Kronos-Moloch is repeated, a composite trinity of Schuler's imagination which represents patriarchy and a "child-devouring morality." The onslaught against Juda and modernity is familiar; the Sun-king Ludwig II is hailed as a reincarnation of artistic glory, a true king who was succeeded by an "Oberförster" (Luitpold). The remaining fragment (*Aeolus, Lucerius, Tiberius*) need not detain us.

Ludwig Klages did not only publish a selection of the fragments; he also included in his 1940 edition a text of the famous series of lectures which Schuler, after initial reluctance, decided to give on *Vom Wesen der Ewigen Stadt* (On the True Nature of the Eternal City). Schuler's mother died in 1913 leaving him penniless, and after the break with George in 1904 Schuler had few associates who could offer material support. In the home of the publisher Hugo Bruckmann he did, however, meet Professor Gustav Willibald Freytag, son of the novelist Gustav Freytag, who was able to offer some financial help (he employed Schuler to bring his library into order). With the outbreak of war Freytag's financial position worsened and Schuler was advised to earn a modest income by lecturing. In 1915 he gave three evening lectures in the home of Graf von Seyssel d'Aix and repeated these in an extended form in the winter of 1917–1918 in Professor Freytag's library. He also lectured in Dresden in the spring of 1918 and, again, in 1922, in the Bruckmann house in Munich (there was also a private reading in the home of the Swedish painter Bertil Malmberg shortly before his death in 1923). Rainer Maria Rilke attended the 1915 readings and wrote an enthusiastic letter to Marie von Thurn und Taxis on March 18 of that year: he also went again to listen to Schuler in 1917, and a letter to Schuler (30 November 1917) expresses his admiration. Speculation that another listener may have been Adolf Hitler has been proved to be false.[14]

What is the argument of these lectures? It is apparent from the start that Schuler is not speaking as an antiquarian but as a man obsessed by Dionysian antiquity, a man overwhelmed by evidence of "cosmic life." The opening address insists: "My lectures speak to the soul, not the intellect. They seek to uncover inner sources of light within the listener. They woo in an erotic fashion: they seek procreation and the birth of light — their intention is, therefore, a religious act" (*CA* 219). Gazing within himself, the speaker informed his audience, he became aware of a throbbing effulgence, a telesmatic, mystical force, an "essential life" pulsing within the blood. (The word "telesmatic" derives from the Greek "telesma," or "completion": it gives us the word "talismanic" and is best understood as meaning "magical," or "numinous"). This living entity, when coming into contact with "cosmic radiance," glows and ignites. This is an erotic moment, and "Blutleuchte" results: it is a heightened state of awareness, or "Ergriffenheit." "Substance" becomes "essence" (or "Telesma") when the blood begins to gleam in ecstatic moments of heroic, or erotic, or magical experience, coming into contact and fusing with the cosmic spirit, becoming one with all that is and has been (*CA* 220). The figure of the hermaphrodite is extolled here, symbolising cosmic nuptials where the "polarised electrodes" of the telesmatic essence engage with an eternal self-impregnation. It was the lecturer's aim to seek out moments of cosmic ecstasy in world history, above all in antiquity. Of great importance here is the swastika: "At the heart of antiquity stood the swastika, the spinning, rotating wheel" (*CA* 222). This symbolised "open life" (das offene Leben), a sense of wholeness or oneness, erotic and glowing. The lecture ended with the lament that world history demonstrates a tragic loss of "Blutleuchte," of consecration and Dionysian celebration: the general mass of humanity is now incapable of experiencing awe and a sense of cosmic wonder. It deplored the "human fleas" that pullulated upon earth, the "atomised" senselessness of modern existence (*CA* 230); the reference to Nietzsche is also a telling one here.

It was the second lecture that greatly appealed to Rilke with its discussion of the realm of death. "Imagine," he wrote to the Princess, "that a man with an intuitive knowledge of Imperial Rome should undertake to explain the world in such a way that it was the dead who were truly essential and the realm of death one vast, unheard-of existence, our own little span of life was a kind of exception — and all this supported by an immense erudition [. . .]"[15] Schuler argued that death was not simply a "reservoir of life" but that those who had passed into the other realm after having achieved "Blutleuchte" would somehow remain eternally "present." Schuler would also use the image of the dark side of the moon for the "other relationship" (Rilke's "anderer Bezug"): death is not a Christian realm of purgatory and punishment but a transfigured complement to existence on earth. The facility with which Schuler moved among the Roman dead enormously impressed the poet who, after Schuler's death, explained to his wife that there was much of this thinker in the *Sonnets to Orpheus*, and that he had placed some narcissi on the altar of a deserted country chapel near Muzot in his memory.[16]

Lecture three emphasises the importance of Imperial Rome as a manifestation of "quintessential being" (*CA* 240). Denigrated and vilified, it nevertheless exhibited a unique florescence. Schuler delights in portrayals of festivals, banquets, baths: the symbolism is phallic and uterine, the salt-cellar holding pride of place as "sperma majorum." Of interest in the fourth lecture is a discussion of Nietzsche's concept of gladiatorial conflict as a canalisation or sublimation of brutality (*CA* 257). Schuler insists that gladiatorial battles were essentially matriarchal, that is, a demonstration of the violence of masculinity and the destructive male urge: the homage to Bachofen is very important, "the first to uncover the matriarchal aspect of antiquity" (*CA* 268). Korybantiasis, "Sonnenkind" and the worship of "lithos psychicos" (Seelenstein) follow, the "sun child," a radiant boy, representing "open life": his beauty is hermaphroditic. Schuler insisted that the Roman emperors were androgynous — Julius Caesar's raiment had long, loose sleeves with fringes, Nero's breast-cloth was derived from female dress, Caligula wore male and female dress alternately, sometimes appearing as a dancer, sometimes as Aphrodite, and Heliogabalus, the supreme "sun child" preferred female dress, exulting in his ambiguity (*CA* 270). The "sun child," surrounded by his dancing copper-clad warriors is the fixed point of a spinning wheel or swastika; his eternal enemy is the Magus, or patriarchal God, the tyrant representing "closed life" (*FuV* 233). The central image of the last lecture is that of Livia sitting before her house as the eagle drops a white hen into her lap, a hen which carries in its beak a blossoming laurel (*CA* 291). The meaning is clear: her womb is to be more powerful than Augustus Caesar's military might. And the lectures end with a threnody, a lament for the decline of Rome and for the rise of Christianity, a religion that extinguished "Blutleuchte" and insists upon the doctrines of damnation and original sin. Yet the final picture is not one of total pessimism — as the head of Orpheus still sang as it floated towards the island of Lesbos, so two contemporary figures gleam as exemplars of some cosmic awareness, two who found death by water: Ludwig II the Bavarian king who was drowned in 1886 in the Starnbergersee and Elisabeth of Austria-Hungary, murdered on the waterfront in Geneva in 1898. And both these noble souls are victims, "crushed by the black wheel which now is master over the earth"[17] (*CA* 304). After speaking these words after the 1922 lecture Schuler slowly walked backwards and declaimed the following verses before disappearing behind a black curtain:

> We shall return. We are not dead.
> Limbs that are swimming in primal red.
> We speak, and our blood is the living page,
> Husks of the sinners in purple rage.
> When the time has rushed in a passionless red

When the time is rotten and full of dread
We come again, through pain and fear —.

(*FuV* 92)

What is to be made of these lectures? Much is impenetrable, much, again, verges upon the bizarre. The Rome portrayed has little to do with the Rome of Mommsen or Eduard Meyer; it is eccentric, tropical, Dionysian, the scene of cults and rituals which represent "das offene Leben." Subsequent world history is darkened by "das geschlossene Leben," by Moloch or Jahwe, a Jewish-Christian world of sinfulness, fanaticism and vindictive aggression. The juxtaposition of sun-child and Magus exemplifies the basic clash between soteriological golden life and dark oppression, between a matriarchal state of wholeness and the violent world of thrusting masculinity. The homage to Bachofen is not peripheral: both Schuler and Klages derived much from the Swiss scholar whose *Das Mutterrecht* (Mother Right) received its second printing in 1897. It was Karl Wolfskehl who first read Bachofen (both *Versuch über die Gräbersymbolik der Alten* [On the Symbolism of Graves amongst the Ancients] and *Das Mutterrecht*); he gave a copy of the former to Klages as a gift, and Klages had it bound in finest snake-skin. Bachofen's *Die Sage von Tanaquil* (The Legend of Tanaquil, 1870), an investigation into oriental practices in ancient Rome, was also a potent inspiration. It is not easy, after almost a century, to imagine the febrile discussions in the house of Wolfskehl and others in Schwabing, discussions revolving around "Blutleuchte," cosmic verities, androgyny and related topics; one source of information (admittedly anecdotal) is Roderich Huch, cousin of the novelist Friedrich Huch, who had moved to Munich in 1899 and had been introduced to the "Kosmiker" by his cousin (Roderich had been hailed as the "Sonnenkind"; he had previously fallen from grace by refusing to stand naked before Stefan George).[18] Huch learned that rapture (Glut), for Schuler, was present above all in heathen peoples, especially the Romans: it was destroyed by Christianity and particularly the Reformation, but might be found in exceptional beings, even in the twentieth century. Women were worthy recipients and vessels of "Lebensglut," their apparent passivity elevating them above arid professional furtherance (Franziska Reventlow was praised for having given birth to an illegitimate son whose father she did not even know). The Jews were singled out for particular opprobrium for insisting on patriarchy, and Dionysian "Rausch" was hailed as an antidote to Jewish legalism. The created world was born from a passive soul: here Nietzsche, worshipped as the great announcer and herald of cosmic fervour, might be criticized for disseminating the doctrine of the will to power. A problem was posed by Wolfskehl who, albeit Jewish, preached matriarchy and celebrated Dionysian festivals in his house, striding through Schwabing with flowing beard and blazing eyes; as a "rapturous Oriental" he was, as we know, rejected because of his Zionism. It is obvious that the term "Jude" (or "molochitisch") has little to do with race or religion but with "Substanz," or general attitude to the cosmos; Luther, condemned by Schuler for his removal from Christianity of the last remnants of heathenism, was called a "Jew," as was Bismarck for his espousal of "Realpolitik." The term "Jew" could only be understood as a secret cipher within a gnostic system which sought to separate those who were open to cosmic epiphanies and those who were not.[19] If Schuler was anti-Semitic then his aversion was eclectic, eccentric, and wholly idiosyncratic. There is no perfervid nationalism here, for it was not Germany that provided the highest manifestation of "Blutleuchte" or "Lebensglut," but Imperial Rome. And the swastika, we remember, is not a symbol of German nationalism, but hangs as a silver jewel in the sky, or burns upon the vulva of the earth-goddess.

It is now appropriate to tackle this most problematic sign and its place in Schuler's Weltanschauung. The swastika was originally an ancient Indian ornament (in Sanskrit the word "svastika" means wellbeing or good fortune); later, however, the sign became associated with esoteric ideas asserting the superiority of Aryan peoples. Klages claimed that Schuler had come across the symbol (a "Hakenkreuz") in 1895 and had given it the Indian name "svastika"; Roderich Huch recalls Schuler's ecstasy on seeing the swastika on a tea service in Wolfskehl's home. We have noted its significance in the *Fragmenta* and also in the lectures. Recent studies have drawn attention to the appropriation of the swastika by occult and völkisch groups in late nineteenth century Germany and Austria;[20] Franz Hartmann used the sign on his theosophical journal *Lotosblüthen* (Lotus Blossoms, 1896–1900); Guido von List used both swastika and triskelion (three-legged) glyphs in such publications as *Die Rita der Ario-Germanen* (The Rites of the Ario-Germans, 1908) and *Die Bilderschrift der Germanen* (The Hieroglyphics of the Germans, 1910), where he argued that the swastika was a symbol of light and fire, now to be associated with the "Armanen," that is, the Nordic, racially pure peoples (it is claimed that he buried eight bottles of wine in the form of a swastika beneath the ruins of the Roman city of Carnuntum); Lanz von Liebenfels, author of *Theozoologie oder die Kunde von den Sodoms-Äfflingen und dem Götter-Elektron* (Theozoology or the Doctrine of the Apes of Sodom and the Electron of the Gods, 1905) propagated the idea of a chosen people and, at

Burg Werfenstein, founded the Ordo Novi Templi, embarking upon a crusade against miscegenation (it was claimed that the swastika was used as a symbol by the Templars); other groups, such as the "Germanenorden" with its doctrine of "ariosophy" or Nordic supremacy, used a curved swastika, superimposed upon a cross, as its heraldic device. The "Thule Society" would foster a semi-religious belief in a race of Aryan god-men and demand the extermination of inferiors: Heinrich Himmler proved particularly susceptible to these notions. A further thrust is provided by those who preached a "Welteislehre" (Hanns Hörbiger),[21] where ice was regarded as the fundamental substance of the universe and where a comparison is made between glacial cosmogony and the cosmology of the Iceland eddas with their references to cataclysms (Muspilheim and Niflheim), and from those who proposed the existence of an ancient race which was supposed to have its origin in the Arctic and then spread southwards across Eurasia.[22] The swastika would then be held to symbolise the Nordic race; the fifteen stars of the Great and Little Bears move in a pattern which, to primitive man, represented a wheel or swastika (the seasonal positions of Ursa minor around the then pole-star, Thurbon, represent this). The astrologer Richard Morrison (who died in 1874) founded an "Order of the Svastika or the Brotherhood of the Mystic Cross," and it was Madame Blavatsky who incorporated the swastika into the seal of the Theosophical Society as symbolising the centripetal and centrifugal powers that preserve harmony and keep the universe in steady, unceasing motion.[23] Occultism, völkisch "ariosophy" and theosophy — the swastika has proved a proud and powerful cipher for disparate believers, feeding into the early days of National Socialism when Adolf Hitler selected the "right hand" swastika to be the emblem for his party, a movement representing, some have claimed, the "Wheel of the Black Sun," an earthly fire recreated by man, or the ancient, counterclockwise movement of the return of the Aryan races to their esoteric centre.

It is axiomatic that Schuler would have rejected "ariosophy" or any emphasis on Nordic polar myth: his gaze was firmly fixed on the Mediterranean, upon Imperial Rome above all. (The reference in Dante's *Paradiso* to the "fifteen stars," the "primal wheel" revolving around the pole, may have been known to him). His reference to the swastika burning on the vulva of the priestess, the crucified wood and nails, is puzzling; a recent study[24] on the swastika helps to throw some light. Heinrich Schliemann discovered in Troy many potsherds and whorls upon which the swastika was inscribed; he claimed that around six hundred objects were excavated which were adorned by this ornament. One of Schliemann's closest collaborators and honorary director of the French archaeological institute in Athens was Emile Bournof, cartographer and polymath who sought to link the swastika to an Aryan, anti-Semitic tradition. His work *La Science des religions* (1888) may be wayward enough, but one page of the English translation of Schliemann's *Ilias* (London 1880) is given in Quinn's study and this page, discussing Bournof, helps us to understand Schuler's swastika.[25] Bournof held that both the right-hand and left-hand swastikas represented the two pieces of wood which were laid crosswise upon one another before the sacrificial altars in order to produce the sacred fire, and the ends of which were bent round at right angles and fastened by means of four nails. At the point where the two pieces of wood were joined there was a small hole in which a thin piece of wood, in the form of a lance, was rotated by means of a cord made of cowhair and hemp until the fire was generated by friction. An idol excavated by Schliemann had the swastika emblem on her vulva: the generator of fire, also of life, are closely parallel. It is almost certain that Schuler read Schliemann's *Ilios. Stadt und Land der Trojaner* (1881) as this would have been compulsory reading for any student of archaeology (as would *Ithaka*, 1896, *Trojanische Altertümer*, 1874, *Troja*, 1883, and *Tirnys*, 1886). Attempts to claim the swastika for Nordic man Schuler would have rejected, but the swastika as womb or well of procreation would have fascinated him.

Alfred Schuler is remote from pan-German irrationalism. His "anti-Semitism," although it may be reprehensibly irresponsible, belongs in a different order from that of Adolf Hitler. Schuler dismissed Christianity as a form of "Judaism for the people," a vengeful and guilt-ridden doctrine; indeed, the Christian "Moloch" may be the more vindictive and sinister of the deities (Nietzsche's analysis of morality in *Zur Genealogie der Moral* is very close here). What would he have made of an incipient Nazi party, the burgeoning swastika flags becoming increasingly apparent in Munich? Did he not believe that it was the swastika rather than the Christian cross which "can, as no other sign, warn and arouse us, light the holy flame in us so that we become joyful sacrifices to the highest [. . .] a victory sign of the new inner-world God?"[26] He died in 1923 before the November putsch: a letter to Kurt Saucke, the Munich book seller, expresses the fear that "the nationalistic tumour [. . .] is the drunken torch of death lighting the masses the way to the slaughterhouse."[27] The brutish ignorance of the S.A. would have appalled him, albeit an awareness of the indebtedness of Italian fascism to Imperial Rome may have led to a tentative support of Mussolini, as it did in Rilke's case. Fascism as "a modern counterpart of earlier hierarchic societies in which authority, stability and inequality had provided the soil of flowering cultures"[28] had its appeal, but the ruthless masculinity of Nazism none. Hitler was no Heliogabalus, and the symbol adopted by the Deutsche Arbeiterpartei, the red of socialism, the white of nationalism and the black of racism was an offensive travesty. Schuler was not, *pace* Aschheim, a Nazi, and it would be appropriate to let Karl Wolfskehl, in his New Zealand exile, have the last magnanimous word: "The figure of Alfred Schuler continues to exist in the wholeness of its mythical reality, in its plenitude, its greatness [. . .] Schuler himself will remain, venerable, wondrous and full of deep significance."[29]

Notes

[1] Alfred Schuler, *Cosmogonische Augen. Gesammelte Schriften*, ed. by Baal Müller (Paderborn: Igel Verlag, 1997), 307–308. This is the first time that Schuler's work has been readily available and all further references to Schuler's writing, unless otherwise stated, will be to this edition under the abbreviation *CA*. Ludwig Klages and three other literary executors published a selection of Schuler's work under the title *Dichtungen* in 1930; ten years later Klages published *Alfred Schuler. Fragmente und Vorträge aus dem Nachlaß* (Leipzig: Johann Ambrosius Barth) which remained the sole source of information on Schuler until Baal Müller's edition (Klages's 1940 selection, when quoted, will be abbreviated as *FuV*). Sections from the *Neronis Domini Fragmenta* may be found in Walter Killy, *Die deutsche Literatur 7. 20 Jahrhundert 1880–1930. Texte und Zeugnisse* (Munich: Beck, 1967), 1088; Schuler's review of Ibsen's *Master Builder*, together with some of the *Kosmoganiae Fragmenta* are included in Walter Schmitz, *Die Münchner Moderne* (Stuttgart: Reclam, 1990). Further quotations from Schuler's *Nachlaß* may be found in Gerhard Plumpe, *Alfred Schuler. Chaos und Neubginn. Zur Funktion des Mythos in der Moderne* (Berlin: Agora Verlag, 1978).
[2] The review appeared under the title "Einige Gedanken über Ibsens neuestes Werk *Baumeister Solness*" in *Die Gesellschaft* 9 (1893), 352–355 (*CA* 214–217); the poem is a sonnet dedicated to the author Leopold von Andrian and was published in the *Blätter für die Kunst* 7 (1904: *CA 141*).
[3] See *FuV* 72–3, also George's poem *AS* from *Das Jahr der Seele* (The Year of the Soul), which specifically refers to that evening and the experience of "worlds of madness." This "römisches Fest" should not be confused with the later "Antikes Fest" which was held in Wolfkehl's house on February 22, 1903 where Wolfskehl appeared as Dionysus, George as Caesar and Schuler as the Earth-mother.
[4] *FuV* 76. The defection, or "Großer Schwabinger Krach" has been sensationalized and trivialized in many memoirs and *romans à clef*. The reasons are

succinctly described in *CA* 28–30 and relate basically to Wolfskehl's Zionism which was anathema to Schuler and Klages despite the latter's admiration for Wolfskehl as the embodiment of an "altjüdische Rasse." George defended Wolfskehl against Klages, and the rift between George and the "Kosmiker" was sealed. For Wolfskehl's position (and magnanimity) see *Briefwechsel. Karl und Hanna Wolfskehl/Friedrich Gundolf (1899–1931)* ed. by Karlhans Kluncker, 2 vols. (Amsterdam: Castrum Peregrini, 1988), vol. 1, 93 and 119. See also Gundolf's letter printed in *Die Münchner Moderne*, op. cit. 479, on the "Zerfall der Kosmischen Runde" where Schuler appears as "der violette Ringelnero." (Wolfskehl did, for a while, carry a loaded pistol to ward off physical attack: he accidentally shot himself in the leg — see *CA* 29). For a more sober account see Gerhard Plumpe, "Alfred Schuler und die Kosmische Runde" in Manfred Frank, *Götter im Exil. Vorlesungen über die neue Mythologie* (Frankfurt a. M.: Suhrkamp, 1988), vol. 2, 213–256, also Martin Vogel, *Apollinisch und Dionysisch. Geschichte eines genialen Irrtums* (Regensburg: Gustav Bosse Verlag, 1960) especially 259–277.

[5] Franziska zu Reventlow, *Tagebücher 1895–1910* (Frankfurt a. M.: Fischer 1976) [Jan. 1904], 277.

[6] Roderich Huch, *Alfred Schuler, Ludwig Klages und Stefan George. Erinnerungen an Kreise und Krisen der Jahrhundertwende in München-Schwabing* (Amsterdam: Castrum Peregrini, 1973) 36.

[7] Theodor Lessing, *Einmal und nie wieder* (Gütersloh: Bertelsmann, 1969), especially 322–329. (Schuler is described as "an oddity, a curious mixture of charlatan and genius, a show-off and a visionary.")

[8] Lessing, *Einmal*, 256.

[9] Gerd-Klaus Kaltenbrunner, "Zwischen Rilke und Hitler — Alfred Schuler," *Zeitschrift für Religion und Geistesgeschichte* 19 (1967), 336.

[10] Richard Hamann and Jost Hermand, *Gründerzeit* (Berlin: Aufbau, 1965), 260.

[11] Ludwig Klages, *Rhythmen und Runen. Nachlaß herausgegeben von ihm selbst* (Leipzig: Johann Ambrosius Barth, 1944), 270.

[12] Michael Meyer, *Ibsen* (London: Penguin, 1985), 397.

[13] Wolfdietrich Rasch, *Die literarische Décadence um 1900* (Munich: Beck, 1986), 170.

[14] Robert Boehringer, *Mein Bild von Stefan George* (Munich: Küpper, 1951) 109, claims that Hitler was present at the first lecture given in Elsa Bruckmann's house in Munich in 1922; Karl-Heinz Schuler has demonstrated without a doubt that Hitler first visited the Bruckmann home in 1924, after Schuler's death. In "Alfred Schuler und der Nationalsozialismus," *Jahrbuch der deutschen Schillergesellschaft* 41 (1997), 383–388.

[15] Rainer Maria Rilke. *Briefe in zwei Bänden*, ed. by Horst Nalewsi (Frankfurt a. M.: Insel, 1991), vol. 1, 566 (March 18, 1915).

[16] Rainer Maria Rilke, 2, 301 (April 23, 1923).

[17] Another example of the poeticising of Elisabeth's death is D'Annunzio's description, translated by Hofmannsthal as *Kaiserin Elisabeth* (Hofmannsthal ed. cit., *Prosa* 1), 369. "Women, strangers, let down the braids of her imperial hair and sprinkled her with water; they found upon her breast two drops of topaz coloured blood, and in her eyes the staring apprehension of that which lay beyond the grave."

[18] Roderich Huch, op. cit., 39.

[19] Steven Aschheim, *Culture and Catastrophe. German and Jewish Confrontations with National Socialism and other Crises* (London: Macmillan, 1996), 59, writes convincingly on Otto Weininger's tortured attempts at defining what it meant to be a Jew. "Judaism was, for him, not a historical tradition or an ethic or racial category. It was rather a Platonic idea, a psychic negative potential of all human beings. There are 'Aryans who are more Jewish than many Jews, and actual Jews who are more Aryan than certain Aryans,' he wrote in his famous *Sex and Character* (1903)." Aschheim is, however, less perceptive when he boldly states that Schuler was a Nazi (73).

[20] Nicholas Goodrick-Clarke, *The Occult Roots of Nazism. The Ariosophists of Austria and Germany 1890–1945* (Wellingborough: Aquarian Press, 1985).

[21] Robert Bowen, *Universal Ice and Ideology in the Nazi State* (London: Belhaven, 1993).

[22] Joscelyn Godwin, *Arktos. The Polar Myth in Science, Symbolism and Nazi Survival* (London: Thames and Hudson, 1993).

[23] Peter Washington, *Madame Blavatsky's Baboon. Theosophy and the Emergence of the Western Guru* (London: Secker and Warburg, 1993).

[24] Malcolm Quinn, *The Swastika. Constructing the Symbol* (London and New York: Routledge, 1994).

[25] Quinn, *Swastika*, 81.

[26] This description of the swastika appeared in 1918 in Eugen Diederich's *Die Tat*; it is quoted in Martin Green, *Mountain of Truth. The Counter-culture Begins. Ascona 1900–1920* (Hanover, NH and London: UP of New England, 1986).

[27] Hans-Eggert Schröder, *Ludwig Klages 1872–1956. Katalog zur Centenar Ausstellung*, Marbach am Neckar (1972), 84. Schröder comments on Schuler's disgust at the vulgarization of the swastika by the Nazis and his subsequent request that an ornamental trefoil be carved instead upon his mausoleum.

[28] J. R. Harrison, *The Reactionaries. Yeats, Lewis, Pound, Eliot, Lawrence. A Study of the Antidemocratic Intelligentsia* (New York: Schocken, 1967), 195–196.

[29] Kaltenbrunner, *Zwischen Rilke und Hitler*, 347.

Ludwig Klages.
Courtesy of Schiller Nationalmuseum and
Deutsches Literaturarchiv, Marbach.

4 : Ludwig Klages

We do not seek the mundane world of men —
Stormgirt we roll in spaces sonorous. . .
— Ludwig Klages

Moloch!
Moloch whose soul is endless oil and stone. Moloch whose
soul is electricity and banks! Moloch whose poverty is the
spectre of genius! Moloch whose fate is a cloud of sexless
hydrogen! Moloch whose name is the Mind!
— Allen Ginsberg

THERE ARE, AS IN THE CASE OF SCHULER, anecdotes in abundance.
"One night," Theodor Lessing wrote in his autobiography,

> the three of us, Klages, Stefan George and myself, were walking along
> the banks of the river Isar when we spotted an old man, down and out
> apparently and blind drunk, staggering towards us. It was obvious that
> he had lost his way and would end up falling in the river. We talked
> about it as we continued on our way. I said "We are obliged to turn
> back and put him on the right path." Klages opined: "There is no
> more blissful end for the wretch than an intoxicated demise." And
> George: "The shadow of a tree is more important than the death of
> this insect. . .".[1]

The Gräfin Franziska zu Reventlow provided a lurid and self-indulgent
account of "Wahnmoching" where "Hallwig" (i.e. Klages) imposed an
imperious regime; her diaries likewise exulted in portrayals of Klages
who was briefly her lover: "O Klages, Klages, demonic, devastating, divine [. . .]"[2] Later it will be the demented Alice Donath, model for the
figure of Clarissa in Robert Musil's *Der Mann ohne Eigenschaften* (The
Man without Qualities, 1930–43) who, exalted, addressed him thus:
"O Klages! Do you not feel that we walk the earth together? That, together, we encircle the sun? That we bear common sorrow? [. . .] Thus
we walk, together, to our destiny! God be with us!"[3] The anecdotes recede and it will be charges of irrationalism levelled against him which
will lend him a notoriety; Thomas Mann will denigrate him, as we shall

see, and Georg Lukács will, unsubtly, condemn him as a precursor of fascism. Of his anti-Semitism there can be no doubt, as much of his writing will bear witness, although it is an anti-Semitism of an eccentric provenance. But Klages is a complex phenomenon, ill served by the effluxions of overwrought ladies and those seeking to equate irrationalism with fascism, and Romantic conservatism with *Lebensphilosophie*. This chapter will attempt an objective appraisal of his work, indicating an indebtedness to Nietzsche's iconoclasm and passion, but also a reluctance to advocate the cult of power, indeed, an indebtedness to writers such as Novalis and Carus, above all to Bachofen, and a deep concern with the preservation of life and the natural world.

What was he? Poet? Psychologist? Philosopher? Graphologist? Exponent of "characterology"? Categorization is difficult in his case. He arrived in Munich in 1893 after studying chemistry and physics in Leipzig and, briefly, at the Technical High school in Hanover. A decisive meeting was that with Stefan George in a Munich guest-house that same year, which led to an invitation to write for the *Blätter für die Kunst* and to submit to George's artistic hegemony. Klages, then twenty one years old, contributed a selection of neoromantic verses ("Early Spring," "Across the White Meadow," "Like the roofs in the park" to name but three of them), also aphorisms ("On the Creative Man") and prose utterances, particularly *Der Eroberer* (The Conqueror). This last portrays a solitary leader, moving on horseback across a desolate plain: he pauses and sits in "lapidary immobility," his features reminiscent of "the splendour of ravaged Dolomites"; his gaze has "the cold gleam of the Northern Lights." Images of metal prevail ("bluish steel, metallic mirror") and we read that the Conqueror "had welded the merciless blade of his hatred in the white fire of lightning." He had longed for light and love but, despised, now turns his hatred upon the world, stamping upon it his indomitable will. Utterly alone, he can subdue half the world, a Tamburlaine-figure with the features of Zarathustra, an archetypal man of destiny.[4] The essay "From the Psychology of the Artist" describes the artist in similar terms: he resembles the man of action, the general, the hero; "On the Creative Man" extols the artist as the embodiment of vital, often monstrous forces. Both these writings betray the presence of Nietzsche, a Nietzscheanism linked with George's aestheticism, with the concept of the artist as spiritual aristocrat, remote in azure loneliness, a superman beyond good and evil. George's appropriation of Nietzsche's *Herrenmoral* attitudes is well known: the young poet Richard Perls described him as an uncrowned king who condescended to give audience, and George himself insisted (in a letter to Sabine Lepsius) that life was only possible for him in the position of absolute authority (oberherrlichkeit).[5] The famous "Nietzsche" poem (1900–01) uses imagery derived from Nietzsche's own "Ruhm und Ewigkeit," places the "Dichter-Philosoph" alongside Christ himself and portrays the lightning hurled from the height into the world of the ignorant and the superfluous. That Klages's reception of Nietzsche was mediated by George at this time (around 1900) cannot be denied. But Klages's attitude to both men underwent a radical change: he became increasingly reluctant to submit to George's imperious demands and, on a much profounder level, became convinced that Nietzsche's concept of the will to power was fundamentally flawed. It was Bachofen who came as a revelation to him, causing a rejection of the worship of both ephebe and *Übermensch*, and diverting his thinking into radically different channels.

In 1894 Karl Wolfskehl came to Munich and made a lasting impression upon Klages: despite the "Kosmiker-Streit" Klages was still able, in the 1940 Schuler edition, to give a sympathetic portrayal of Wolfskehl whereas George is abruptly rejected a being merely a lover of young men and a seeker after sterile rhymes. It was Wolfskehl, as has been noted, who had read Bachofen's *Das Mutterrecht* and *Versuch über die Gräbersymbolik der Alten* and recommended them to Klages; *Das Mutterrecht* proved especially fruitful. Klages steeped himself in the book for five weeks on end, inaccessible to his Schwabing colleagues; it was this work that Klages regarded as the most precious volume in his library. (Later, in February 1919, Klages visited Bachofen's widow who still lived in Basle and who gave him a photograph of her husband as well as the unpublished manuscript of her husband's account of his journey to Greece; Klages would go as far as to say to a Swiss friend that he, Klages, reckoned the work of Bachofen to be amongst the greatest spiritual creations of mankind and the guiding star of his life). *Das Mutterrecht* became compulsory reading in "Wahnmoching"; again, Franziska zu Reventlow supplies anecdotal evidence for its popularity, when she has "Dr. Sendt" (i.e. Paul Stern) explain the following in her *Herrn Dames Aufzeichnungen* (Mr. Lady's Writings):

> Everything beginning with the prefix Ur [original or primitive], has a particular resonance here — Ur-time, Ur-night, Ur-forces, Ur-shudder and so on. And remember — the difference between "cosmic" and "molochitic" is the same as between "matriarchal" and "patriarchal" [. . .] According to Bachofen, a well-known scholar [. . .] the most primitive form of life is "hetaeric," and here in Wahnmoching we consider this "enorm," colossal. Hetaerism is the expression of the blind, procreative Earth, honoured in cultic chthonic festivals.[6]

Herrn Dames Aufzeichnungen may be rejected as *Trivialliteratur* but it rightly emphasises the importance of *Das Mutterrecht,* which became the bible for the esoteric pan-gnostic circle which sprang up around Schuler and Klages, a circle that increasingly reflected an anti-Christian bias, a rejection of modernism (associated increasingly with Judaism) and a quest for Dionysian community. There is still Nietzsche here, but a Nietzsche modified by Bachofen's *Das Mutterrecht.*

Bachofen's book profoundly influenced not only the "Kosmiker" in "Wahnmoching" but also, through Franziska Reventlow, the Utopian colony in Ascona which she visited in 1910. (Ascona became notorious after Otto Gross had moved there and attracted a motley collection of outsiders, eroticists, anarchists and those who sought to reject the authoritarianism and paternalism of Wilhelmine Germany).[7] It was believed by many that Bachofen had discovered an older and better civilization, unlike the one around them in 1900, based on gynaecocracy (women's rights, women's religion and so on), but the book has a far more polyvalent, a much less simple argument. It begins with the conviction that the power of myth is irrefutable and that its study is vital to the modern age (the book first appeared in 1861). Myth is not formless, like shifting sand; there are laws and precepts to be learned as there are from any discipline. There follows a tribute to the dark mystery of pre-Hellenic times, a period which should not be rejected as primitive but praised for its fecundity: later developments, although necessary for the development of the human race, lacked the earlier cultic quality. Socrates sitting at the feet of Diotima, following only with difficulty the poetic flight of her mystic revelations, was indeed an awesome image, yet Bachofen sees that there must be a necessary progression from inchoate, chthonic, female-based wisdom to the pellucid radiance of paternity, as there is a progression from Hetaerism (indiscriminate copulation) to the cult of Demeter, of ordered matriarchy and agriculture. But this was a slow process, Bachofen concedes: woman was not, he writes, adorned with all her charms to wilt in the arms of one individual, and the temptation to relapse, to return to the world of the fecund swamp, is ever present.

It was the cult of Dionysus which brought a new direction into the struggle between Hetaerism and Demeter (and here Bachofen's description of Dionysus differs radically from that of Nietzsche, approximating more to Hölderlin's concept of Dionysus as "the creative god").[8] Dionysus appears as the conqueror of matriarchy, particularly of its degeneration into Amazonian excesses. Dionysus is the implacable enemy of all that is unnatural (the mutilated breasts of the Amazon), seeking to propagate marriage, the return of woman to motherhood and the recognition of the splendour of his own phallocentric nature. Yet Dionysus is also to be seen, Bachofen writes, as the god of women, the source of their sensual and suprasensual desires, the centre of their whole existence — and hence it is they who recognise him in his true glory. He transfigures, in the beauty of his youth, both Amazonian truculence and hetairic lubriciousness, but, Bachofen knows, the revelation of the phallus brings with it a threat, a temptation to revert to telluric sexuality.

Dionysus is the god who approaches the status of Apollo, Dionysus, in whom the male principle enters its highest manifestations, the phallic potency now enriched by an abundance of fertility cults celebrated by women. He rises as a prince of light — and yet he cannot aspire to the highest, the purest form of illumination. This is reserved for Apollo in his immaterial radiance. The physical thrust of paternity, seeking copulation, is presided over by Dionysus, but the spiritual aspect of paternity, of the male principle, is Apolline. At the dawn of Hellenism a motherless virgin, Pallas Athene, leapt from the head of Zeus to rule over pure, incorporeal paternity; the movement from matriarchy to patriarchy coincides with the highest religious development in mankind, a movement away from the physical to the metaphysical. And Bachofen's ambiguity is apparent here: he must greet the spiritual hegemony of Zeus and the patriarchal principle, but his style is quickened by an awareness of the fascination exerted by gynaecocracy in all its manifestations. The cult of Apollo has a hyperborean origin: virgins brought votive offerings annually to Delos, where it was established. Salvation comes from the North, and from the North there comes the true "Lichtheld" — but the womb of the fertile South constantly beckons.

Bachofen's *Das Mutterrecht* is a fascinating as well as a difficult book, not simply the account of the anthropologist but the hymn of an ardent, if restrained, lover of Greek myth. Most striking are is portrayals of the symbolic meaning of the earth, the sun and the moon, particularly the latter. The earth represents the extramarital, natural, telluric principle; the sun represents patriarchy; the moon represents the mediator, moving on the boundary between the telluric and the solar realms. It is the purest of the material, transient bodies and the impurest within the celestial realm. The moon steps before the sun as woman before man; the moon is female the earth male (here Bachofen quotes from Genesis chapter 37, verses 9–10). That which is above the moon is eternal and incorruptible, like the sun; that which is below is transient and corruptible. As opposed to the Sun the moon is the female, conceiving entity, but as opposed to the earth it is the male fructifier, sending forth its watery beams upon the earth. The body (soma) is of the earth; the soul (psyche) is of the moon, whilst the spirit (nous) has a solar provenance. Bachofen is most eloquent on the symbolic meaning of milk and honey for woman (the anointing of the female genitals before copulation) and wine for man; his erudition will provide a whole fund of symbols and images whose diffusion was indeed remarkable. Another term deriving from Bachofen is "Pelasgian," relating to the ancient, prehistoric world of the Eastern Mediterranean: this will play a considerable part in Klages's major work *Der Geist als Widersacher der Seele* (The Mind as Adversary of the Soul).[9] It is the Pelasgian, pre-Hellenic world which is the supreme beneficiary of chthonic mystery, and the memory of that sunken world will forever be a protection against a sterile Hellenism, a structural mythology alien to Sibylline utterances. Both the fecund swamp *and* the ordered world of Demeter were inimical to Christianity, Bachofen concludes, for Christianity asserted the power of masculine spirituality. But ancient rites lived on despite the attempt made by Christianity to extirpate them, and the Knights Templars with their "baphomet" harkened back to earlier rituals (the chapter on Ludwig Derleth will have more to say on this). And one sentence from *Das Mutterrecht* struck Klages with the force of revelation: the quotation from Paul's First Letter to the Corinthians, Chapter 15, verse 46 which, in German, runs as follows: "Nicht das Geistige ist das Erste, sondern das Seelische, nachher das Geistige." It was not the "spiritual" realm which was fundamental, but the realm of the "soul": the Authorised Version juxtaposes here the "spiritual" and the "natural." For Klages the terms "Geist" and "Seele" define the basic dichotomy; the world of abstraction, of analysis and logic may well represent a striking achievement, but there will be a great impoverishment if the ancient substratum is denied.[10]

It is not difficult to understand the impact that this book, through its second edition (1897) made upon Schwabing (and later Ascona). There is the inevitable trivialization and vulgarisation: the worship of the womb of Franziska Reventlow, the cult of woman as the origin of creation (with Gustave Courbet's painting of 1866, *L'Origin du Monde*, as a suitable pendant). Bachofen had indeed portrayed woman as the "Urprinzip," the basic, maternal, "given" substance: woman "is," but man "becomes"; woman is eternal and immutable, but man is less fixed, hence closer to death. The cult of chthonic creativity reached preposterous levels in Schwabing: Schuler is reported to have rounded upon his mother and reprimanded her for not knowing what a womb was. But Klages was drawn above all to the rich nexus of interlocking images or "Urbilder" which Bachofen provided, the images of moon and water, honey and wine, tree, sun and a whole host of others, redolent with symbolic force. A sunken world was rediscovered, suffused with divine immanence, a Pelasgian world, a world from the deepest unconscious layers, of powerful resonances, admitting the paramount importance of "Seele" as opposed to "Geist," emotive personality as opposed to sterile ratiocination. The points are set here for the future direction which Klages's thinking will take, and it will be an anti-Semitic, anti-Christian direction for Judaism, in its imposition of a patriarchal God, is seen as inimical to Pelasgian gynaecocracy. And how could any religion whose aim it was "to bring to nought things that are" (Paul, Corinthians I, Chap. 1 verse 28) satisfy on a profound level? From Nietzsche, Klages had learned that Christianity was a nihilistic, a *décadent* religion, and it is to Nietzsche that we must now return.

Like Schuler, Klages valued Nietzsche's mythic regeneracy and vitalism, his emphasis on violent destruction and new beginning, on the birth of the new after the defeat of the moribund. Richard Hinton Thomas has written of "the enormous and varied debt which Klages owed to Nietzsche"[11]; in *Die psychologischen Errungenschaften Nietzsches* (Nietzsche's Psychological Achievements, 1926) Klages speaks of Nietzsche's influence in terms of typhoons, earthquakes, and volcanic eruptions, as dramatic as the impact of a work by Böcklin or as a fearful journey:

> Scarcely have we begun to read Nietzsche than we find ourselves forced into a magic carriage which rushes at vertiginous speed through endless landscapes hurling us into the depths of the earth one minute, then flinging us on to icy glaciers and mountain peaks, and everything is shot through with a harsh and brilliant light, often terrible and threatening, always violent and overwhelming.[12]

Nietzsche is a philosopher, a prophet, a poet, a stylist, a rhetorician, but he is extolled above all as a psychologist or, to use the term which Klages preferred when referring to himself, a "Seelenforscher" or "Seelenerrater"; it was with Nietzsche, Klages claims, that "Seelenforschung," or "soul research" really began. Nietzsche's transvaluation of all values was the crucial fulcrum for Klages who seized upon the relationship between "Geist" and life. If life is the highest good what is its relationship to the intellect, to logic? Is ratiocination to be defended? Klages explains that one can take sides for or against logic — "one takes the latter stance if one is on the side of Life, which is alogical and unintellectual. Life and the intellect go different ways and, indeed, according to Nietzsche the intellect is a disease of life" (*EN* 4). Nietzsche was right, Klages argues, to attack the fanciful notion that "there could be a *cogitare* without a *vivere*, a cognition without experience" (*EN*

23). Nietzsche, like many of the Romantics, had longed for a truth to be communicated without the need to resort to analytic knowledge; he longed to communicate meaning without implicating his vision in those processes of despoilment and falsification which inevitably attend the illness of consciousness and analytical language; Zarathustra would use the image of "Geist" cutting into the quick of life itself and thereby causing irreparable harm (4, 134). For "Geist" is like a sword plunged into the heart of a tree and which cannot be removed lest the tree be damaged — yet how could a tree be deemed healthy with a blade in it? One of Nietzsche's most brilliant images concerning the need for *vivare* over the deadening accumulation of factual knowledge occurs in *Vom Nutzen und Nachteil der Historie für das Leben* (Of the Benefit and Disadvantage of History for Life); called to account for failure to living life to the full the accused must learn that "It is not justice that is in session in this court, and even less is it grace which delivers the judgement: it is Life itself, that dark, pulsating, insatiably desiring force. . ." (1, 269). Yet there is a profound problem for Klages in one important point: Nietzsche's concept of the will to power. If life is defined in terms of violent and drastic subjugation, then it betrays a world characterized by "Geist," for "Geist," in Hinton Thomas's words, "dispossesses everything it turns its attention to and claims it for its own."[13] Nietzsche explains: "Life itself is *essentially* appropriation, wounding, subjugation of that which is alien and that which is weaker; it is suppression, hardness and an imposition of form, annexation and, at its very least, exploitation [. . .]" (5, 207). If this is the case, then the will to power, as life's highest manifestation, is akin to "Geist," indeed, indistinguishable from it, and Nietzsche the orgiast, the disciple of Dionysus, is also the thinker who insisted on the primacy of power, control, and domination, seeing the ego not as a magic crystal but as an authoritarian radiance. If the will to power is a will to destroy, so it will also be a will to kill life and hence paradoxically, akin to Christian morality and any life-denying creed. *Die psychologischen Errungenschaften Nietzsches* contains a virulent attack upon the Judaeo-Christian tradition which Klages sees as a vindictive belief bent upon world domination. He follows Nietzsche here and quotes from *Zur Genealogie der Moral* (Genealogy of Morals) and *Götzendämmerung* (Twilight of the Idols) on Christianity as a religion of hate, a religion of the hangman; in Christianity Judaism found its most sublime and cunning continuation, a religion of vindictiveness and resentment, propagated by an ascetic priesthood. To object that is was the Jews who insisted upon Christ's crucifixion is unsubtle: this was a supremely political act, a means of apparently denying Christ's example whilst at the same time ensuring that the bait would be swallowed and that the world would be conquered by three Jews (Jesus, Peter and Paul) and one Jewess (Mary).[14] As Hellenic man had striven for *kalokagathia* (the cult of beauty, and goodness in beauty), so mediaeval man sought salvation in a denial of this world: Christianity becomes a life-denying aberration, a corrupt and destructive creed, a tool of that "Geist" which breaks as an extra-cosmic force into life, conquering the soul of man and, through technical mastery over the earth, destroying life itself. "By their fruits shall ye know them"; Klages never ceases to stress the bloody history of Christianity, beginning with the destruction of temples, the barbarism of autos da fé, the violence of the crusades, the cruelty of the conquistadors, the destruction of Moorish civilization in Spain, St. Bartholomew's Night, the Thirty Years War, the enslavement of "Naturvölker," and the capitalization of the whole planet. A religion of hatred, then, a continuation of Jahwe's wrath by more subtle means, where an insidious morality triumphs over life, morality as a form of will-to-power over others, a formidable self-aggrandizement on the part of "Geist." And Nietzsche? "To use the shorthand of myth," writes Klages, "Nietzsche was a battlefield between Dionysus and Jahwe," (*EN* 210), a man consumed by an unbearable tension, the man who extolled life above all, but destroyed life in his insistence on life's raptorial energies.

In 1901 Klages, after receiving his doctorate, informed his father that he would never take up a career as a chemist and explained that he was planning to found an institution devoted to psychology and "characterology"; in 1905 he founded in Munich a "Psychodiagnostisches Seminar," lecturing on graphology, the psychology of crime and, "Über Geist und Seele." Of great interest was the work of Carl Gustav Carus (1789–1869), doctor, psychologist, and painter whom Goethe had greatly esteemed, and whose *Psyche* (1846) Klages published in a new edition. Carus could be said to have elaborated on Novalis's critique of rationalism, and on that poet's conclusion that man's search for knowledge, his acquisitive intelligence had led to his alienation and separation from nature. An extreme castigation of the intellect is found in *Die Lehrlinge zu Saïs* of 1800 (The Apprentices at Saïs) where one of the acolytes explains that "Thought is only feeling's dream, feeling that has expired, a pallid and feeble life."[15] In Novalis the idea emerges that not only analytical thought, but the power of reflection and consciousness itself drove man from the springs of life into the arid desert of a world without harmony. Carus made explicit the metaphysical implications of this view: "The higher intelligence develops, the brighter the torch of science shines, the more the sphere of the miraculous and the magical contracts."[16] To Carus, as to other German Romantic philosophers of nature, the advance of a rational and scientific culture was synonymous with the decline of the "cultic." Once a utilitarian reason began to perceive the pragmatic value of things, once consciousness was capable of articulating distinctly in terms of cause and effect, then the realm of magical order in which the self felt secure in the world recedes, giving way to a universe divorced and estranged from man. Romantic writers such as Novalis, Carus, and Eichendorff had a profound effect on Klages's thinking: *Vom kosmogonischen Eros* (The Cosmogonic Eros) will have as its motto the statement by Novalis that "the exterior world is an interior one raised to the condition of mystery." Klages exhibits in his lectures and writings a profound concern for life, its mystery, vulnerability and uniqueness; his "characterology" sought to define the typology of the attitudes and structural features to be found in different egos, studying the constant struggle between "body-sensuality" and "mind abstraction." His essays on signs, gestures and expressions became increasingly influential, and it was above all his feeling for unconscious life, together with his awareness of the dangers of abstract conceptualization, which put him very much in the vanguard of those who rejected subjugation in all its forms. On October 10, 1913, the "Freier Deutscher Jugendtag" was celebrated on the hill known as the Hoher Meissner near Kassel: this was, as Martin Green has told us, a gathering of various youth groups to demonstrate an alternative commemoration of the Battle of Leipzig, rejecting utterly the chauvinism of military and governmental circles.[17] Links between Klages and Ascona have already been mentioned: the "Freier Deutscher Jugendtag" was called into being by Eugen Diederichs who elicited from Klages an important essay for the occasion, *Der Mensch und die Erde* (Mankind and Earth). The emphasis in this work as elsewhere is on the arrogance of technology (Klages was appalled at the sinking of the *Titanic*) and the destructiveness of "Geist," whose baleful influence is seen in the destruction of nature, of the countryside, of organic living, and of life itself. A commercial rationality is castigated which (in 1913!) has changed the face of the earth in the name of Mammon and Progress. It has decimated, even annihilated, entire animal species, whole tribes of primitive peoples who become the victims either of callous genocide or alcohol, syphilis or the blessings of Western civilization. Communal rites and feasts have practically disappeared Klages explains: fauns, nymphs and shepherds dance no more. A vulgar Americanization, a vicious utilitarianism have drained the soul of its vital energies; we are left with a world adorned with specious glitter and bereft of any life-sustaining rites or symbols. For Klages there was no doubt at all that we are living in an age witnessing the destruction of soul, and that progress was synonymous with decadence and civilization with desolation, a "life in death" ruled over by a despotic, ghostly reason. An unfettered lust for murder was deeply etched into the countenance of Western culture, before whose poisonous breath all things withered and died, a culture whose "race of rational and righteous men left everywhere the disease of their avaricious hands."[18]

In 1921 Klages published his most rapturous evocation of life as an ecstatic intoxication, *Vom kosmogonischen Eros*. This book stresses above all the need for the "reality of images" and adumbrates a "cosmogonic Eros," particularly in connection with pagan traditions. Klages's examination of the ancient concept of Eros, as mediator between God and man, develops the distinction between earthly and heavenly love, between sensual attraction and the ecstatic enthusiasms of the soul. Similar to Martin Buber (in his *Ekstatische Konfessionen*) Klages extols rapture, mystical ecstasy and the soul's ability to express itself in defiance of sterile conceptualization. We are on familiar territory here: there is a rejection of what Klages thought of as the abstract, rational love of Christianity and Platonism and the emphasis on the connection of love with looking, seeing, gazing and the illumination of the individual in erotic incandescence. Eros is not to be understood as promiscuity, but is a force akin to magnetism that pulses through all, making inner feelings become outward reality. It is through vitality of feeling, through transport, that the pernicious influence of Geist is overcome: it is not through the cultivation of concepts but the vital enmeshment of *images* that life achieves its highest potential. A Pelasgian antiquity is posited, for it was in Bachofen that Klages had learned of the various traditions which were current among the Greeks with regard to the pre-Hellenic inhabitants of their country, and the inclination of the Greeks to use the general name "Pelasgian" to describe them. Bachofen associated the Pelasgians with Thrace (*M* 42) and portrayed the crime of matricide as the most heinous in their civilization (*M* 89). For Bachofen it was in the cultivation of mysteries that the legacy of the Pelasgian world found its safest refuge against the masculine spirituality of the "this-worldly" rationality of the Hellenes, a rationality averse to mystery (*M* 366). The epithet Pelasgian or Pelasgis attained the meaning of "ancient," a word linked by some scholars to "sea" (pelagos) or to "stork" (pelargos) as a symbol for the creative element of the watery regions (*M* 160–161), or simply a corruption of the term Vlachs or Wallachians ("Velakski"). But for Klages the Pelasgians represent a people close to nature and having a rapport with things which has not been clouded by arrogant, analytic reason; they are not impeded by individualism but one with the awesome flux of existence surrounding them.

Quoting Hesiod, Klages tells of the oldest, Orphic mysteries, of how Chronos created a silvery cosmic egg out of ether and the bottomless abyss.[19] From the egg sprang the hermaphroditic god Phanes-Eros-Dionysus who contained within himself the seed of all future gods. Gaia, Echidna and Uranos were created by auto-impregnation. The focal point of worship for the Boethians was a massive, unhewn stone at which, every five years, festivals in honour of Eros were celebrated (*KE* 39): it was at such a stone that the mad Emperor Heliogabalus worshipped in Emesa.[20] This deity is not to be understood as a charming rococo *putto* but as a rushing whirlwind, a vitalism that pulses through creation. Klages extols "Rausch" — intoxication or rapture, a feeling of entheos, of sated, triumphant being. This "Rausch" may be experienced at the simple sight of a beloved object, heterosexual or homosexual, or at the sight of an animal or plant; it may be experienced no less deeply when perfume is inhaled, or when wine is tasted or music heard; it may be served consciously, or in a narcotic trance. And Eros "celebrates his origins in the rustling of a vernal wind, before the glory of the starry firmament, in driving hail, on a sun-parched mountain pass, in the roaring of the surf, in the flaming ecstasy of 'first love', but no less rapturously in the embrace of shattering destiny" (*KE* 58–9). There is an urge to pour forth, a radiant ejaculation, an abundance without restraint. There is no constraint, no dearth but an exuberance of thrusting fullness, "a golden pouring flame, a bursting pregnancy." There are three forms of chaotic "Rausch" — erotic, heroic and magic: the first is present in every shuddering awareness of life's glory, the second in races such as the Pelasgians, the third in the worship of ancestors, in funeral cults and astrology (*KE* 79): this will be greatly expanded in Klages's major work *Der Geist als Widersacher der Seele*. It is Nietzsche, Goethe and the German Romantics who are hailed as the great explorers of "Rausch" — but this pantheistic ecstasy did not last; it was threatened by that extra-spatial, extra temporal power with which we are already familiar.

The cosmos is polarized into soul (psyche) and body (soma), but the obtrusive intervention of "Geist," the power of abstraction, analysis, separation, splits the soul from the body by means of *noesis* (comprehension by intellect alone) and *boulesis* (a purposive, rather than an instinctual will: *KE* 69). Now life is subjugated and crushed beneath the yoke of concepts (*KE* 69), and it is only through ecstasy that the mastery of "Geist" is overthrown, for ecstasy is not "Entleibung" but "Entgeistung" (*KE* 27), the removal not of body, but of spirit. Again

Klages insists that it was Christianity that destroyed "Rausch" and erotic wonder; it annihilated "Rausch" by diluting it into *agape*, insisting on a tepid, general "love of one's neighbour," even of "the rabble"; it also abstracted love to a Platonic ideal (*KE* 49). Klages takes Nietzsche's aphorism "Christianity gave Eros poison — he did not die, but became degraded into vice" (5, 102), to hammer home Christianity's disgust with joy and sensuality. Saulus/Paulus again meets especial opprobrium because of his vindictive nihilism: I Corinthians, chapter 1, verses 27 to 29 are quoted ("But God has chosen the foolish things of this world to confound the wise [. . .] That no flesh should glory in his presence.") as is 1 Romans, Chapter 7, verse 23 ("For I sce another law in my members, warring against the law of my mind, and bringing me into captivity to the law of sin which is in my members": *KE* 94). Christianity encourages a morbid introspection, a "Geist" that inhibits and destroys. Judaism is a more blatant Moloch, or Moloch-Jahwe, demanding the piacular sacrifice of sons and daughters, a rapacious, patriarchal spirit demanding submission (*KE* 73). We have already noted the paradoxical equation of Judaeo-Christianity with the will to power, for asceticism is close to lasciviousness, a perverse desire to mortify flesh and exult in laceration. This, Klages claims (*KE* 95–96) is an example of "de-eroticised sexuality," for Christianity is choked with flagellants, martyrs, castrati and those whose cruel self-mutilation would be deeply offensive to the Pelasgian world.

The fierce hostility to Christianity is prompted also by Klages's belief that the Church has encouraged believers to neglect, even despise, the visible world in favour of an imaginary future world, so that this life is regarded simply as a place of passage. It may be interesting here to consider the similarities between Klages and Rilke. I have already referred to Rilke's admiration for Schuler; Rilke's famous letter to Hulewicz, his Polish translator (November 1925) speaks of the rejection of Christian attitudes and the need for a new "terrestrial consciousness" (we also remember Rilke's suggestion, in the *Brief des jungen Arbeiters* [Letter of a Young Worker] that we must, like St Francis, replace the cross with the Hymn to the Sun). "Nature," Rilke writes, "the things we associate with and use, are provisional and perishable; but so long as we are here, they are our possession and our friendship, sharers in our trouble and gladness, just as they have been the confidants of our ancestors. Therefore not only must all that is here not be vilified or degraded, but, just because of that very provisionality they share with us, all these appearances and things should be, in the most fervent sense, comprehended by us [. . .]."[21] Rilke also insists, in the Eighth Duino Elegy, that there is a fundamental defect or limitation in mankind, the fact that our awareness of Being, or existence, as an object, as something distinct from ourselves, prevents us from identifying ourselves with it and achieving a condition of pure Being, or "openness" (das Offene), the "nowhere without naught": in this "open" world there is no time, no nagging awareness of inauthenticity or future, no end, no limit, no separation or parting, and no death as the opposite of life. With Klages we have noticed a juxtaposition between a Pelasgian antiquity and the modern, post-Christian era; in the former man was unaware of consciousness, experiencing the full force of the world as a stream of images, each with a powerful symbolic radiance. "Symbols," writes Klages, "are glyphs of ecstatically observed images" (*KE* 129); Pelasgian man did not experience allegorically, but symbolically. The sensual urgency of life, moving in all its forms, a world in awe of natural phenomena, suggested by an animistic vision animated and made dynamic by ancestral spirits and traditions — this is extolled both by Rilke and Klages. The modern (Christian) world, in contrast, is a world not of images but of concepts or precepts, a world under the sway of "Geist" and distracted by the shadow of death as judgement. It is only in moments of "Rausch" that modern man casts aside ratiocination, purposefulness, morality and achieves liberation and awareness of that cosmogonic Eros which transfigures all; this remarkable book ends, as is fitting, with the aquatic uproar of the second act of Goethe's *Faust II*, the tumultuous paean of praise for that deity who creates and sustains life: "So herrsche denn Eros, der alles begonnen!" — "let Eros be master, the Lord of Creation!"

At the outbreak of the war in 1914 (a war which appalled him and which he could never support) Klages moved to Switzerland, living with various friends until, in the spring of 1920, he moved to the home of Camilla Meyer, daughter of the poet Conrad Ferdinand Meyer (1825–1898), and lived in her house, with interruptions, practically until his death in 1956. His financial situation was parlous: the Psychodiagnostisches Institut in Munich had been closed and he was forced to earn his living by lecturing and writing on a variety of topics — on graphology, character, dance, rhythm, and consciousness. A writer who studied Klages closely, particularly *Vom kosmogonischen Eros*, was Robert Musil: I have already referred to Alice Donath and her mental illness, also her role as Clarissa in *Der Mann ohne Eigenschaften* where Klages appears as the figure Meingast. During the writing of this famous novel Musil was much drawn to the relationship between waking thought and mythical archetypes and rejected the prejudices of European man concerning the power of myth. Where the arts become artificial, and life so mechanical the human soul is left impoverished; in his enthusiastic praise of Döblin's epic poem *Manas* (1927) Musil explains that

> There are not many questions that are so important for literature as that which concerns the way one could give back to it the intoxication, the divinity, the verse, the feeling of being more than life-size, without plaster-of-Paris monumentality and without artificially obscuring the achieved illumination of our spirit.[22]

Vom kosmogonischen Eros had a powerful influence on Musil's own refinement of the notion of love, its varieties and their relations to biological drives and spiritual conditions; Musil was fascinated by an Eros which was not simply directed to one object (transient and carnal), but cosmic, pulsing through existence, a *Fernliebe* that approaches mystical panpsychism.[23] The diaries abound with references to Klages and the *Eros kosmogonos*, particularly during the years 1920–1921 where we encounter the statement: "In ecstasy the spirit does not free itself from the body but the soul from the spirit."[24] References to "Rauschgötter" and "Pelasgertum" also betray the presence of Klages. The editor of the diaries, Adolf Frisé, emphasises Klages's importance, but the treatment of "Meingast" in *Der Mann ohne Eigenschaften* is far from complimentary. Musil sought a "taghelle Mystik," a bright mystification of the day, and no chthonic "Urschoß"; intellectuality may be the expression or tool of a desiccated life, but a dark irrationalism is manifestly dangerous.[25] Meingast argues that the idea of redemption has always been anti-intellectual, and that it is not to be confined to religious feelings: since the word "lösen" (loosen) has corporeal implications it indicates that only acts can redeem, "Erlebnisse" that involve the whole man. Because man has become over-intellectualized it follows that under certain conditions the woman must assume the instinctive leadership. Under Meingast's influence Clarissa turns to eroticism of all kind, equating herself with the bi-sexual god proposed by Meingast. She seeks disciples, but only finds them in the lunatic asylum; Ulrich's suspicions are proved, tragically, to be true.

Klages devoted his remaining energies to the completion of his magnum opus, the monumental *Der Geist als Widersacher der Seele*: volumes one and two appeared in 1929 and volume three in 1932. The times were not propitious for such a vast and idiosyncratic study and, after 1945, Klages was either ignored or uncomfortably associated with an irrationalism which was held to be a precursor of National Socialism. The 1960 student edition in one volume, over one thousand five hundred pages long, scarcely helped to make his name better known. This chapter will close with a brief discussion of the work's central ideas and will assess the relationship between Klages and fascism, seeing him not as the advocate of a power-hungry Weltanschauung but, essentially, as a backward-looking Romantic. His wayward anti-Semitism is deplorable, but the need to prevent the world from sliding into Rilke's "Tun ohne Bild," a mindless Americanization (Klages's picture of a multi-storey tourist hotel next to the Pyramids is a telling one) has much that is admirable in it. The introductory motto, taken from Omar Khayyám, runs as follows: "Reicht dir ein Weiser Gift, so trink's getrost, / Reicht Gegengift ein Tor dir, gieß es aus!" (Take poison from a wise man, drink at ease / But pour away the antidote from fools!). This gnomic utterance hints, we assume, at Klages's unsettling, obsessive, insistence on the pernicious influence of "Geist," and we are encouraged not to listen to the counterarguments of lesser men.

The work is best seen as a vast *summa* of all that has gone before, and the central premise is already known to us. There is a fundamental dichotomy between head and heart, rendering the human personality a place of contradiction. Life and mind ("Geist") are two completely original and contradictory powers, neither derivable from the other nor from any third entity. Body and soul ("Seele") are indivisible, but into this union the mind intrudes, like a wedge, with the intention of separating them. This "Geist" is something extra-spatial, extra temporal (ein außerraumzeitliches Seiendes, logos, pneumo, nous) which is fundamentally life-denying; the body is "entseelt" or "de-souled" and the soul "entleibt" or "excarnated."[26] Klages states apodictically at the end of the eighth chapter of Book One that history is nothing but the triumph of "Geist" over life and, bleakly, intimates that the destruction of life is inevitable. The historical process of mankind (also called "progress") is the victorious battle of the mind against human life and will end with the logical destruction of the latter (*GWS* 69).

For Klages, as for Nietzsche, the fullness of life, its flux, variety, and richness is the highest good. Klages is not alone here in his worship of life; Heinrich Rickert claimed, in his *Philosophie des Lebens* (Tübingen, 1920) that the word "life" had the same talismanic quality for many of his contemporaries as did the word "nature" for the youthful rebels of the *Sturm und Drang*. "Lebensphilosophie" postulated the primacy of immediate experience, or "Erleben," a pre-reflexive, pre-analytical awareness of the world, and its adherents praised the power of "Schauen," of holistic vision. Like Nietzsche, Klages observes a historical continuum, comparing primitive man, living still in a mythologically suffused universe, with the enlightened man of civilization. Nietzsche knew that thought relies upon life, not the reverse, and any philosophy which questions life must be questioned by life itself. But, as we have seen, Klages cannot follow Nietzsche in accepting life as "Wille zur Macht": for him "Geist" and power are synonymous and exult in the destruction of life. ("Our book," he writes, "finds the key to what the spirit basically is not in the intellect but in the will" — *GWS* 1420.) This imperious spirit has caused the destruction of nature, an over-intellectualization and mechanization that threatens life's vitality. It isolates, separates and arrogates to itself the power of the intellect, and the coldness, sobriety and rigidity of modern life is the sign of the spirit's triumph. The rhythmical flow of life is interrupted, inhibited, and the bond between soul and life is lost. The soul is the principle of life itself, the capacity to receive the flow of images that rain down upon it. Vital images, and an empathic, observing soul are necessary for the fullness of life, for life is grasped not conceptually, but emotionally. For the soul the world is a series of images (Bilder) which constantly change, move and flow, and observation is the activity of the soul which surrenders to a multiplicity of phenomena. The soul experiences in time and space; it remains passive before the reality of images which present themselves. And the true Eros of man is kindled, ignited, by the reality of images, whilst the soul, "empfängnisbereit," or ready to conceive, allows the true reality of images to act upon it, undisturbed by reflection or critical analysis. There is, Klages held, a magic in the interaction of soul and the pulsing, rhythmical flow of images, and it is primitive people who are praised above all for experiencing this, for their susceptibility, their openness to the cosmos, to myth, to the world of wonder and terror. But modern man, enslaved by ideologies and a drive to conquer the planet, has destroyed the harmony between soul and world, and *Der Geist als Widersacher der Seele* is an enormous lament for the loss of that Pelasgian golden age which flourished before the "Geist," that *actus purus*, began its triumphant conquest.[27]

Klages owes a considerable debt to certain aspects of the work of Goethe and, as has been noted, to the German Romantics. Goethe, for him, was the man who, throughout the whole of his long poetic life, responded vitally to the powerful natural images around him and recreated them in his art. He refers specifically to Goethe's dithyrambic prose-poem *Die Natur* (1782), to Görres, to Eichendorff and above all Novalis, whom he quotes extensively. "Whose heart does not leap and hop with joy when that powerful feeling, for which language only contains the two words love and passion, pours through his life a fragrance dissolving all within it and, trembling in a sweet terror, he sinks into the dark, beckoning womb of nature, his poor personality consumed by the leaping flames of joy, and nothing remains but the burning focus of immeasurable procreation! What is this flame which bursts from everywhere? A fervent embrace, whose sweet fecundity melts in passionate drops upon us . . ." (*GWS* 898). For life, as it were, fights back through the work of great writers who are able to by-pass the strictures of "Geist" and respond to life without restraint or ulterior purpose. Klages points particularly to the florilegium of genius which flourished at the end of the eighteenth century in Germany, to Arndt, Hölderlin, Beethoven, Novalis, Görres, Kleist, to the brothers Grimm, Eichendorff and Carus who represented what he calls a "telluric transition" from the desiccated rationality of the Enlightenment and who still had knowledge of the "world-creative" power of love; he also draws attention to the 1890s. "This was the last, the ultimate wave [that is, the last assertion of life as against "Geist"], because essential existence perished with them. Perhaps men have never experienced and suffered more passionately the shudders of existence as they did then. The horizon flamed in the fiery dusk of departure, a final, irrevocable sundering [. . .] Even Nietzsche confused that woeful, powerful radiance with the gleam of a new dawn. I have given place to such a description merely in order that the reader might know that we are calling the last bearers of earth's essence the dithyrambic panegyrists of destruction. They were surrounded by lemurs, and vampires, and their work was never completed. The earth smokes as never before with the blood of the slaughtered and the *simian* strut with the spoils that have been plundered from the shattered temples" (*GWS* 923).

The attack upon Christianity is pursued with ever increasing ferocity in *Der Geist als Widersacher der Seele*: it is rejected as a perverse doctrine, exulting in mortification, damnation and the destruction of the senses (*GWS* 758); a further section (*GWS* 1230–31) speculates on the reaction of an alien from a distant (and happier) star to the images associated with Christianity, images redolent of blood, violence and degradation. Saulus/Paulus, we notice, is again vituperated; a discussion of the four "epic" peoples — Indians, Persians, Greeks and Germans also refers to the Semitic races, and compares the vitality of the Arabs to that of the Vikings (*GWS* 1242). But Jahwe is condemned for infiltrating the resentful, oppressed under class of the Roman Empire and, through Paul, preaching a doctrine which, in its hatred of the world, nevertheless exerts a baleful influence upon it. Klages shows himself to be an implacable enemy of Paul, of Christianity, of the Jewish acquisition of world power (*GWS* 1267–68). The Jew subsumes modernism, and Klages looks backward to the Pelasgian age which we have already described. The last part of *Der Geist als Widersacher der Seele* is devoted to that world where "Geist" did not inhibit soul, where life was not a will to power, being itself a cosmic power in which man participates.

This was a world without "history," for history is but a demonstration of the spreading of the phantoms of "Geist," with sterile formulae replacing "Urbilder." There are, Klages explains (*GWS* 1258), three Pelasgian types: the prehistoric ancestors of the European cultural nations, the extrahistorical peoples who survived untouched by Western civilization, and the true poets of all peoples, not personalities as such but the receiving organs of the world's glory, souls who transcend the jejune constraints of "Geist." Many pages are devoted to Bachofen and "gynaecocracy," to elemental symbols (tree, water and moon) and, above all, to the Magna Mater and the female principle. The oldest wisdom of humanity, we learn, was always the possession and privilege of women, the sibyls, Valkyries, and swan maidens, and it was the exaggeratedly masculine West, under the influence of "Geist," exemplified above all by Jewish American capitalism, which displaced this earlier knowledge. We should approach the world as lovers, not predators, to listen to the "primeval song of the landscape," but ideologies and exploitation now triumph over the earth, and Klages's vast threnody draws to a close.

What is one to make of this long, obsessive book? Does it not seem paradoxical that a volume of over one thousand five hundred pages should lament the power of thought over life? Obviously, Klages must respect the power of argument, but he insists that reason is never to be elevated to the highest position; "Geist" should be the servant of life and not its master, clarifying growth, but not impeding it. Klages sought, in the manner of Goethe, a biocentric philosophy, not a logocentric one, seeing the fulfilled personality as achieving a balance between "Geist" and "Seele," a "Verlebendigung des Geistes" where "Geist" has ceased to be an instrument of the Will. It is impossible for modern man to achieve the almost somnambulistic certainty of those who lived in mythical accord with earth and cosmos; we are *knowing*, but must ensure that we do not become emotionally stunted in our cerebral solipsism. Klages, as we have noted, shares the preoccupation of those associated with *Lebensphilosophie:* there are links also with expressionism, with Gottfried Benn, also D. H. Lawrence. With regard to Lawrence, Martin Green points out that Klages, for all the advocacy of the feminine, was a "masculinist" who was interested in the erotic (but not homosexual) love that could arise between men and in the way in which power and authority could be carried and engendered by that love (Lawrence treats this theme in *Aaron's Rod* as well as *The Plumed Serpent*).[28] In *Vom kosmogonischen Eros* Klages warned of how often the attempt to transform the procreative and heterosexual instinct into erotic magic ends with the tragic defeat of the lovers; sympathy is purer and deeper between people of the same sex, and the symbol of such love is the Dioscuri, the heavenly twins. It is also "Blutbrüderschaft" (blood brotherhood) which links Klages with Lawrence, and here we approach the dubious notion of "thinking with the blood" and a fascistic irrationalism.

I have briefly referred to Lukács's criticism of Klages in *Die Zerstörung der Vernunft* (The Destruction of Reason), a rejection of him as a protofascist; Lukács's claim that Klages was admired by Rosenberg is erroneous, however, as anyone who has read what Rosenberg wrote on Klages will be well aware.[29] The violent, masculine thrust of fascism was anathema to Klages, as must be apparent from our discussion; there is no "Führerprinzip" in Klages, as there was in a thinker like Paul de Lagarde. Klages abhorred armed struggle; his hostility to "Geist" and ambition, his aversion to technological civilization, to authoritarianism, to logic, to stultifying morality and his praise of the chthonic is an outright condemnation of any creed which extolled power, regimentation and subordination to a ruthless ideology. Thomas Mann was premature in his inference that Klages was implicated in the triumph of National Socialism. In a letter to his mythologist friend Karl Kerényi (20 February 1934) Mann thanks the latter for the recommendation to read Aldous Huxley (whose essays Mann greatly admired) and D. H. Lawrence, for whose "hectic sensuality" Mann felt little sympathy; a reference to J. C. Powys led to a discussion of the atavistic tendencies in much contemporary writing and Mann explains:

> In present day European writing there is a kind of rancour against the development of the human cerebrum which always seems to me to be nothing more than a snobbish and stupid form of self-denial [. . .] I am no friend of the anti-intellectual movement represented in Germany particularly by Klages. I feared and fought it early because I saw through its brutally anti-humanistic consequences before they became manifest.[30]

If the "anti-intellectual movement" had connotations of violence and barbarism then Hinton Thomas is correct in stating that the "anti-human" consequences of men's thinking were as least as great a concern to Klages as they were to Mann. In April 1938 Alfred Rosenberg delivered a lecture at the University of Halle entitled "Gestalt und Leben" which was later published in the *Nationalsozialistische Monatshefte*: in it Rosenberg objected to Klages's concept of the deleterious intrusion of "Geist" into human life and rejected the idealisation of "Pelasgertum," describing it as a sinking back into a formless chaos, chaotic as regards both race and soul, into conditions which can never be regarded as desirable. To talk in this way about a near-Eastern tribe, its ecstasies, deities and matriarchy, to argue that its way of life is desirable and exemplary for life as a whole, and to condemn Nordic Hellenism seems to us to be a dangerous enterprise and by no means suitable to further a genuine, real existence — it can only bring confusion.[31]

A concerted attack against Klages followed: he and his circle were denigrated as "belonging to the most loathsome manifestations of contemporary life" and it was recommended that "the whole crowd of them" be incarcerated.[32]

The anti-Semitism remains however and cannot be denied; the figure of the Golem represents for Klages "the Satanism of Jahwe in the form of a human being: it imitates, outbids and destroys. The Jew appears as a servant yet soon conquers; the Jew creates a 'Golem-as-machine' to destroy the earth, enslaving millions in the name of progress."[33] With Christianity as its most sublime manifestation, Jahwe-Moloch is seen as an insidious and vengeful deity bent on hegemony and holocaust. This has nothing to do with race, but "Substanz," as the chapter on Schuler has already explained, but Klages also descends to sneering calumny: the 1940 edition of Schuler's work is zealous in its scrutiny of Stefan George's Aryan origins, his preference for Jewish acolytes, his choice of a Jewish publisher (Bondi); Maximin, the young man worshipped and deified by George as the incarnation of pure beauty is (erroneously) called "Kronfeld." The height of Jewish insolence is seen, according to Klages, in the use of the ornamental swastika by Bondi. It is difficult to decide whether those anti-Jewish jibes are sincerely intended or used as a ploy to facilitate publication in Germany in 1940. In *Rhythmen und Runen,* the so-called *Nachlaß* which appeared in 1944, Klages's attack on Moloch and Christianity is continued and Germania is extolled, not in any crudely chauvinistic sense, but as the place where the soul, in contrast to the "morbid exaltation of the Orient" and the "form-inhibited, plastic, Southern manifestation of the Greeks" is "more severe, hyperborean [. . .], restless, deeper, more cosmic."[34] There is no slum-begotten National Socialism in this late work but a hopelessly Romantic longing for forest and myth, for "Schauer" and a Hölderlin-inspired purity, for life in its wholeness and authenticity, unalloyed and lovely in its transience.

Klages remains an uncomfortable and controversial figure. His intense individualism has a forbidding quality about it; his insistence on the mind's ravages alienates him, as does the vehemence of his denial of Christianity. Many find his extensive *œuvre* incompatible with his critique of logical analysis; it was Theodor Lessing who commented that Klages had wished to pick from the tree of life, and reaped only from the tree of knowledge, and there is much that is valid in this statement. Those concerned today with man's abuse of the natural world, the effects of thoughtless technology and industrial pollution may find in him a spokesman; otherwise he speaks to few. The first motto for this chapter, taken from *Rhythmen und Runen*, tells of a defiant loneliness, a preference for cosmic emptiness. The thinker who extolled Eros and Magna Mater is remembered above all for an obsessive dichotomy and a steely fire which burns without warmth.

Notes

[1] Th. Lessing, *Einmal und nie wieder* (Gütersloh: Bertelsmann, 1969), 310.

[2] Franziska Reventlow, *Tagebücher 1895–1910,* ed. Else Reventlow (Frankfurt a. M.: Fischer, 1976), 277. The atmosphere in Schwabing is described after the "Kosmikerstreit" of 1904. Wolfskehl ("Carlo") is portrayed with sympathy and his plight is regretted: a physical attack by Schuler is (implausibly) suspected. Klages, her lover, is both feared and adored.

[3] Karl Corino, *Musil. Leben und Werk in Bildern und Texten* (Reinbek bei Hamburg: Rowohlt, 1988), 392.

[4] *Der Eroberer* has been reprinted in Killy, *Deutsche Literatur 7*, 1086–1887.

[5] Heinz Raschel, *Das Nietzsche-Bild im George-Kreis* (Berlin and New York: De Gruyter, 1984), 30.

[6] Franziska Reventlow, *Herrn Dames Aufzeichnungen, oder Begebenheiten aus einem merkwürdigen Stadtteil* (Berlin: Buchverlag der Morgen, 1990), 72–73.

[7] Martin Green, in *Mountain of Truth. The Counterculture Begins. Ascona 1900–1920* (Hanover, NH and London: UP of New England, 1986) gives a lively portrayal of the communes of Ascona.

[8] Seth Taylor, *Left-wing Nietzscheans* (Berlin: de Gruyter, 1990) comments on Nietzsche's personal acquaintanceship with Bachofen. He is correct in stressing that there is no reason to assume that Nietzsche took over the symbols of the Dionysian and the Apollonian from him, as these have a long tradition in German literature.

[9] The word "Geist" is notoriously difficult to translate into English. The original meaning is "spirit" in a theological sense, that is, holy; in the eighteenth century this was superseded by the meaning of "intellect," the ability to impose a human, rational pattern upon the world. Amongst Romantic thinkers the word "Geist" came to mean that quality which represents the highest

manifestation or quintessence of a people (Volksgeist): it also represented an ideal concept as opposed to that which was merely empirical. Klages used the word to denote abstraction, a force inimical of life. (See Roy Pascal, *From Naturalism to Expressionism*, 297–305 for a useful discussion of the term.) I shall keep the word "Geist" in this discussion of Klages as "mind" or "intellect" do not have the sense of creative energy that "Geist" does. It is also important to remember that, for Klages, "Geist" was frequently inseparable from "Will," hence imperious and predatory.

[10] J. J. Bachofen, *Das Mutterrecht* (Basel: Benno Schwabe Verlagsbuchhandlung, 1897 edition), 22. (Hereafter *M.*)

[11] Richard Hinton Thomas, "Nietzsche in Weimar Germany and the Case of Ludwig Klages" in *The Weimar Dilemma. Intellectuals in the Weimar Republic*, ed. Anthony Phelan (Manchester: Manchester UP, 1985), 71–91.

[12] Ludwig Klages, *Die psychologischen Errungenschaften Nietzsches* (Leipzig: Johann Ambrosius Barth, 1926), 11. (Hereafter *EN.)*

[13] Hinton Thomas, in *The Weimar Dilemma*, ed. Phelan, op. cit., 80.

[14] The passage in Nietzsche (5, 286–287) runs as follows: "Which of them has *prevailed* for the time being, Rome or Judea? But there is no shadow of doubt; just consider whom you bow down to in Rome itself, today, as though to the embodiment of the highest values — and not just in Rome, but over nearly half the earth, everywhere where man becomes tame, and wishes to become tame — to *three Jews*, as we know, and one *Jewess* (to Jesus of Nazareth, Peter the Fisherman, Paul the carpet-weaver, and the mother of the first of these, called Mary). This is very remarkable — Rome has been defeated, without a doubt."

[15] Novalis, *Schriften*, ed. Richard Samuel. Stuttgart: Kohlhammer, 1960. Vol. I, 96.

[16] C. G. Carus, *Romantische Naturphilosophie* (Jena: Eugen Diederichs, 1926), xvi. Of great interest would also have been Carus's differentiation, in *Über Lebensmagnetismus,* (1857) between the two modes of looking at the world, that which was "biozentrisch" and that which was "logozentrisch," with the former providing the deeper awareness.

[17] Green, *Mountain of Truth*, 140.

[18] August Wiedmann, *The German Quest for Primal Origins in Art, Culture and Politics 1900–1933* (Lewiston/Queenston/Lampeter: Edwin Mellen Press, 1995), 175.

[19] Ludwig Klages, *Vom Kosmogonischen Eros*, 4th ed. (Jena: Eugen Diederichs, 1930), 38. (Hereafter *KE.*)

[20] It was believed that the stone of the Great Mother at Pessinus in Phrygia, the Stone of Emesa and the stone set into the corner of the Kaaba at Mecca were of divine origin, emanating from the Most Holy whose seat was the Pole

Star: see Joscelyn Godwin, *Arktos. The Polar Myth in Science, Symbolism, and Nazi Survival* (London: Thames and Hudson, 1993), 144.

[21]Rainer Maria Rilke, *Sämtliche Werke* (Frankfurt a. M.: Insel, 1966), vol. 6, 1115.

[22] Robert Musil, *Prosa. Dramen. Späte Briefe*, ed. by Adolf Frisé (Hamburg: Rowohlt, 1957), 616.

[23] Renate von Heydebrand, *Die Reflexionen Ulrichs in Robert Musils "Der Mann ohne Eigenschaften"* (Münster: Aschendorff Verlag, 1966), 136–141.

[24] Robert Musil, *Tagebücher*, ed. by Adolf Frisé (Reinbek bei Hamburg: Rowohlt, 1976), Heft 21, 617.

[25] Marie-Luise Roth, *Robert Musil. Ethik und Aesthetik* (Munich: Paul List, 1972), 106.

[26] Ludwig Klages, *Der Geist als Widersacher der Seele*), 4th ed. (Leipzig and Munich: Johann Ambrosius Barth and H. Bouvier, 1960), 62. (Hereafter *GWS*.)

[27] As August Wiedmann has observed, Klages went to extraordinary lengths to describe the world of living images, images revealed to primordial sight. Klages constantly reminds us that, originally, man lived through and by images and that thought and feeling were "imagistic" through and through. Moon, tree, plant, pond, sea, sky clouds, not to mention a myriad of forms, colours, sounds, movements and rhythms — each was a carrier of expressive meanings, each and every one was vibrant with life. A sharp distinction is drawn between a profane world of objects (*Dingwelt*), a reified, objectified reality, and a sacred *Bilderwelt*, a world of images. "This and only this resplendent 'Bilderwelt' of immediate existence was the true 'motherland' of the human soul, and not that encrusted frozen *Dingwelt*, the lifeless 'fatherland' of a raiding, willfully matricidal spirit" (Wiedmann, 181).

[28] Green, *Mountain of Truth*, 207.

[29] Georg Lukács, *Die Zerstörung der Vernuft* (Berlin: Aufbau Verlag, 1953), 430. See also Alfred Rosenberg, *Der Mythus des 20. Jahrhunderts* (Munich: Hoheneichen Verlag, 1936), 137.

[30] Thomas Mann, *Gesammelte Werke in 13 Bänden*, vol. 11, 631.

[31] Hans Eggert Schröder, *Ludwig Klages. Die Geschichte seines Lebens. Zweiter Teil. Das Werk 2* (Completed by Franz Tenigl, (Bonn: Bouvier, 1992), 315–318.

[32] Schröder, *Ludwig Klages Centenar Katalog*, 109–110.

[33] Schröder, *Ludwig Klages. Das Werk (1920–1956)*, 678–679.

[34] Ludwig Klages, *Rhythmen und Runen. Nachlaß herausgegeben von ihm selbst* (Leipzig: Johann Ambrosius Barth, 1944), 211.

Ludwig Derleth.
Courtesy of Schiller Nationalmuseum
and Deutsches Literaturarchiv, Marbach.

5 : Ludwig Derleth

Too late, Schwabing, no use running,
Jesus-Bonaparte is coming. . .
— Roderich Huch

You laid about you with a valiant sword
And now stand merciless, and will not yield.
But will you never leave that killing-field
And listen to love's true and powerful word?. . .
— Stefan George

"SOLDIERS! I GIVE YOU AS PLUNDER — *the world*!" Readers of
Thomas Mann's *Doktor Faustus* will doubtless remember the figure of Daniel zur Höhe, introduced in chapter thirty four as a member
of the Munich circle around Sixtus Kridwiss, that leader of a group of
disenchanted scholars and poetasters who disturbed the narrator deeply
by their arrogant rejection of reason and humanity. Daniel zur Höhe is
described as the author of a work entitled *Proklamationen* which had
appeared before the First World War, a work consisting of a series of
highly charged, gnomic utterances; Serenus Zeitblom explains:

> The signatory of these proclamations was an entity by the name of
> Christus Imperator Maximus, an imperious energy which enlisted
> death-devoted soldiers to conquer the planet, issued communiqués in
> the manner of military orders and stipulated its demands in a ruthless,
> self-satisfied tone. It preached poverty and chastity and never tired of
> demanding absolute and unquestioning obedience, its fist hammering
> upon a table.[1]

The reader may well experience a sense of déjà-vu or déjà-lu here:
Daniel and his proclamations were the subject of Thomas Mann's story
"Beim Propheten" (At the Prophet's), written in 1904 and published
later that year in the *Neue Freie Presse*, Vienna. It was the result of a
visit to the atelier of Ludwig Derleth in Destouchesstrasse 1. The facts
are well established: in the company of his future mother-in-law, Frau
Pringsheim, Thomas Mann attended the readings on the evening of

Good Friday, 1904. Derleth had not been present, but the proclamations were declaimed by his sister Anna and the disciple Rudolf Blümel. The description in the story of the invitation cards (the eagle bearing a dagger in its talons), of the room (the lectern and the monastic and militaristic accoutrements) and of the readers closely match the facts; "Daniel" may not have been present, but the description of the "Daniel" in *Doktor Faustus* ("a gaunt thirty year old, dressed in a garb of clerical black buttoned up to the throat, with a profile like a bird of prey and a staccato manner of speaking") leaves the reader in no doubt that Derleth is the author. There were, in fact, three readings (or "Herausschreiungen") in all. The work was published on Harry Graf Kessler's recommendation by the Insel Verlag as *Die Proklamationen* in December 1904; a second slightly modified edition, appeared in the Musarion Verlag as *Proklamationen* in 1919.

Derleth was born in Gerolzhofen, Lower Franconia, in 1870; he arrived in Munich in 1889 to study philosophy and theology and rapidly became one of Schwabing's initiates, that bohemian quarter notorious as a breeding ground for perverse and irrational doctrines, a meeting place for those who yearned in overwrought and unbalanced visions for redemption, epiphany, catastrophe, and apocalypse. We have met these initiates before; although Ludwig Derleth may appear a more peripheral figure, remote from the turbulence of the "Kosmiker," his ruthless pose and merciless comminations make him an important and fascinating writer.[2] Derleth's first poetry, together with prose sketches, was published in the bibliophile quarterly *Pan* in 1896. Such pieces as "Anadyomene" and "Putrefaction and Flame" are stylized poems, utterances, aloof and hierogrammatic, and the prose utterances "Of light and the Great Darkness" and "Eleusis" are reminiscent of Theodor Däubler and fit well into the solar mythologizing of our post-Zarathustra generation. Further poems were published in Stefan George's *Blätter für die Kunst* ("The Emerald," "The Leader" and "The Cohort"), highly wrought pieces which are practically indistinguishable from the early work of Ludwig Klages. It would be false, however, to rate Derleth simply as an acolyte of George, derivative and ephemeral: Harry Graf Kessler expressed the opinion in a letter (5.11.1897) that "you are chosen to be one — and perhaps the greatest — of our German poètes maudits"; the Dutch poet Albert Verwey dedicated his *Michael* to him, and C. J. Burckhardt was later to single him out for fulsome praise. But it is not as a "poète maudit" that he would be remembered, for the path that he chose to pursue would lead into a realm remote from jejune aestheticism.

Derleth was obsessed by the belief that he was to be the Savonarola of his age that he was destined to preach a ruthless and imperious Christianity. The influence of the Rosicrucian Sâr Joséphin Péladan, self-styled "Grand Maître de l'Ordre de la Rose Croix du Temple et du Gral" whom Derleth visited in Paris encouraged the latent anti-materialistic vision. Péladan saw in Rosicrucianism a symbolic façade disguising Catholic truths; for him the order favoured a fervent Catholic ideal. It was this as well as Péladan's journey to the Holy Land in 1889 (where, he claimed, he had discovered the authentic tomb of Jesus in the mosque of Omar) which reinforced Derleth's own zealotry. On July 20, 1903 he set off on his journey to Rome, arriving at the time of the announcement of the new pope, Pius X, who was to succeed Leo XIII. Derleth hoped that a cosmic, elemental, world religion, a new, merciless and inexorable Catholicism might be founded, where incense and gunpowder, organ music and ordnance would herald the attack on the citadels of complacency and mediocrity. On his return to Munich he was fired solely with the all-consuming desire to found an Order, a fanatical sect determined to expunge millennia of human domesticity — and the *Proklamationen* were the opening salvo. He subsequently moved with his sister to the fifth floor of Mariastrasse 2, taking with him the lectern carved with an eagle from which the perorations had been declaimed, certain pictures of Napoleon, of the head of the Medusa, and of the Virgin Mary. And here he would remain, apart from sporadic journeys to Rome, to Vienna, to the Near East and finally to San Pietro di Stabio in the Ticino, Switzerland, where he died in January 1948. His life's work, the vast *Der fränkische Koran* (The Koran of the Franks [i.e. of the western peoples]), some 1900 pages long in the 1971 edition of *Das Werk*, is probably the most massive block of unread fiction in twentieth-century German literature. The work became so unwieldy that Derleth was forced to publish Part One in 1932; it met with scarcely any interest, one exception being Karl Wolfskehl who spoke enthusiastically of the work later when in exile in New Zealand. Certain fragments of Part Two (to be listed later) were published toward the end of Derleth's life, others posthumously, but the bulk remained unknown until 1971. A gigantic vision, then, a "Koran" or recitation, taking in the whole of Western culture and one which also betrays a fascination with the Near East, the world of the Templars, and with the Holy Land, the crusading zeal of Urban II, the later fanaticism of the Assassins and the Mahdi, subject of an early poem by Derleth (now lost). It is a work so extraordinary that it may indeed take pride of place in a literature not deficient in eccentric nimiety. And yet this strident Catholicism, this "deus vult" which combines uneasily with a Nietzschean despotism is surely not as remote as Mombert's interstellar odysseys or Däubler's aurora borealis. I shall attempt here to explore Derleth's oeuvre, to push into virgin territory and establish the work's parameters.

A church militant — this remained Derleth's most cherished ideal. His worship of Mary will have nothing of the prurient sultriness of decadence, nor of Hölderlin's rapt and incandescent invocation of Rome and the Vatican in the last fragmentary utterances; it is a cult of absolute stringency and fervour, an obsession and fanatical glorification, an intransigent dedication far exceeding the neo-Catholicism of a Bloy or a Bernanos, a Péguy or a Claudel, a Chesterton or a Francis Thompson. The sincerity may be admired, but its excessive ardour becomes disquieting: the announcement of the new pope, Pius X in 1903, brought little comfort to Derleth, who awaited a more draconian form of Catholicism, and a more intense cult of Mary, than ever before. It is tempting to seek similarities between Derleth and the papal paranoiac Baron Corvo (that is, Frederick Rolfe), a man similarly obsessed by siglas, blazons, and other ecclesiastical accoutrements in his cult of Sanctissima Sophia. Like Derleth, Rolfe had eked out a penurious existence as schoolmaster and yet had also sensed he was destined to be "an artificer of transcendent genius."[3] In Derleth's case a desire for grandeur is fed not only by an extreme Catholicism but also by a Nietzschean vitalism:[4] an imagination kindled by the apocalyptic images of the Book of Revelations, by examples of Roman glory, by the cult of the Borgias and also by *Thus Spake Zarathustra* produces a strange and unsettling rhetorical universe. The synthesis of Christ and Zarathustra, attempted by many German writers before 1914 (and later attempted by the eponymous hero of Joseph Goebbels's novel *Michael*) demonstrates the eccentric channels through which religious yearning flowed when deprived of more orthodox formulations. The fusion of prayers for redemption and shouts of command, the excesses of the church militant, above all the confusion of militaristic metaphors and literal exhortations to destroy — these characteristic traits of Derleth's work lend a forbidding, alien, aspect to his writing that appeals to few readers.

Die Proklamationen, some forty pages long, provides an obvious starting point. "I awoke, and three signs appeared to me: the lightning, the eagle and the star. I, Ludwig Derleth, stand alone, and all have joined against me. I declare war in the name of Jesus of Nazareth [. . .]."[5] An arresting opening, and one which announces that "All regiments, workshops and magazines of the world — we decimate." Passages redolent of *Zarathustra* are frequent: "It is better not to be born than to be slothful. If you are light, then shine in the darkness

[. . .]" (1, 45); "I shatter your tablets of stone and pour my commandment into your blood [. . .]" (1, 68); "You are impatient? You long for a new deed?" (1, 68). The New Testament, *Zarathustra*, and the *Book of Revelations* are strangely blended:

> And many people were standing on the mountain tops and gazed at the cloud in the distance. And the Lord spake: "See!" And the faces of those who were blinded by the light turned to the emptiness. And the Lord spake: "Hear!" And the trumpets blazed and the drums roared and the trombones sounded. And the Lord cried: "Massacre!!" (1, 51)

The constant references to tumult, uproar, thunder and collapse betoken an obsession with dislocation and havoc deriving from *Götterdämmerung* rather than Christianity; it should be borne in mind that Derleth studied the New Testament in Greek during the winter of 1898–99 and recast most of it in a manner that stressed the harshness of Christ's injunctions. The references to dissension and the sword (Matthew 10, 34–5), the cursing of the fig-tree (Mark 11, 14 and 20), the sending of fire on the earth (Luke 12, 49) and the insistence on the highest ideals were those aspects of the gospels which Derleth extolled: they had, of course, provided Nietzsche with many of the images and precepts to be found in *Zarathustra*.

The idea of a church militant informed the basic tenor of Derleth's vision, a church more Roman and more Catholic than any that had previously existed. His Savonarola pose has been attested; rejecting the frivolity of Schwabing at the turn of the century he preferred instead to condemn and denounce, "a warrior-Christ who, armed with sword, cross and flaming brand set forth on his crusade against the world and its degeneration."[6] Ignatius Loyola springs to mind; Christus Imperator Maximus demands absolute obedience, and his disciples proclaim: "We elevate the fruitful ideal of submission above the democratic structures of the world [. . .]" (1, 54); "We are disciples, and are known as followers and know that we must devote our whole beings to this battle, body and soul" (1, 48). The highest examples of obedience are cited as "The Roman infantry, the Corps of Assassins and the Society of Jesus" (1, 54). These disciples, drilled to fanatical acceptance of gnomic decrees, are priests and storm troopers, moving with smoking, bloody swords against a moribund world; from on high a "raving voice" exhorts: "Bathe in blood! Gorge yourselves on blood! Intoxicate yourselves with blood that you may not resemble the pale, ghostlike armies of Hades" (1, 64). And the shock troops, these columns of fanatics hardened in the fires of combat, "destroy the rabble and shatter their government" (1, 70). Not only the state, but the Church itself, flawed by democracy and compromise, must likewise be destroyed: "The priest kills the steer and the axe strikes the pontifex. Your kingdom is at an end . . . Red madness today celebrates its masterpiece with deeds and fiery incense [. . .]" (1, 82). And the reader, stunned by hyperbole and martial uproar is possibly not surprised that the Roman emperor Caligula is hailed in preference to the meek who, for Derleth, will never inherit the earth.

> The Lord spoke: "See the Emperor who suffered in madness, that I should lead him to the elect. Verily I say unto you: shattered goblets of stone shall be transformed into vessels of the elite in the will of the Lord." And the beloved amongst the disciples found Caligula waking in a bad sleep, dreaming that he was bathing in black streams of blood in a hot sultriness [. . .]. (1, 67–8)

Derleth's Caligula, like Nietzsche's Cesare Borgia, is an exemplification of the will to power, a figure who transcends the traditional categories of good and evil. Yet he is summoned by the Lord of *Die Proklamationen* to be His servant, for the one who does not shrink from blood is the one who will execute the Lord's commands. The highest synthesis would be that between the ecstatic visionary and the man of action, a *miles gloriosus* who would follow Christus imperator maximus through the bloodiest battle; amidst an ever-increasing tumult of peroration he announces:

> Let My will enlighten the obedient ones, let a secular dictatorship be founded. Let Europe be overwhelmed by our common desire to resist its insurrection. Let us hurl the crushing weight of our power against disintegration and destroy industrious England throughout the world. (1, 80)

Disintegrating Europe is to be welded into a ring of steel, and one country above all is singled out as being the arch-enemy to be chastised and obliterated — England.

Derleth's aversion to England owes much to Nietzsche, who castigated its utilitarianism, cant, lack of music, food, and much else besides. Like Nietzsche, Derleth looked to France and above all Italy for his spiritual home (although, of course, for Nietzsche Rome was "the most indecent spot on earth for the creator of Zarathustra": 6, 340). Following George, Derleth believed that the Mediterranean world was the *fons et origo* of world civilization; the Greek world of beauty, so important for George, was eclipsed in Derleth's case by a radical and uncompromising Catholicism. Christus Imperator Maximus desired the conquest of Europe and the destruction above all of "industrious England," the head of a world empire, traditionally empirical, pragmatic and suspicious of drastic solutions. It is highly unlikely that the political tension between Great Britain and Imperial Germany should have impinged upon Derleth's vision: his objections were of a different nature. Parliamentary democracy must be anathema to such a mentality as his, and he extolls Napoleon rather than those who defeated him:

> We distance ourselves from that insolent, unholy people [i.e. the British] and demonstrate our superiority over the rulers of the mob; as kings we distance ourselves and in the depths of our blood we cherish that glorious desire, a desire akin to the highest, purest love, a desire which inspired Napoleon the Great and carried him through sleepless nights as he planned dominion over state, church and planet. (1, 48)

We have a striking example of that mythologizing tendency so prevalent among many German writers at the turn of the century, the preference for the forcible *idea* or *image* rather than the historical *fact*; Ernst Bertram's comment in his famous book on Nietzsche, that "All that has happened seeks its image, all that is living its legend, all that is real its mythical equivalent" seems particularly appropriate here.[7] Derleth will not create his own world of mythical resonances as did Däubler and Mombert, but will use the world of Catholic symbolism and hagiography, fuse it with his own eclectic view of world history and, after the perorations of the proclamations had receded, create his own Koran or recitation, a vast vision of Frankish civilization. High up in his Munich atelier, surrounded by portraits of Alexander, Hannibal, Sulla, Augustus, Mohammed, Francis of Assisi, Loyola, Wallenstein, Napoleon, and Nietzsche he devoted his life to the writing and completion of his enormous epic.

Part One, *Des Werkes erster Teil* (1932) consists of a "Proömion" and nine sections, encompassing 486 pages. This poem gives witness to the holy seriousness with which the poet approaches his great task: the work will speak for him (he trusts) when he is no longer living. The central section is the praise of Rome ("O aromatic Rome of seven hills," 2, 10), city of fragrance, bride of the Great King, chalice of joy; should the poet be untrue then let his hand decay upon its stump, his heart burst, his blood gush forth, the light decay and the "golden songs fall silent." The Vatican is placed firmly in the centre of Derleth's universe and from it radiate energies and fields of force which pulsate through the cosmos. The lines of verse and prose are urgent, stately and rhapsodic in turn, expressing a fervent and immediate vision. The hammering and dynamiting of *Die Proklamationen* recede, but the proud stance remains, indifferent to the yelling and the barking of the mob: "die kämpfende Muse," the "fighting Muse" is hailed (2, 12), companion to Mars, with "whirring bow and ringing lyre." The poet's attitude is sacerdotal and his "Wortgebäude," his linguistic structure, will be an edifice of praise, a testament to God's glory.

Section One may be called a solemn credo, devout and fervent witness to the Catholic ecclesia in a series of prayers and exhortations. A "Veni creator Spiritus" stands as an introduction, a rock-like affirmation.

> Let us offer sacrifice to the great Spirit
> Whose will is triumphant
> the Supreme Ruler of Being, the King of Eternity
> the Lord of Infinity
> the omnipotent Creator of Heaven and Earth
> the Great Giver, the Benefactor of Life
> the Sublime Ruler, Lord of Divine Princes
> the Father of Worlds, the Fount of the Spiritual Hosts
> the Wonder beyond the Solar Path
> inconceivable to Reason
> accessible only in the Fire of Ecstasy.
>
> (2, 14)

God is the "Creator of Light / Orion's belt, Ursa Major and Aldebaran" and the poet beseeches Him to "shatter the silence of my night" (2, 19), to speak and overwhelm. Christ is giver of the living bread, guardian of immortal wine, mirror of holy grace; He is hope of the strong, shepherd of the gentle herd, palm of life and salt of earth. This note of fervour continues for many pages, interspersed with the Latin of the Vulgate ("Benedicat nos Dominus noster Jesus Christus," "Summo materiatori patri optimo maximo"). The section culminates in an intense Mariolatry:

> O Virgin, blessed mother of Our Lord
> thou Mistress of Bliss
> thou peace most yearned for by the storm-tossed
> thou fulfilment of all desire
> thou radiant golden crown of all beauty
> thou pilgrimage of all graces
> thou holy chalice of pure senses
> thou golden palace of the new covenant
> thou courtyard of the spiritual Imperium
> thou deepest mystery of all love

thou Name, known only to that heart which is sealed by thee
thou Harbour, trust of the wing'ed soul. . .

(2, 67)

This fervent plenitude is reminiscent of the Baroque; closer in time is
the poetry of Prince Emil von Schönaich-Carolath-Schilden, whose
collected works appeared in 1907 and whose "Ver sacrum" is quoted
almost word for word (2, 56). But Derleth's voice is unmistakable, in-
sistent, ardent, and earnest; the exclamatory swell of supplication rising
in an expressive hymn.

The second recognisable section begins on page 70 ("The world of
baseness closes round, / the path to Paradise is steep [. . .]"). And
then, in rhythmical *vers libre*, a journey is portrayed, a venturing-forth
by sea to exotic realms in which the traveller, a fusion of argonaut and
crusader, leaves the inauthentic turmoil of existence to seek contact
with divine forces. The realms are those of myth and faery, Atlantis and
Avalon: there are echoes of Homer ("the rosy-fingered dawn"), Hölderlin ("the north-east blows" — a deliberate borrowing from the latter's *Andenken*) and *Zarathustra* (the wandering of the prophet across
islands and mountains). A mysterious figure (the Old Man of the
Mountain — 2, 89) hints at the "corps of the Assassins" referred to in
Die Proklamationen, but the venerable sage of the *Der fränkische Koran* is an icon of verdant growth, a spirit of the forest living in umbrageous isolation. The journey takes the reader to the island of the lotus
eaters, but there can be no mere escapism here as in Tennyson: in images strikingly akin to those used by Rilke in his Tenth Duino Elegy the
"foothills of extinguished hope" are portrayed, those outcrops of polished primeval suffering, a petrified yearning. The loveliness of Tahiti is
glimpsed, the Tinian of Hölderlin, the Pallau of Gottfried Benn, but
there can be no earthly goal.

Section three (2, 95) leaves the sea and reflects the tranquillity of
Perchtoldsdorf near Vienna, where Derleth composed it. The prevailing
mood is one of lightness and harmony, of Spring and growth: the wanderer returns to a landscape of Hellas and Franconia where Ulysses-
Derleth exults in the burgeoning of fig, peach and hyacinth, and the
song of nightingales. A *chinoiserie* is also present in the portrayal of the
white porcelain bridge, also of waterlilies and the delicate temple (2,
101): the reference to water-colours, Indian ink and pearls are vividly
reminiscent of Hans Bethge. There is a decorative reminiscent of
Jugendstil, element here, compounded with a nature-mysticism reminiscent of Johannes Schlaf or, indeed, Waldemar Bonsels; the stanza
beginning "Now climbs the golden sun-sacrament" (2, 107) with its

description of sunlight, grass, pebbles, water beetles and dew-spangled cobwebs seems to derive from the final section of Jens Peter Jacobsen's *Gurresange* (Songs of Gurre), made familiar by Schoenberg. It may seem improper to refer to Jacobsen, the convinced follower of Darwin, in connection with Derleth's work, but Jacobsen combined close observation of nature with an ecstatic sense of wonder which found expression in pantheism. The *Gurresange* ends with an evocation of sunrise and effulgence, a sense of awe and joy which is not remote from Derleth's vision here. And the section ends, surprisingly, with an exhortation to read and absorb Shakespeare's *As You Like It* and *Twelfth Night*— Derleth's aversion to hyperborean Britain is here forgotten, and Shakespeare's two comedies are extolled. A light scherzo, then, refreshing indeed after the forbidding solemnity of much of Derleth's writing.

Section four (2, 132) is an extended hymn of praise to Dionysus and the gift of wine. Nietzsche's cult of Dionysus is obviously the starting point for Derleth, but English readers will catch echoes of Fitzgerald's Omar Khayyám translation (the misformed jug blaming the potter, the references to Djamshid's cup, the description of wine as an alchemist, the desire to be buried in a vineyard); the seventy two pages are, as it were, drenched in wine, seeing it as a life-enhancing sacrament. The symposium of Socrates alternates with wine festivals in the Rhineland, Franconia and the Mediterranean; the joys of Tokay are portrayed, also Falernian wine, as are Malmsey, Burgundy, Muscatel and mead (there is even praise of stout, porter and ale — 2, 137). The tone is, for Derleth, surprisingly colloquial at times ("They were the sons of Bacchus, one by one / Boozing away and all as drunk as lords"): there is also a delight in listing jugs, chalices, pots and amphora, all made of various metals (pewter, silver, etc.) and stoneware. A gigantic carnival is underway with much cooking, frying, feeding and general excess, with the abbot of St. Dionys leading the way in "troughing, feeding, hogging" (2, 139): there are also "buxom wenches and dainty poppets." Even "the old man of Königsberg" (Immanuel Kant) succumbs to Sicilian wine, deserting the grey mists of the North and seeing metaphysics lying inebriated in the gutter (2, 152). A glorious bacchanal, then, a praise of inebriation with wine as the great redeemer. Dominik Jost[8] speculates that there are reminiscences here of the "antikes Fest" held in Wolfskehl's home in Schwabing in 1903; there is, however, more of a medieval feel to this section, an awareness of wine as fruit of the earth yet at the same time suffused with divine significance. The belief in the sacramental nature of reality never left Derleth, who sensed a correspondence between the mundane and the transcendental spheres. For him it was the great error of Protestantism to have curtailed severely the plethora of symbols and sacraments that transfigured the medieval world, thus rendering the gulf between nature and spirit ever wider. Nietzsche's attack against Protestantism and Hölderlin's late preoccupation with Catholic themes may have played a part. Derleth knew that it was the wisdom of the Catholic church that it considered the pagan foundations on which Christianity was built and saw the need of preserving them. For bread and wine may be seen as a memory of fertility rites, the perpetual harvest of the fields being offered in sacrifice to those forces which conceived it. The wine, the blood of Christ, was the sap of nature, the juice of life infusing warmth and strength into all that subsists. And life dominated by the church is a feast, a constant correspondence between God and man, touched at all points by the numinous. It is D. H. Lawrence who is a most unlikely commentator here, a man remote from Derleth and yet strangely similar in the following comment:

> The old Church knew that life is here our portion, to be lived, to be lived in fulfilment. The stern rule of Benedict, the wild flights of Francis of Assisi — these were coruscations in the steady heaven of the Church. The rhythm of life itself was preserved by the Church, hour by hour, day by day, season by season, year by year, epoch by epoch, down among the people, and the wild coruscations were accommodated to this permanent rhythm. We feel it, in the South, in the country, when we hear the jangle of bells at dawn, at noon, at sunset, marking the hours with the sound of Mass or prayers. It is the rhythm of the daily sun [. . .] Oh what a catastrophe for man when he cut himself off from the rhythm of the year, from his union with the sun and the earth.[9]

And Derleth, in a transport of ecstatic inebriation, expresses a similar idea in the jocular utterance: "But he who does not feel, in a draft of good wine, the presence of the Holy Spirit — to him we wish that nothing but water and abstinence should pass his throat!" (2, 150).

Section five (2, 206) is the most fervent and extended example of Mariolatry in modern German literature, exceeding even the rapture of section one. The Virgin is extolled as an erotic experience but also as a expression of transcendental love. She is a goddess, pure and blessed, a Virgin and immaculate Mother, a precious pearl without blemish; the strophic utterances are suffused by a glowing sensuousness, by colours of gold, purple, ivory and chryselephantine. The poet loves Her for she is "the Daughter of eternal days"; she reflects the light of dawn, holding mirrors to the cherubim, herself the "specula sine macula," the unspoilt image of God. The verse here attains that hymn-like grandeur

which characterizes Rilke's second Duino Elegy, and there are also
echoes of Novalis in the description of the poet laying his head upon
the Virgin's breasts, resting upon their rosy tips (2, 211). The reader is
forcibly reminded of that anonymous twelfth-century poem which
praises thus the Virgin's breasts: "Tua sunt ubera / vino redolentia, /
candor superat lac et lilia, / odor flores vincit et balsama" (Your breasts
are as fragrant as wine; their whiteness whiter than milk and lilies, their
scent lovelier than flowers and balsam wood).[10] The *Song of Songs*,
Solomon's great love poem, is also not far: the poet's hymns are "rich
with aromatic spikenard" as he greets the "Beloved One, the Lily of the
Field" (2, 225). and we are also close to Ecclesiasticus 24, 15: "I gave a
sweet smell like cinnamon and aspalathus, and I yielded a pleasant
odour like the best myrrh, as galbanum, and onyx, and sweet storax,
and as the fume of frankincense in the tabernacle."[11] The image of the
pearl in the "traubigen Ohrgehäng" (2, 242) refers in all probability to
the picture in the ruins of S. Maria Antigua in Rome where St. Anne,
the Virgin's mother, carries in her arms the baby whose earlobe, in Oriental fashion, has a jewel hanging from it;[12] there is also the strange image in a late Hölderlin fragment of a golden earring whose shadow lies
across the Virgin's cheek like a grape upon dun-coloured foliage.[13] The
poet, an enraptured hierodule, elevates his gaze to the loveliness of the
Virgin and intones a radiant doxology. Yet he knows also that Mary,
symbol of intercession and divine love, is present in each erotic manifestation for love is both sacred and profane. The Virgin is Love, the
"Urfeuer" (primeval fire) of all planets and souls: Eros anticipates her
and is present in all acts of procreation (2, 220). She arises in radiant
splendour and pagan beauty from her bath, and the poet is transfixed
by the beauty of her nakedness. The line "All things speak to me as a
symbol of Her" (2, 214) is Goethean, seeing the Beloved incarnated in
all aspects of nature. She is present in mystical androgyny as morning
and as evening star; she is hailed as "Venus verticordia," a tribute,
surely, to Richard Dehmel and his "Metamorphoses of Venus." Her
most modern manifestation is as an elegant woman, glimpsed in a large
conservatory beneath palms, wearing a black hat with a spray of emerald green colibri feathers and an embroidered satin jacket, holding a
sprig of jasmine and kissing the opulent lips of a tropical poppy (2,
236).

Derleth is here looking back on a long tradition, seeing in Mary the
ultimate fertility symbol; there is no steely asceticism but a fervent conviction that Mary is present in every manifestation of erotic fire, of vernal growth and fruitful blessing. There is an irrepressible exuberance in
this section, an affirmation and rejoicing in the glory of womanhood

and sexuality, no gnostic rejection of matter but an exultant affirmation. The Northern sundering of sensuality and transcendence is here utterly rejected, and Derleth's Mariolatry here reaches its triumphant climax. But such a joyous pleroma is cut short by the next section — no warmth and joy, but an awareness of failure and unfulfilment.

Crucial to section six (2, 254) is the knowledge that "The great god Pan is dead," a quotation taken directly from section eleven of Nietzsche's *Geburt der Tragödie*. Nietzsche is here referring to the death of tragedy, that is, of Dionysian ecstasy and exultation; the quotation is taken from Tiberius who recounts that sailors heard the fearful news of the death of Pan as they passed a lonely island. Their reaction is the reaction of those, Nietzsche writes, who hear that Dionysus and his life-affirming *acceptance* of tragedy are no more. Derleth is here expressing the triumph of Schopenhauer's world of pessimism, of Apate and Maya, those principles of illusion and deception, of denial and resignation. Nietzsche had overcome Schopenhauer, turning life denial into radiant affirmation despite the prevalence of pain, and this acceptance of life he baptised "Dionysian." In section six Derleth laments the death of Pan/Dionysus, of turbulent life affirmation; he regretfully admits the grey veil of sadness, the nexus of inconsequential phenomena that envelops us. There is no longer an ecstatic god of energy and praise, but a world of tepid half-heartedness. Many images reinforce the sense of loss: the house is grey and deserted, the sun is cold, the garden is despoiled. The golden falcon has fled and the "goddess of darkening grief, of woe-begottenness" holds sway (2, 262). The death of Pan is the death of joy, and the city of Dis is portrayed, a place of ash and sterility, a Waste Land. "O light of the sun, why hast thou betrayed me?" (2, 352) — with this mournful question the section ends.

Where is the Christology here in the lament for Pan/Dionysus? Derleth's work stands in a long poetic tradition exemplified above all in Hölderlin, a tradition that suggests an esoteric relationship between Christ and Dionysus. The bread and wine of the Christian Eucharist are not unrelated to the body and blood of the wild Greek god; both Christ and Dionysus know the wonders of wine, and the miracle of Cana and the mast which brings forth foliage are but manifestations of a similar mystery. Born of divine father and a mortal mother they are both *suffering* gods who overcome death to rise again. In the Incarnation the ancient myth is used, transformed. Hölderlin had attempted a synthesis of Christ and Dionysus as he sought to bring the spiritual climate of Ancient Greece to Germany, but Christian, particularly apocalyptic, tones come increasingly to the fore in his poetry and finally predominate, whilst Dionysus is driven underground. In the late fragments, poised on the brink of mental collapse, Hölderlin, son of the Protestant Tübinger Stift, greets the Madonna and a vision of the Vatican arises "in a green night"; that other son of the Protestant manse, Friedrich Nietzsche, will finally insist on Christ and Dionysus as adversaries (6, 375) whilst he himself, in the last insane letters, calls himself "the Crucified" and "Dionysus." In *Denys l'Auxerrois* (translated into German in 1903), Walter Pater portrays Denys as a monk, a Dionysus redivivus as the *spiritus rector* of a Gothic cathedral, forming the heathen pan-pipes into a massive organ, an instrument traditionally associated with Christian piety; Gerhart Hauptmann would likewise describe Strasbourg Cathedral as "perfect Dionysus" and delight in a portrayal of pagan and Christian synthesis in the Seventh "Adventure" of his *Till Eulenspiegel*.[14] For "the great Pan is not dead" — naggingly the god returns again and again into many a piece of modern fiction, and he will reappear in chapter six of this book.

Two critiques follow (sections seven and eight), a *Kritik der Wissenschaft* (Critique of Knowledge) and a *Kritik der Geschichte* (Critique of History): both are written in prose. These two long essays are essentially broadsides against analytical science and a lack of transcendental awareness (which, Derleth believes, will ultimately lead to nihilism) and attack what he regarded as the hopeless vulgarity and senselessness of the modern age. *Kritik der Geschichte* has an undeniably Nietzschean ring about it, a blistering attack against democracy, egalitarianism, tastelessness and the lack of any hierarchy, of any "spiritual aristocracy." The reference to the "rabble" (2, 412) and "the image of the last man" (2, 445) stem directly from *Thus Spake Zarathustra*; abject conformity, complacency and the lack of nuance are especially deplored. Where there are still monarchs these are rejected as puppets and grotesque travesties: we remember the picture of Napoleon that decorated the Munich garret. The prophet of *Die Proklamationen* rises again, a voice declaiming in thunderous promulgation. The vision is theocentric yet strikingly similar to Nietzsche's, the fear that, once the divine ground of being no longer holds, then the "earth is unhooked from its sun," and disintegrates in an outer darkness.

The last section, section nine (2, 448), ends with an apparition of a mountain, a journey to the heights of the earth and a mystical self-purification: the echoes of Dante and of Goethe (*Faust II*) are apparent. The pilgrim meets three figures, Death, the Seraph, and the Fisherman; Death flees before the radiance of the dawn and the Seraph, Virgil-like, accompanies the wanderer into the realms of light. He, Derleth, knows that is task is "to find the land where the Best is King;" (2, 453); he sees in a vision the constellation of Cassiopeia with its delta of stars, (and "D" is his own initial) and he is called to announce Christ's majesty (2, 457). The Fisher of Men leads him upwards in a radiant apotheosis, where the poet, absolute in light and sublimity, knows that all earthly things are but a symbol — "ein Gleichnis" — and as poet-prophet his task is to interpret this. The book (or, rather, its first part) ends with images of height, radiance and transparency, of kneeling and accepting, of adoration and knowledge of the One true Christ. There is, however, no humility but confidence and self-assurance.

Der fränkische Koran (Part One) was greeted by a resounding silence, the times, apparently, being inauspicious. A few grudging comments referred to its largeness of scale and its "baroque opulence," and it was unfavourably compared with George's Hellenic severity. George himself made no comment although Wolfskehl, as we know, was enthusiastic, praising its syncretic view of world history. Would a second part ever appear? What would it contain? Who would read it? The convulsions of the next decade and a half, of the years remaining to Derleth were not conducive to the completion and sympathetic reception of works of such enormous scope and mythopoeic Christianity. In 1935 Egon Wellesz used texts from the *Der fränkische Koran I* in his *Fünf kleine Männerchöre*, but otherwise it seemed as though Derleth had completely disappeared from the cultural scene or, rather, the scene imposed by the *Reichsschrifttumskammer*. We hear of journeys to Haifa and Baalbek, Damascus, Palmyra, and Constantinople. Derleth was also to move from Perchtelsdorf with his wife Christine and settle in San Pietro di Sabio near the Swiss-Italian border; it was here that the bulk of that which would compose *Der fränkische Koran* (Part Two) would be written. It is this mass of material which makes up volumes three to six of the 1971 edition of his work.

Das Buch vom Orden (The Book of the Order, 3, 9–117) continues the praise of discipline and order, and the creation of a fanatical brotherhood which we observed earlier. Derleth was an admirer of Karl Gutzkow's *Die Ritter vom Geiste* (The Knights of the Spirit 1850–51), a nine-volume account, covering some 3000 pages, of the exploits of one Dankmar Wildungen who believes he has a claim to the German Order of Knights Templar and sets about the foundation of a new order, the Order of the Knights of the Spirit. Johann Wilhem Friedrich von Meyern's political novel *Dya-Na-Sore oder die Wanderer* (Dya-Na-Sore or the Wanderers) in five volumes (1787–1791), a description of secret societies in Tibet and India, and containing many plans for reform, also appealed to him. *Die Proklamationen* had already extolled obedience and purity; now St. Francis is placed besides St. Ignatius

Loyola, clothed in "the diamond armour of chastity." Heroism, with Nietzschean overtones, is of the highest importance here: the tone is authoritarian, aloof and serene. *Das Buch vom Orden* begins with the statement that all evil and suffering in the world stems from a primeval rejection of that divine hierarchy which God had established at the beginning of time, a hierarchy with its priesthood, warriors and servants. Without this theocratic structure a necessary disintegration followed — here the echoes of the Romantic writer Novalis (*Die Christenheit oder Europa*) are discernible. A state without its divinely ordained hierarchy (there are comparisons, 3, 13, to a golden beehive) is a meaningless charade, doomed to collapse and barbarism. A philosopher-priest rules and educates: hieratic myths are enacted in an acropolis of granite, adorned with pillars of agate holding a gigantic globe of lapis lazuli (3, 28).[15] The soldier priests are like young eagles (an emblematic bird for Derleth with both pagan and Christian connotations) and their training, physical, mental and spiritual, is portrayed in detail (3, 55). The importance of music is stressed above all, a transcendent art and one capable of expressing arcane mysteries. A steely idealism is promoted, a body tuned to physical perfection and a mind dedicated to the highest goals, suffused by a radiant fervour. Such terminology — obedience, physical prowess, fanaticism, idealism — has a disquieting ring when one considers the times in which this book was written. It is tempting to compare Derleth's vision with that of Georg Adolf Josef Lanz von Liebenfels (1874–1954), founder of a *Neutemplerorden* of blond, blue-eyed men (the Ordo Novi Templi) situated in Burg Werfenstein in Upper Austria. Lanz von Liebenfels had been a member of the Cistercian Order between 1893 and 1899 in Heiligenkreuz but left the brethren and in his journal *Ostara* (1905–1931) preached the need for the cultivation of a master race which must needs be separated from the lower orders, the "Äfflingen." The new doctrine was to be called "Ariosophie" or "Arioheroik"; Lanz also translated the bible in a highly idiosyncratic manner stressing, like Derleth, the harshness of Christ's message. But the reader is relieved to find that, in Derleth's Order, the neophyte studies the enactment of works dealing with Indian legends of reincarnation, Greek myths, Islamic stories, and Christian mystery plays. There is no swastika flying here, and no concept of Germanic-Nordic supremacy.

The next two sections, *Die Posaune des Kriegs* (The Trumpet of War) and *Die apokalyptische Schlacht* (The Battle of the Apocalypse) are characterized by violence and uproar: Derleth's penchant for scenes of martial strife and glory is here clearly exemplified. *Die Posaune des Kriegs* (3, 121–192) portrays a youthful nobility which has turned away from the blandishments of civilization and devotes itself to a crusade, a holy battle to cleanse the world of degeneration and complacency. There is an Oriental flavour in this section; we remember the early poem "Der Mahdi" and Derleth's predilection for the more militant manifestations of Islam. And the very title of his life's work, the reference to the Koran, testifies to the awe in which he held the Arab world, its cruelty, wisdom, fanaticism and splendour. This section of his work extols the dedication of the Knights — and they are closely modelled on the Knights Templars who believed the greatest blessing that can be envisaged is to die in battle. Derleth's whole oeuvre is sustained by the belief that Christianity must resort to violence to achieve its aims: as early as 1902 a diary entry argues that "Christianity is inconceivable without force (puissance),"[16] and Nietzsche's innumerable references to war and struggle ("If one has renounced war then one has renounced the greatness of life" (6. 84) could be one example) must have played their part. Neither Nietzsche nor Derleth advocate crude militarism for the conflict they extol is a spiritual one, an attack against baseness and pusillanimity in Nietzsche's case and a materialistic godlessness in Derleth's. How far the pronounced and prominent military metaphors may be held to be irresponsible is another matter; suffice it to say that Derleth believed that Christianity was a heroic faith, a religion imbued with the need for self-sacrifice and ruthlessness. *Die Posaune des Kriegs*, in rhythmical prose, portrays the conversion of cloisters into barracks (3, 123), the rejection of silks and the donning of armour and the great movement eastwards to defeat the foe (3, 143). The mobilisation of the despised and the rejected (3, 130) shows that Derleth held that the energy of the criminal is preferable, when channelled into the right direction, than the tepid subservience of the meek — a view that Zarathustra would have applauded. His strident, bellicose tone may derive from Nietzsche; there are also echoes of Claudel's *Tête d'or* (1890) and the occasional descent into sub-Rilkean kitsch: "And they peeled the host-white body of the youth from his brazen armour, the body which had still exuded an ambrosial perfume after the enemy had flung it upon a pile of rotting corpses" (3, 149). *Die apokalyptische Schlacht* (The Battle of the Apocalypse: 3, 197–220) portrays the cosmic battle, the forces of darkness (die Unterirdischen) rising to defeat the Sons of Light; the section is basically a reworking of the Book of Revelations, a description of Michael's struggle with Satan, the unleashing of the Four Horsemen of the Apocalypse beneath a sky dark as bronze, dark as congealed blood (3, 206). The tone is chiliastic and peremptory and the brief but violent account ends with a "final command," and exhortation to "dynamite the planet!" (3, 229) to give way to the new

Sun — Jesus of Nazareth. Again, the shouts of command are greatly reminiscent of *Die Proklamationen*, that rich and disturbing seed-bed in which much of the later work has its origin.

It is with relief that the reader turns to *Das Buch der Geschichte* (The Book of History: 3, 225–286) and *Der Tod des Thanatos* (The Death of Thanatos: 3, 273–362) after the deafening explosions of battle. The former is a sombre portrayal of inadequacy and confusion, criticizing above all the Babylonian confounding of tongues, the Vanity Fair of life without meaning or authenticity. "Nemo contra hominem nisi homo ipse" — it is human frailty which has blighted the earth and made man wretched. More substantial is *Der Tod des Thanatos*, a long essay, interspersed with poems, which Derleth published in spring 1946 on the advice of the theologian Hans Urs von Balthasar, author of *Die Apokalypse der deutschen Seele* (it was reprinted in 1969). Balthasar greatly admired Derleth's ardent Catholicism: he had read the first version in 1942 and condoned, even though he did not emulate, Derleth's more Nietzschean attitudes. It would be the publisher Josef Stocker of Lucerne who insisted on the removal of the statement "With Jesus of Nazareth against Christianity" and also the claim "I speak the language of the Catholic Church which does not yet exist. The Vatican is only an enclave of the great Catholic Church."[17]

Der Tod des Thanatos has as its first section a further attack on human fallenness and depravity, an onslaught against vileness and brutality where the divine image has been eroded by bestial coarseness: one sees "half-rational creatures and faces devoid of all divinity, apes, dogs and jackals" (3, 275), a race of inferior stock that breeds without respite (3, 281). It is only the acceptance of Christ which will transfigure and redeem: "The true ens realissimum, the image of the divine kingdom, is the Catholic community" (3, 296). The central section explains what the death of Thanatos means: the Greeks portrayed death as a naked youth with upturned torch, but death is overcome by Christ's descent into hell, a shattering of the brazen doors of Dis (3, 307). Christ is the "supreme, imperial General of all times" (3, 308 — again we remember *Die Proklamationen*). Although the heathen adversary is defeated, Derleth insists that Christianity's strength lies in its rootedness in the pagan, sensual past; one of the central theses of his theology is the sensual nature of Christianity (we remember section four of *Der fränkische Koran I* and its praise of wine and the earth), the importance of Christ's incarnation in human flesh and the concept of the resurrection of the body. Christianity is not an abstract idea (3, 312–313): its insistence on the body of Christ and the womb of Mary helped it to absorb the earlier pagan theogonies and transfigure them. What emerges with increasing clarity is Derleth's contention that the classical, pagan world is just as important as the world of Judaism as a prerequisite of Christianity (3, 325). Of supreme importance is the fact that the Hellenic element triumphed and that the New Testament was written in Greek, not Hebrew (Derleth reminds us of the ancient belief that it was Hercules, in the guise of Simon of Cyrene, who helped Christ carry the cross to Golgotha.). Derleth may well have remained aloof from the political events around him, but his tendency to ignore the role played by Judaism in Christianity is much of its time. Hans Urs von Balthasar also suggested the removal of utterances from *Der Tod des Thanatos* which might be construed as anti-Semitic. The book ends with a zealous exhortation to mankind to change, to accept Christ and to repent, a skilful rhyming of "Glockengeläute" and "Metanoiete" (3, 361).

Die himmlische Basilie (The Heavenly Basilica) is the shortest book of *Der fränkische Koran* (3, 367–370), being little more than a long paragraph intent on denying the reality of a political struggle in favour of a spiritual war (it was published in the journal *Wort und Wahrheit* in 1947). *Advent* (3, 375–429, published posthumously in 1968) is more serene in tone than many of the other books and extols the fusion of east and west in a manner not dissimilar to that vision at the end of Novalis's *Heinrich von Ofterdingen* where the child of Heinrich and Mathilde, signifying a golden age, unites and reconciles. More weighty is *Die seraphinische Hochzeit* (The Seraphic Nuptials, 4, 9–52). In the Spring of 1937 Derleth completed this discrete section of *Der fränkische Koran* (Part Two) and gave it the tentative title *Die Legende vom Bruder Immerwach* (The Legend of Brother Ever-Wakeful); against his normal practice he sought to publish it as a separate work. It is a quietly lyrical meditation on the saintly life of Brother Ever-Wakeful and characteristically Derleth in its fusion of Franciscan piety and Nietzschean imagery ("the laughing lightning," "the glittering serpent of the abyss" etc.). Ever-Wakeful moves inexorably towards transfiguration: his body ("gleaming white as a pearl," 4, 90) is placed within a coffin of cedar wood. This peaceful and contemplative portrayal gives way to a more full-blooded description of heavenly joy in *Das Paradies* (4, 101–125) when Derleth's imagination exults in portrayals of richly sated colours, of birds, fish, and animals in a new Garden of Eden, radiant in blissful light. Androgynous union is portrayed, also a fusion of religions and mythologies, embraced and sanctified by Christ's blessing. Even the people of Israel, we notice, are welcomed, that people "whose ancient race may be proud of the richest progenitor, a folk on whose ancient tree the mother of God blooms as a mystic flower" (4, 124). In the midst of abundance and profusion there is a fullness of both life and spirit and, in a humorous aside (how rare in this writer) the poet sees himself welcomed to the feast and handed the sparkling wine: "The crystal chalice gleams and pearls with ambrosial wine [. . .] It is Ludwig Derleth for whom the wine is poured" (4, 121–122). There is no *inopia entis* here, no decay, no fallenness — an ecstatic vision prevails. In *Das sybillische Buch* (The Book of the Sybil), however, (4, 129–167) the vision is darker, more restrained: the poem descends into a chthonic realm of archetypal pictures (4, 131) deriving from multifarious mythologies, gorgon-like monsters and vast landscapes; he is accompanied by "das Weib Melancholie" past a Böcklin-like Island of the Dead (4, 155); he finally addresses the sphinx who points towards a Day of Judgement.

The *Poem der Magischen Natur* (Poem of Magical Nature: 4, 171–196) was published in 1958 in the *Ludwig Derleth Gedenkbuch*; it is a sensuous and glowing invocation of earth's glory and richness. A garden is portrayed, radiant as "an emerald jewel between the breasts of a royal bride" (4, 172); the earth is extolled as are other continents, other tellurian potentialities, other stars and constellations, fragrant with balsam and incense. There are telling references (4, 175) to the "Zarathustra-Religion," a life-enhancing cult of affirmation, nobly blessing and striving for life's highest manifestations. Derleth's ideal of a hierarchic order of monks is again present, a brotherhood devoted to prayer and agriculture. The earth is abundant in the fecundity, but it is man who neglects to see this: there is water, wood, ore, corn, flour, wool, stone, life, light and divinity. A final picture portrays a transfigured nature: the amethyst takes on the perfume of a violet (4, 191), and the earth blooms in purple and emerald. There is no stridency in this section but an ardent faith in the earth's majesty and ripeness.

The fourth volume of *Der fränkische Koran* (Part Two) ends with three short books, *Vom Wingert zu Kelter* (201–223), *Die Wandlungen der Pandora* (227–252) and *Der Liederdichter* (255–300), none of which had previously been published. *Vom Wingert zur Kelter* (From Vineyard to Winepress) consists of the ecstatic, rapturous experiences of a nun, a Hildegard of Bingen or a St. Theresa of Avila in which the image of the winepress is used to convey the nun's engulfment by grace as her heart is "pressed" in the chalice of the Eucharist. A lightning bolt shatters her earthly darkness (4, 222) and a blood-red, fire-red heart appears before her. The imagery is sexual: the nun's heart throbs and bleeds in a tempest of love as Christ overwhelms her. It is the next book which expresses the relationship between the sexes on a secular level — although for Derleth there is nothing which is "merely" secular: the relationship between man and woman, in its highest manifestations, is suffused by a great spirituality. *Die Wandlungen der Pandora* (The Metamorphoses of Pandora) deals with woman as helpmate, servant, companion: her destiny is an ecstatic fusion with the soul of her partner. Zarathustra's praise of woman as "pure and fine, like a jewel irradiated by the virtues of a future world" (4, 85) is evident in the imagery used by Derleth to convey woman's purity (4, 236): she is "as pure as the spring, as newly fallen snow, as gold liquid from the crucible, as a blossoming damson tree, as a mirror forged by the silversmith"; there are also obvious borrowings from the notorious misogynist Otto Weininger (woman has no "Wesen für sich," and it is only through man that her highest potential is achieved). The portrayal of woman active in a domestic milieu (4, 241), owes much to the Swiss writer Gotthelf (1797–1854) whose work Derleth greatly admired. The portrayal of Pandora and her transformations may be remote from the feminism of the late twentieth century: the poet who lived with a wife who adored him and a sister who worshipped him, who was steeped in the Catholic culture of the South and intrigued by many aspects of Islam can hardly be expected to sympathise with the movement towards female emancipation that blossomed in Germany in the 1920s if, indeed, he had ever been aware of them. His last book, *Der Liederdichter* (The Poet of Songs) is Goethean in its praise of nature, and a persona reminiscent of Lynkeus der Türmer (*Faust II*) gazes out in rapt adoration, greeting both occident and orient, the luminous diadem of the Pleiades and the earth itself as it spins, intoxicated, around the solar orb (4, 285). A dynamic feeling is conveyed in this section, and an equipoise remote from martial clamour and also from labyrinthine introversion. *Der fränkische Koran* is here, one feels, at its climax — but another vast section, consisting of some 740 pages in two volumes, will follow.

Albert Verwey, one of George's circle, called Derleth "the martyr of the Absolute, a hero striding towards the edges of madness";[18] the critic Jan Aler writes that Derleth's work "floods, thunders and roars along like the 'Great Stream of Becoming' [. . .] His work is reminiscent of the extravagant titanism of a Mombert or a Däubler, of the sublime linguistic torrents of a Claudel or a St.-John Perse";[19] Karl Muth, founder of *Hochland*, talks of "that tangled undergrowth from which the forest of this linguistically beautiful, but totally formless poetry, arose."[20] An almost monomaniacal voice speaks in solemn peroration, proclaiming a litany compounded of Nietzschean imperiousness, Christian idealism, and an Oriental fanaticism: what the gaunt priest of "Wahnmoching" proclaimed the sage of San Pietro di Stabio expressed in a work so vast that only the most dedicated reader could hope to penetrate. The landscape of both volumes of *Der Heilige* (The Holy One) is, however, comparatively familiar — it is that of *Thus Spake Zarathustra* with its pseudo-orientalism, its Jugendstil topoi (jewels, island, maidens), a Böcklinesque world of cypresses, caverns, and sunrise. In the first section a saint or prophet is described, stepping into an emerald green garden at the side of a lioness (5, 9); he lives in an azure loneliness, remote from the market place. He is visited by neophytes who praise his isolation (5, 11), a prophet whom God's eagle visits and feeds. Three gifts, he proclaims, are indispensable — love, freedom and light: these are sent by the gods (5, 13). If *Die Proklamationen* and much of *Der fränkische Koran* call to mind Nietzsche's vision of "the Roman Caesar with the soul of Christ" (11, 289), then *Der Heilige* portrays a Zarathustra at rest, with lion and eagle. The hammering, liturgical insistence of the earlier work is remote as the prophet moves through the dappled green-gold light ["Grünlichtergefunkel"] of the forest (5, 19). The image of water carried as a crystal ball derives from late Goethe (the poem *Paria*) and there is much of Goethe's orientalism in the portrayal of gardens, fountains and vegetation. The prophet moves with his disciples through the market-place, praising the quiet serenity of the strong, the pure in heart who need no outward display, and condemns the "windbags and sophists" (5, 47) who preach an anarchic lawlessness. It is "the resting Will" which he extols (5, 59), the "fruitful womb of all that is." The vocabulary is increasingly redolent of Zarathustra ("conquer," "invincible," "eternity"): the martial imagery, however, so dear to Derleth, recedes — this is not the Lord of Luke 12.49 but a sage who blesses the greatness of heroic magnanimity (5, 80). "Nothing sanctifies more than the power to help" (5, 102); a golden radiance envelops all. The prophet makes gnomic utterances extolling greatness of spirit, self-overcoming, nobility of gesture and purpose; it is only the dwarf who longs for self and vain display (5, 179). The first section draws to its close with the exhortation to love the earth and not to lose oneself in aetherial realms as poets are wont to do — we should not seek the laurel but the crown of thorns (5, 213), an emblem not only of suffering but of blessing and sanctifying.

The second section of volume five begins with the praise of woman. Again, a Jugendstil landscape emerges through which the prophet and his disciples pass; a glimpse of the Circassian women (5, 236) is greatly reminiscent of Zarathustra's praise of the dancing girls. The prophet teaches purity and companionship, respect and understanding, and extols above all the realm of androgyny (5, 281). There is no flirtation with decadence here but a vision, shared by other twentieth-century writers, of a condition of union and transcendence, Trakl's "Ein

Geschlecht," Musil's sibling hermaphroditism in *Der Mann ohne Eigenschaften*, Rilke's "der weibliche Mensch," Schuler's esoteric androgyny and its importance, as we shall see in Däubler. There are echoes of Theophrastus and Ovid, and also of the Cabbala and Leo Hebraeus who posited an androgynous God who reveals himself through his female principle, Holy Wisdom (sophia): Boehme's Adam Kadmon is not far. Boehme leaned heavily on the language of Paracelsus and resorted to alchemical terminology to express complex psychological states; he may well have known of the importance of the Hermetic Androgyne in alchemical experiments, and the fusion of two complementary principles during the Magnum Opus; the "chymical nuptials" of the King and Queen (i.e. the fusion of sulphur and mercury) was a deeply cherished ideal. Derleth himself drew on alchemical terminology, particularly in *Der chymische Herkules*, a short utterance to be included later in *Der Heilige* (6, 222–227) which portrays the realm of minerals and the "clavis magica" which liberates the souls of metals and creates King Gold and his Silver Queen. (The unification of the fixed and the volatile, the male and female elements, was looked upon as being an important step toward the final purification of the material world.) The section ends with a vision of reconciliation of inner and outer, with the tormenting Erinnyes becoming the Eumenides, the good spirits which heal and bring concord.

The last two books (6, 9–376) portray the prophet's movement toward death and transfiguration. Faithfulness is extolled as an aristocratic virtue (6, 14) and envy deplored (6, 26); Scribes and Pharisees are condemned for their shallow pedantry (6, 45); duplicity is excoriated, as is the black magic of a Medea (6, 79). Silence is welcomed as a fructifying condition (6, 104), yet language, the Word, the Logos is hailed as the womb of all that is (6, 115); scientific knowledge is castigated if it cannot spread warmth as well as light (6, 124). Derleth uses an expressive, rhythmical prose, interspersed with short, strophic utterances: the imagery is frequently sensuous (dawn as a purple lining on the hem of a black robe) and ornate, delighting in descriptions of temples, parks, oases and pilgrimages. The final part (part four) contains oblique references to Christian soteriology, but there is nothing zealous or proselytising: fishers of men are referred to (6, 159) and there are reminiscences of the earlier *Koran* on the emphasis on the need to transcend vulgarity, the need for communion and consummation. Man's fallenness is admitted, especially his abuse of the natural world and the animal kingdom (6, 192); the prophet speaks thus of the four paths open to him: He who strives upward will go the way of fire; he who strives downward will go the way of water; he who goes outward will go the way of dust; he who goes inward will go the way of thought. (6, 207). Suffering is greeted as a source of joy in a truly Nietzschean manner (6, 250), and a glimpse of a great harmony is celebrated. In exalted prose the prophet greets God as the God of life as of death (6, 312), death being simply the transformation of one form of matter into another. A "Mahl" or Last Supper, not specifically Christian, but *necessarily* Christian marks the climax of the book, and an empty tomb: the prophet has passed through death and returns to the cave of the lion. With this *Der fränkische Koran*, and Derleth's whole oeuvre, is finished.

In describing the Daniel of *Beim Propheten* Thomas Mann wrote of the strange regions, strange minds, strange regions of the spirit which were lofty and spare, effluxions of pale young geniuses sitting with folded arms, inwardly consumed, hungry and proud. Here is ice and chastity; no compromise is valid here, no concession, no half-way house, for the air is so rarefied that the mirages of life no longer exist. Here reign defiance and an iron consistency, the ego supreme amidst despair; freedom, madness and death hold sway. And after the reading, these sermons, parables, theses, laws, prophesies and exhortations the visitor expresses his reservations: although Daniel was a genius — the isolation, the freedom, the spiritual passion, the magnificent vision, the belief in his own powers all bore witness to this, even the approximation to madness and crime — something vital was lacking. Perhaps the human element? A little feeling, a little yearning, a little love?[21]

Thomas Mann did not, could not, have known the complete *Koran*, but knew his Schwabing and the spiritual ethos engendered there. So did Albert Verwey who could describe Derleth as "Gods Veldheer," worshipping "de reinste Jonkvrouw," but also saw the dangers of such a monomaniacal devotion. True, there are tender moments in the work (and how could there not be in nearly two thousand pages?), and the *Der Heilige* contains, as we know, moments of serenity and equipoise. But the Napoleonic pose, the arrogation of judgmental powers, the confusion of crusade and Cassandra, the cultural criticism endorsed by Nietzsche, the alternation of mystic rapture and military dynamics, the prayers and perorations, spread over long, sonorous stanzas of prose leave the reader stunned and disorientated, lost in a Jugendstil world which merges with medievalism and Roman imperialism. Its giganticism is very much of its time and it stands as a garish monument on the literary landscape of the first half of the twentieth century. The more tolerant commentator might draw attention to the odd stained-glass window in this crazy edifice which deserved praise and comment; the less favourably disposed would ignore the monstrous edifice entirely.

Yet the journey of exploration is fascinating for those who feel "a pious Catholic with Nietzschean ideas" an intriguing phenomenon and likewise the attempts to build a "Dionysian Christianity." "With Jesus of Nazareth against Christianity" — a remarkable motto indeed but one which might well have been found in Nietzsche's *Nachlaß*. And the fact that such an Antichrist could have found such an acolyte is worthy of our attention.

Notes

[1] Thomas Mann, *Gesammelte Werke in 13 Bänden*, vol. 6, 483.

[2] See *Die Münchner Moderne*, 476–478 for Franziska Reventlow's satire on "Christus Imperator Maximus" and His peroration.

[3] R. S. Furness, "Proclamations and Papal Paranoiacs. A study of Derleth, Baron Corvo and Joséphin Péladan," in *Kritische Fragen an die Tradition. Festschrift für Claus Träger* (Stuttgart: Hans-Dieter Heinz Verlag, 1997), 187–207.

[4] Dominik Jost, *Ludwig Derleth. Gestalt und Leistung* (Stuttgart: Kohlhammer, 1965), 50, gives details of Derleth's reading of Nietzsche. See also R. F. Krummel, *Nietzsche und der deutsche Geist: Ausbreitung und Wirkung des Nietzscheschen Werkes in deutschem Sprachraum vom Todesjahr bis zum Ende des Weltkrieges* (Berlin and New York: De Gruyter, 1983), 183 for Pieter van der Meer de Walcheren's references to Derleth as "a pious Catholic with Nietzschean ideas!"

[5] Ludwig Derleth, *Das Werk* (Bellnhausen/Gladbach: Hinder und Deelmann, 1971), vol. 1, 45. All references to Derleth's work will be taken from the six volume edition.

[6] Rolf von Hoerschelmann, *Leben ohne Alltag* (Berlin: 1947), 124.

[7] Ernst Bertram, *Nietzsche. Versuch einer Mythologi* (Berlin: Bondi, 1919), 6.

[8] Jost, *Ludwig Derleth*, 127.

[9] D. H. Lawrence, "A propos of 'Lady Chatterley's Lover'" in *The Cambridge Edition of the Letters and Works of D. H. Lawrence. Lady Chatterley's Lover*, ed. by Michael Squires (Cambridge: Cambridge UP, 1993), 322–323.

[10] Marina Warner, *Alone of All Her Sex. The Myth and Cult of the Virgin Mary* (London: Picador, 1985), 192.

[11] Warner, 99.

[12] Warner, 30.

[13] Friedrich Hölderlin, *Werke. Kleine Stuttgarter Ausgabe* (Stuttgart: Kohlhammer, 1953), vol. 2, 217.

[14] Peter Sprengel, *Die Wirklichkeit der Mythen. Untersuchungen zum Werk Gerhart Hauptmanns* (Berlin: Erich Schmidt Verlag, 1982), 154–155.

[15] There is much that is reminiscent of Fidus here, particularly the latter's fantastic plans for the construction of temples, inspired by Dornach and Bayreuth. As early as 1895 Fidus had planned Temples of Lucifer and a Temple of the Earth; this was to be surrounded by a moat and a holy grove and contain Halls of Feeling, of Knowledge, of Submission, of Longing, of Love, of Silence and of Darkness. There was also a Temple Without a Door for those initiates who were privileged to possess an astral body. See J. Frecot, J. F. Geist and D. Kerbs, *Fidus 1868–1948. Zur aesthetischen Praxis bürgerlicher Fluchtbewegungen* (Munich: Rogner und Bernhard, 1972).

[16] Anne Ratzki, *Die Elitevorstellungen im Werke Ludwig Derleths und ihre Grundlagen in seinem Bilde vom Menschen, von der Geschichte und vom Christentum* (Cologne: Walter Kleikamp, 1968), 57.

[17] Jost, 150 and 151.

[18] Albert Verwey in *Ludwig Derleth Gedenkbuch* (Amsterdam: Castrum Peregrini, 1958), 38.

[19] Jan Aler, "Ludwig Derleth. Ein katholischer Mystiker, der auch auf Nietzsche und Kierkegaard hörte," *Duitse Kroniek* 33 (1983), 133.

[20] Karl Muth, *Hochland* (May 1934), 178.

[21] Thomas Mann, *Gesammelte Werke in 13 Bänden,* vol. 8, 370.

Theodor Däubler.
Courtesy of Schiller Nationalmuseum
and Deutsches Literaturarchiv, Marbach.

6 : *Theodor Däubler*

Beyond the North, the Ice, the Now
Beyond the realms of Death,
Remote, away,
This is *our* life, our happiness!

— Nietzsche

Nocte media vidi solem
[I saw the sun shining in the middle of the night]

— Apuleius

It was Vienna which came as a revelation to me, where I experienced
something ineffable — music [. . .] I was fascinated by the shattering
effect of Beethoven's Ninth Symphony, and twice captivated by Wagner's *Siegfried*. From then on I could only brood in lines of poetry,
and then to think in the same: it was music which gave shape to
phantom images within me. The German language became my
mother tongue once more."[1]

This was Theodor Däubler's account of the beginning of *Das Nordlicht* (The Light of the North), an epic which, he continues "I
started at the foot of Mount Vesuvius, and in German." It was not an
Impero del Sole which the young citizen of Trieste and Fiume started to
compose, but *Das Nordlicht*, with Siegfried the sun-god as godfather,
conquering and slaying the "monster of elemental chaotic night"[2] and
kissing Brünnhilde awake in an ecstatic climax which is ablaze with
light. Vienna was also the city of Gustav Mahler, the artistic director of
the Vienna Opera, and it was not only Mahler as conductor but also as
creator of vast symphonies that Däubler experienced him. It is tempting to compare Mahler's monumental orchestration with the vastness
of Däubler's cosmic sweep; the Third Symphony especially, with its
rapturous sense of panic — or Nietzschean affirmation — seems to feed
directly into the *Pan: Orphisches Intermezzo* section of *Das Nordlicht*, as
we shall see. This is also the symphony that movingly incorporates the
"Midnight Song" from *Thus Spake Zarathustra* into its fourth move-

ment, a song of deep isolation but one in which the contralto voice glowingly accepts a vision of eternal joy. Music released a flood of images seeking expression in German, images and resonances revolving around a personal solar mythology on a vast and idiosyncratic scale. *Das Nordlicht*, loosely constructed, took some twelve years to complete. It was written during Däubler's extensive journeys throughout Europe and in Florence, where Däubler had settled in 1909, the critic Arthur Moeller van den Bruck undertook to do the proof-reading. (The sculptor and playwright Ernst Barlach gives an amusing account of "the majestic, ten-ton incarnation of the Däublerian stellar-spirit sitting at a greasy marble-topped café table with Moeller.")[3] The first version, the so-called Florentine version, comprises some thirty thousand lines; it was published by Georg Müller in three volumes in 1910. The "Geneva Version" (*Genfer Fassung*), somewhat modified, was published by Insel in two volumes in 1921–22; the much shorter "Athens Version" (*Athener Fassung*) was published in *Dichtungen und Schriften* by Kösel in 1956.

What is the theme of this enormous oeuvre? Däubler himself offers an explanation:

> I was overjoyed to feel that the earth contained within it much of the sun and that this solar element combined with us to fight against gravity, striving to be joined once more with the sun. Everywhere. Even in the ice. Especially there, at the poles, where the night is deepest and lasts longest — especially *there* we find this powerful longing! There is a gleaming penetration between that sun which has been released from the bonds of earth and the divine sun itself — and this causes the polar light within the month long darkness of the poles! The earth is longing to become a radiant star again.[4]

It is the aurora borealis which fascinates Däubler, not australis: there is a link here with the Romantic poet Novalis for whom the North was a spiritual realm, the "Reich Arcturs" of Klingsor's fairy-tale, the realm of Polaris as a place of transfiguration and transcendence. It is also of interest here to recall that the miner in Novalis's fragmentary novel *Heinrich von Ofterdingen* finds that gold is the elemental equivalent of the solar essence. There is a long alchemical tradition here; Däubler may have known Eugen Diederich's edition of Novalis's collected works which appeared in 1899, or assimilated certain Romantic concepts which had been disseminated by Georg Brandes and Ricarda Huch. Josef Görres, likewise, praised the North, extolling its "transparent, clear aether [. . .] where ideas glittered in stellar radiance!"[5] It is clear that there is nothing *völkisch* in Däubler's concept, nothing of the Nazi boreal obsession, the preoccupation with the North as a realm of Aryan man before the hypothetical shift in the earth's axis, nothing of a World Ice Theory that portrayed the Nordic ancestors of the Teutonic peoples surviving the disintegration of a "tertiary" moon, the last ice age and a great flood. The writer who was born in Trieste of Swabian and Silesian-Irish stock, who spoke Italian fluently and responded enthusiastically to the melodious Greek spoken by many of his classmates, who lived for long periods in Italy and Greece and travelled widely in the Near East had no time for pan-German nationalism or Nordic fanaticism: *his* North was the realm of spiritual illumination. And it should come as no surprise that *Das Nordlicht* is a vast poem of praise to the Mediterranean (to Italy above all), to Egypt, Persia and India. A vast panorama, one that takes the reader on a vertiginous journey through time and space, exulting in the power of light, of solar light, which ultimately is identified with spirit.

Das Nordlicht consists of two recognisable halves, *Das Mittelmeer* (The Mediterranean) and *Sahara*. The first half consists of some 615 pages in the "Genfer Fassung" and includes "Prolog," "Die Hymne der Höhe" (The Hymn of the Height), "Venedig" (Venice), "Rom," "Florenz," "Der Traum von Venedig" (The Dream of Venice), "Perlen von Venedig" (The Pearls of Venice), "Neapel" (Naples) and "Pan. Orphisches Intermezzo." These various sections were written between 1894 and 1909. The second half, *Sahara* (622 pages) is made up of four main sections: "Ansang" (Song), "Der Weltbruch" (The Fractured World), "Das Ra Drama" (The Drama of Ra) and "Der Ararat." This last section has the following subdivisions — "Die indische Symphonie" (The Indian Symphony), "Die iranische Rhapsodie" (The Persian Rhapsody), "Die Alexandrinische Phantasie" (The Alexandrian Fantasy), "Roland," "Drei Ereignisse" (Three Events), "Die Auferstehung des Fleisches" (The Resurrection of the Body), "Der Ararat speit!" (Ararat Erupts!), "Lieder im Seelenschein" (Songs in the Soul's Illumination), "Der flammende Lavabruch" (The Flaming Lava-flow) and "Der Geist" (The Spirit).

The prologue explains that the aurora borealis represents the light of the sun imprisoned at the earth's centre; light spreads out from the fiery kernel and flickers with an azure radiance at the North Pole (1, 52). The debt to German Romanticism has been noted, also the approximation to depth psychology: within the human psyche resides an untapped pool of images, a fecund reservoir of archetypal patterns. The "Hymn of the Height" exults in Wagnerian images of "Wildwabernde Fackeln," of flickering light upon basalt and granite. The fading moon is not mourned for the moon, which should have been a mediator of sunlight, is dead (1, 73); the earth produces a new moon from its own light, the boreal source. The moon is deceptive for its light is borrowed from the sun; Bachofen, it may be recalled, admitted that the moon, in sending forth its watery beams onto the earth, had a haunting power, yet also saw it as a passive entity when compared to the sun. Its "Licht-flimmerschleier," or veil of shimmering light, is milky and sad and this mediator between telluric and solar realms is essentially sterile. It is to the sun that Däubler turns, the sun glittering on the waters of the Adri-atic, and it is Venice which is the first Italian city to be greeted, that city that Nietzsche associated always with music, with the South and with shuddering, tremulous joy (6, 291).

In the autobiographical fragments contained in *Wir wollen nicht verweilen* (We shall not tarry), published by Georg Müller in 1914, Däubler insisted that he was a Venetian: the first artistic style that he understood was Byzantine, and the miracle of his youth was the experi-ence of St. Mark's (*DuS* 35). A "decadent" Venice of "ironic moon-light," of lapping water is acknowledged, but "I decided to seek the sun — I had seen through my Romanticism and had sufficient power to reject it" (*DuS* 41). The following section of *Das Nordlicht*, "Venice," greets the gleaming light cast over the sea by the rising sun, extols the golden glory of St. Mark's and hails the gods of Greece, Dionysus above all (1, 104): it is Dionysus who has risen, "sonnentrunken," from the waters. A reference to Aphrodite (1, 112) may be puzzling, as the goddess is not associated with this city; Däubler, however, celebrates the love between sun and sea, light and water, and there are echoes of the glorious days of the Serenissima, the celebration of Ascension day when the doge was rowed out to the lagoon by the Lido in his ornate gondola to perform the symbolic rite of throwing a ring into the waters and espousing the Adriatic. Light, water and gold — this is the opening of *Das Rheingold* with the Rhine maidens delighting in the sun's rays, the deeply glowing gold beneath the water, the light striking down into the darkness. It was in Venice that Wagner dreamed, one night before his death, of bewitching water-maidens disporting themselves in liquid radiance; here Däubler emphasises the fusion of libido (sun) and water (Venice), but his next city, Rome, will exemplify the union of light and stone.

For Bachofen the sun represented patriarchy and the spirit (nous) had an unambiguously solar provenance. In the next section, "Rom," Däubler hails the sun as "Verschwenderin der Liebe" (1, 146), as "squanderer of love," the sun being grammatically feminine in German. It is sun and stone which are juxtaposed here, for Rome is characterized by massive architecture, reflecting its former grandeur. Alfred Schuler had sought to emphasise the more ancient, chthonic, "feminine" aspects of Rome; for Däubler it is an essentially masculine city, virile in its power, illuminated by a quickening radiance. As Venice united the people with the sea, so Rome unites them with its own power. Däubler, like so many of his contemporary writers, was drawn to the figure of Nero, that exemplar of decadence, who cannot stem the growth of Christianity, the subterranean religion of the Catacombs deriving its precepts from "the desert God of the Semites" (1, 159). The sickly moon rising as a blood-shot eye (1, 146) seems to derive from Oscar Wilde's *Salome*; Nero and his barbaric acts of cruelty, together with the burning of Rome are very much part of the stock-in-trade of fin de siècle writing, but Däubler portrays them with gusto rather than prurience. He also delights in portrayals of circus and bacchanal, but is keenly aware of "the fearful gnawing" (1, 190) at the foundations, the subterranean rumblings presaging a new religion. (Schuler had lamented the triumph of the Semitic Christ; *his* vestal virgins deliberately extinguished the sacred flame lest it fall into the hands of the Christians). A "Lichtgott" or god of light will emerge and ultimately conquer Rome, a city which, after painful convulsions, emerges as the seat of popes, the site of councils and dogmatic pronouncements. Däubler also portrays the rise of France and the construction of Gothic cathedrals; the triumph of the Nordic spirit is also acknowledged (1, 267) with Protestantism, German abstraction and German music as paramount. The final tribute to Rome is an evocation of the Roman carnival (1, 277), a Goethean echo, perhaps, before the ideal voyage across Italy continues.

If water is the symbol of Venice, and stone is the symbol of Rome, so bronze is the symbol of Florence: as liquid as water and then as hard as stone it has the task of reconciling these opposing forces. Florence becomes the city of art *par excellence* because it is born from the union of opposites, not only water and stone, Däubler implies, but soul and body, flux and form, spirit and matter. Tuscany is greeted with rapture, its warmth, light and fragrance: the city of Florence is its jewel. The poet focuses upon the baptistery (1, 325), the thirteenth century edifice adorned by the beautiful bronze doors of Ghiberti where the glories of creation are carved in gleaming splendour and glowing metal. The Florentines gazed with special pride on these magnificent creations which must have shone with all the brightness of their original gilding when Michelangelo pronounced them worthy to be the gates of heaven. Donatello's David is also extolled in his nakedness (1, 324) as bronze, triumphant, suffused with sunlight. In this city dominated by beauty no bleak asceticism is possible, and Savonarola finds his cruel death (1, 328). To detach the spirit from its physical form must needs be a futile task, for the two are one: in perfected mortality man becomes immortal. This is what draws Däubler to Tuscany, and many painters are evoked (Giotto, Paolo Ucello, Masaccio and many others): his lyrical meditations reflect the fascination that the Renaissance exerted at this time on many German writers and thinkers from Nietzsche onwards, through Jacob Burckhardt to Thomas Mann, whose *Fiorenza* dates from 1905. If Thomas Mann sought to show the dichotomy between morality and art, the ethical and the aesthetic, Savonarola, prior of San Marco and Lorenzo de' Medici, then Däubler attempts simply to show that asceticism has no place here; there can be no desire to fuse Christ and Savonarola and infer that the spirit ultimately gains power over life. The light turning the bronze doors of the baptistery to gold demonstrates the fusion of spirit and substance in a sacramental effulgence.

Before Naples is reached, the last stage of Däubler's Italian odyssey, two short insertions devoted once more to Venice are inserted, "The Dream of Venice" and "Pearls of Venice," a series of sonnets. These were not included in the earlier edition of 1910: it would seem that Däubler was unable to shake off the fascination exerted by the Queen of the Adriatic and turned to her once more. "The Dream of Venice" is a sensuous portrayal of milky lagoons, chryselephantine clouds and heavy, perfumed night, night as a naked mooress with a dark mass of pubic hair (1, 354), surrounded by grey snakes, rises from a black swamp. The "Pearls" are more restrained, more haunting, and show a remarkable similarity to the poetry of Georg Trakl whose own "In Venedig," written after a visit to the city in 1913, seems close, with its dark swarm of flies, its sadness and its memories. Trakl had made the visit on August 16 with Karl Kraus, Peter Altenberg and others; he had already met Däubler during the latter's visit to Innsbruck on November 22, 1912, where Däubler had read from *Pan: Orphisches Intermezzo* (to be discussed later). Trakl and Däubler had spent some time together on the following day, and Däubler's "Goldene Sonette I" from the collection *Der sternhelle Weg* (The Starlit Path, 1915) seems quintessentially Trakl:

> Vertändelt ist das ernste Gold der Garben.
> Auf alten Mauern schlafen rote Schlangen
> [. . .]
> Das Jahr vollendet seinen Kranz der Farben. . . .
>
> (*DuS* 234)

("Squandered is now the earnest gold of sheaves.
The red snakes sleep upon the ancient walls
[. . .]
The year completes its wreath of colours. . .)

To return to *Das Nordlicht*, the sonnet "Verstumpfen" (Dulling: 1, 372) tells of sickness and flies; "Sonderbar" (Strange: 1, 376) talks of dead, silver masks in silent waters; "Byzanz" describes silent moonlight playing on mosaic floors (1, 387). The pearls of Trakl's "Rosenkranzlieder" (Songs of the Rosary) are not far, brown pearls, but for Däubler grey, cool, or lilac, and harbingers of sickness ("Das schnelle Ende" [The rapid end] 1, 403). The "Pearls of Venice" fit awkwardly into *Das Nordlicht*, but the reader, if he has persevered, will not be surprised at the manner in which Däubler fills his baggy *monstrum* with the most disparate elements.

Neapel is a short section greeting, again, the sun and love which carries us towards the glowing orb (1, 450). (Nietzsche, incidentally, had visited Naples in 1876 in his search for the "Islands of the Blessed": the poem "Sanctus Januarius," inserted into Book Four of *Die fröhliche Wissenschaft* (The Joyful Wisdom) hails the flaming spear whose heat melts the ice of winter.) A shadowy drama is now enacted: a "Weib" is portrayed, a female pendant to the lyrical ego, together with her child, a "son of the cosmos." This "cosmic child" is a Euphorion figure, but he is not killed tragically by seeking to rise as Daedalus did; he is, rather, "killed," as is his mother, by the poet's "Gedanke," or thought. It seems that hubris is responsible here, an arrogance which seeks too much; an eruption from Vesuvius (1, 457) presages the disaster. Telluric fire, bursting forth as a volcano, devastates rather than brings illumination: the ego, likewise, can destroy through imperious demands. The contrite poet longs for salvation, far removed from this "Schreckenstätte," this fearful place of horror (1, 466); the blasted landscape around Vesuvius, the scorched and blighted rubble, cannot but drive the poetic impulse into remoter realms. And now we approach *Pan: Orphisches Intermezzo*, a section which, written in the years 1902–1903, is a work in its own right, a paean of praise to panic forces. It is an important utterance, reverberating with a Nietzschean presence, an ecstatic dithyrambus: it was from this that Däubler read aloud in Innsbruck and Trakl, it is reported, clutched his brow and affirmed that "Pan has awoken!"[6]

"Pan erwacht. Der Sommer marschiert ein" ("Pan Awakens. Summer marches in") — this is the first movement of Mahler's Third Symphony, a symphony that Mahler contemplated calling "Die fröhliche

Wissenschaft" or "Pan".[7] It is noteworthy that the composer also commented that *Zarathustra* was born from the spirit of music, that it was *symphonic* in construction. This vast movement, lasting some forty minutes, contains an orgiastic and corybantic march of immense proportions, expressing summer's victory in the midst of the warring forces of nature. The movement is so enormous that the listener cannot hope to obtain a clear perspective of it, and Mahler's giganticism is here akin to Däubler's. Däubler's grotesque neologisms and frequently bizarre rhymes have the same jarring effect as Mahler's theatricality and alienating juxtapositions, but the cosmic sweep of both composer and poet cannot but overwhelm and amaze.[8] For both, Pan awakens, and uproar ensues: the Arcadian deity, goat-like and giver of fertility, rests at noon, but awakens to herald triumphant affirmation. In Däubler's own words: "Pan ist der Versorger der gesamten Weltrhythmik auf Erden" (1, 39) — Pan is the provider of the secular rhythm of earth. He is the god of nature, and is hence beyond moral categorization. This *Intermezzo* interrupts the human flight towards the sun to portray worldly, pagan entities: Pan fuses with Silenus and with Dionysus in rapture and ecstasy. Däubler is close to Nietzsche here in equating Pan/Dionysus with an amoral life-force: the death of Pan, as recorded in *Die Geburt der Tragödie* (there is a legend that sailors heard the cry of lament as they passed a lonely island: see also Derleth 2, 254) is tantamount to the death of the deepest affirmation of existence. But here Pan is very much alive and the poet exults in his presence: "O Pan . . . oh ancient forest, thou symbol of life!" (1, 489). Pan-Zarathustra announces the following creed: "We are divine, for we chastise and destroy! / And if we plunder and annihilate / The order of the world is not disturbed!" (1, 492). Further Nietzschean images prevail: "He who seeks eternity must clothe himself in fire!" (1, 511). and the portrayal of woman as "a deep, deep well / In which the man sees clear and pure / His own reflection" (1, 515). The description of panic Arcadia moves to Orpheus and Eurydice, also to the Maenads swinging the thyrsus, the staff tipped with a pine cone and wreathed with ivy borne by the votaries of Dionysus. In the "Genfer Fassung" which we are using a "Hymn to Nietzsche" is inserted here: a Bard sings of the joys of earth ("Earth is a lovely girl whose breasts are full," 1, 572) and proclaims the message: "Listen, o Man, Pan now is awake! / O Dionysus, fiery throbbing soul! / I believe in vengeance, chance and power! / My ego is that which annihilates Death!" (1, 574).[9] This figure climbs into high mountains leaving Orpheus (who rejects the "petrified moon," 1, 589) to build a solar altar in the crystalline clarity of midday. An unmistakable Mombert landscape is created here (the naked youth), fused with

Nietzschean pseudo-biblical imagery (the lion full of golden bees). And the *Intermezzo* ends with ecstatic joy, a shout of praise to Dionysus-Bacchus interspersed with stammering exultation: "Evoë, Evoë!" (1, 601), "Pan! Pan! Pan!" (1, 604). It is *this* earth that is praised, bathed in the lambent rays of the sun; Dionysus, as "golden god" (1, 615) blesses and affirms.

Thus ends the first part of this remarkable sun-pilgrimage, a journey southwards through cities and landscapes, art and mythology, where a "lyrisches Ich" expresses and experiences a sun-intoxicated world. The reader, disorientated, responds with amazement to the cataract of elemental images, to literally hundreds of quatrains, to sonnets, to strophes and lines of differing length, to capricious patterns and a vast variety of prosodic forms. There is a sense of vast oceanic churning, of unrestrained battering and inundation. And what of the theme itself, the title? The aurora borealis flickers and shimmers intermittently, or disappears altogether, driven underground or becoming invisible in the hard, clear light of the Mediterranean. Yet if it symbolises a longing for spiritual illumination it cannot fade, even in the most brilliant day, or at the greatest distance from the pole. The cosmic traveller seeks "the Pentecostal I" (1, 15), the state of pure spirit where all division is transcended, and in the second half of Däubler's verse epic he moves from the Mediterranean world to more exotic realms, above all to the East, to seek a fiercer exposure to that fearful light. The Italian cities of Part One at least acted as stepping stones; from now onwards the terrain becomes even less familiar. Part Two is called *Sahara*.

A poem introduces the work, and immediately presents uproar — the earthquake (the "dragon's snorting roar") which demonstrates once more the need felt by the earth's molten interior to burst outwards towards the sun (2, 9). The fiery lava of speech is also extolled, the speech of a prophet such as Moses; as flickering light transfigures him, so the Northern light plays across the pole. The desert as a place of exposure and vision, of glittering stars — this is acclaimed in the next section, "The Fractured World" which centres on man and religion, a world of "cathedrals of flame" 2, 29) where the puny power of reason is transcended. Regretting the utilitarianism of the age (and, probably, his parents' free-thinking agnosticism), the poet laments "I am a son of the age / Which praises reason too highly" (2, 29). He waits for an epiphany, for engulfment by numinous, quickening forces. A "testamentary dance of death" (2, 38) is included as the pace quickens, a rapid succession of biblical images culminating in the "Dies irae, dies illa / Solvet saeclum in favilla, /Teste David cum Sibylla . . ." (2, 44). Apocalyptic images predominate, of splitting earth and seas of fire; the poet, gazing at the destruction, announces abruptly that it is "as sinner and as Christian" that he experiences the turmoil (2, 50). Again, it is "sunwards" that man is seen as flying, away from heaviness and gravity, that gravity which was Zarathustra's implacable enemy. There are pictures of flood and desert, and the "lyrisches Ich" now gazes at Sinai and Egypt. *Das Nordlicht* here seems to be a gigantic elaboration of Hölderlin's spiritual journey, from Teck to Tinian, from Lauffen to Patmos, from the umbrageous woods of Swabia to the harsh, burning landscape of Asia Minor.[10] The next section, "Das Ra-Drama," moves on to Egypt.

The quick iambic trimeters and the obsessive rhyming on "Saïs" introduce a light, tripping tone, but the issues are profound — the cult of Ra, that hawk-headed sungod, most venerated in the fifteen and sixteenth dynasties in Thebes. During the eighteenth dynasty Ra became Amon-Ra, king of the gods. In this dynasty Amenhotep III instigated a movement towards new religious thought which culminated in the monotheistic cult of the Aton, or sundisk; this was supported and proclaimed by his son Ikhnaton or Amenhotep IV. (In religious iconography the sungod Amon-Ra was depicted as a disk with rays terminating in hands which held the symbol of life.) The brief triumph of Amenhotep IV is portrayed by Däubler (2, 178–182) in the incantations of his mother: he is extolled for banishing the "flickering shadows" and preventing the worship of meaningless avatars (2, 179). It is inevitable that Däubler should be drawn to the monotheistic sun-worship of Amenhotep IV who rejected the Nilotic worship of crocodile and hippopotamus; the blazing solar disk over Egypt fascinates and burns with a pitiless energy. A "classical dance of death" (2, 128–136) reminds us of the barbaric chaos of ancient Egyptian mythology where sphinx, owl, snake and mummy haunt and gibber: this is the world that Amenhotep IV sought to destroy. But in the reign of Tutenkhamon both king and people reverted to a polytheistic orthodoxy; the glories of the eighteenth dynasty were forgotten as Egypt declined, its beliefs mocked by the later Romans as primitive absurdities. The "ankh," symbol of life (the sun's gift to the world) would, however, be preserved, transfigured into the Christian cross.

Eclectic and, indeed, eccentric as Däubler's portrayal of Egypt is, it is in a tradition which was drawn to the mysteries of Saïs, that city associated with the veiled goddess Isis, daughter of the sungod Ra and sister-bride of Osiris. The cult of Isis was one of the most active during the declining years of paganism, and the myth of Isis may well have prepared the way for Christian monotheism, the goddess herself changing to become a precursor of the Virgin Mary. During the Renaissance Isis reverted to a native goddess yet also, as a divinity of fertility, she heralds the conception of Christ. In the seventeenth century, as a result of Athanasius Kircher's study of hieroglyphics, the fascination exerted by Egypt grew, reaching its peak in the freemasonry of the eighteenth, as exemplified in Mozart's *The Magic Flute*. For the Romantics Isis had two more aspects: she was Nature, the universal mother, yet also the goddess hidden from the uninitiated by a veil. Her invisible face became the crystallization of all mysteries and taboos: in Schiller's "Das verschleierte Bild zu Saïs" (The Veiled Image in Saïs) the hero is given due warning not to raise the veil; in Novalis's "Die Lehrlinge zu Saïs" (The Apprentices of Saïs) there are two dénouements — in the first the one who lifts the veil sees himself, in the second he sees his beloved. Gérard de Nerval, as heir to the German Romantics, made the myth of Isis one of the central themes in his work; the theme of the unveiling of the goddess occurs also in Rimbaud and Flaubert. Däubler had never studied systematically, but his immense and catholic reading led him to many myths and legends. Ra and his daughter ruled triumphant in Saïs: both sungod and nature-goddess are extolled in a hieratic veneration. In *Das Nordlicht* Däubler jokingly suggests that Ra is "uranisch"; that is, homosexual in his patriarchy (2, 140); the "lyrical ego," one suspects, transcends conventional sexuality, and the shadowy "Weib" who haunts various sections is more of an eidolon than an ideal, an anima who, ultimately, is absorbed into the glowing solar vision.

Däubler's portrayal of Egypt lacks the magisterial erudition of Thomas Mann;[11] there is a quirky obsession that is also far removed from Rilke's awed reaction to Karnak. The next section is "Der Ararat" which is divided into ten subdivisions: the journey continues, moving south eastwards towards India and Persia. Again, it comes as no surprise that Däubler should be drawn towards this mountain; there is a poetical fitness in the legend that Ararat was the resting place of Noah's ark inasmuch as the huge, broad-shouldered mass, more dome than peak, is about equally distant from the Black Sea and the Caspian, from the Mediterranean and the Persian Gulf. Around Ararat there are many legends associated with the Flood; the Garden of Eden is placed in the valley of the Araxes; Murand is the burial place of Noah's wife, as Arghuri was the place where Noah planted the first vineyard. (Armenian monks believed that no one was permitted to set foot on the secret summit of Ararat: it was scaled in 1829 by a German explorer.) But Däubler's imagination does not rest here: it is India that he now invokes.

The *Indische Symphonie* portrays an exotic landscape, a sense of teeming life: Däubler's predilection for assonance here reaches an almost grotesque (and certainly untranslatable) intensity. ("Und Dschungeln umgeben von urstummen Muscheln, / Wo munter die Unkenbrutnumen sich tummeln / Und suchen, sich Lustsucht durch Brunst zuzutuscheln, / Unsummen Unsummen von Brummeln und Hummeln," 2, 240). Däubler here is drunk on elemental sounds, overcome by the magic of the dark, seductive "U" sounds akin to the "Ur" which Thomas Mann describes in all its sonorous portentousness.[12] India is compared to "einem riesigen Herzen;" (2, 225), a gigantic heart: its grandiose, exuberant mythology expresses an irruption of eternity into history and the descent of its gods to earth is described in epics which are the chronicles of a time when men communicated with the divine in a natural way. The *Mahabharata* is extolled (2, 256), the monumental poem from the heart of the Hindu tradition. Its nine thousand couplets, we learn, call for a positive attitude to the world, a way of surviving in a time of catastrophe without losing contact with whatever it is that enables man to live and fight in a meaningful way. Siva is also hailed (2, 259), the god who occupies an important place in all Hindu mythology and worship, the patron of dance and theatre whose exploits are widely reproduced on the walls of temple and in painting. Siva is associated with the lingam, an upright stone: his compassionate traits are, however, often obscured by his more fearful aspects, for he haunts funeral pyres at night and is also the god of destruction. Däubler never travelled to India although it was a fashionable goal for many German artists and writers before the First World War — Melchior Lechter, Waldemar Bonsels, Hermann Graf Keyserling visited the subcontinent, as did Hermann Hesse (1911). But Däubler's "lyrisches Ich" had no need of steamers such as "Prinz Eitel Friedrich" of the Norddeutscher Lloyd to convey him from Genoa to Bombay; India is grasped imaginatively and immediately (Däubler would also admit (2, 18), that he read the names of the various Indian gods from the stained glass in the French Naval Museum in Paris). What is important in this chapter is Däubler's attitude to Buddha. Buddha is described as resembling the moon (2, 254), of being the opponent of the sun; he mildly denies the physical and seeks ultimate extinction. The moon is likewise compared to the lotus (2, 262), with dreamy forgetfulness and loss of all desire. Däubler's *Mit silberner Sichel* (With silver sickle), published in Dresden-Hellerau in 1916, continues to juxtapose sun and moon, seeing the latter as capricious and over-sophisticated. "Folly, too, comes from the moon. It has induced us to invoke idols, for the sun is far too rich, radiantly living and effusive: it needs no reverence, nor likes to be exalted; its priesthoods have been imposed upon it by the moon" (*DuS* 194). The reader may be wryly amused by the claim that the sun need not be exalted, for Däubler's heliocentric belief is persistent and obsessive; suffice it that Buddha, his moonlight and lotus flowers, fade, and the journey to Persia begins.

Die iranische Rhapsodie exemplifies the profound fascination that Zoroastrianism has exerted on the European mind. Mazdaic Zoroaster, the founder of the ancient Persian religion as taught in the Avesta, became known to the Greeks and the Jews; Zoroaster was introduced into the Biblical tradition by assimilation. It was held that Balaam and Zoroaster were one, and that Balaam's prophecy of a star coming forth out of Jacob (*Numbers* 24, 17) makes Zoroaster a prophet of Christianity: he is also seen as one of the Magi who, having seen His star in the East, came to worship the divine child. This favourable conception the Church fathers had of Zoroaster is contrasted by another which saw him as the legislator of a rival religion, a creator of magic and a dabbler in necromancy. In the eighteenth century Zoroaster was reinstated as lawgiver and sage, and Alessandro Scarlatti, Rameau, and Mozart emphasized Sarastro's role as guardian of Enlightenment and freedom. In the nineteenth century he was romanticized and associated with fire and light, illuminating the darkness (Victor Hugo); in Nietzsche he is the prophet-proclaimer of the *Übermensch*. Däubler portrays the land of the Medes and the Persians and calls on Ahriman (2, 271) and Ormuzd (2, 285), the latter, Ahura-Mazda, as the primal spiritual being, the former as the evil spirit associated with darkness, filth and death. (The chanting of "abra abra abrakada dabra" (2, 271) is actually out of place here, associated as it is with the Greek word αβραξαδ, in Greek notation associated with the number 365 and the 365 orders of spirits which emanate in succession from the supreme Being.) Däubler extols Mazdaism but also sees the triumph of Jehova (2, 322), and the section ends with Ararat again, a triumphant paean and the ultimate ascent of the mountain (2, 341).[13]

Let us pause briefly before tackling the final quarter of this remarkable offering. It has been Däubler's aim to extol the sun, and its northern manifestations, as the spirit; he belongs here in a Romantic tradition unadulterated by *völkisch* speculation and remote from Gottfried Benn's "Mythos vom Norden,"[14] that concept of ice, spirit, and anti-Rationalism which Benn briefly entertained. The first stage of his poetic odyssey consists of an Italian journey with Venice, Rome, and Florence hailed as epiphanies of solar radiance; the Naples episode hints at violence (eruption) and pride. In *Pan* the longing for spiritual illumination is interrupted by an exultant paganism; the lyrical "I" now

moves to embrace other religions, seeing them as fascinating examples
of the human need to worship. An eccentric syncretism prevails, with
the monotheism of Amenhotep IV fusing with aspects of Zoroastrianism; Däubler praises Buddha but also rejects him for preaching denial
and Nirvana. There are echoes of Bachofen in the identification of the
sun with patriarchy; the moon is frequently equated with femininity.
The references to a "Weib" remain sporadic and diffuse: there are hints
that this "anima" figure fades before the glories of spiritual illumination. *Das Nordlicht* now moves towards the portrayal of the triumph of
Christianity and a vision of transcendence: the next section, *Die alexandrinische Phantasie*, fuses the legends of Perseus and Andromeda
with St. George. Perseus slew the fearful Medusa; legend has it that after sailing along the coast of Philistio (Palestine) he caught sight of a
beautiful woman, naked except for a few pieces of jewelry, chained to a
rock at the water's edge. She is threatened by a monster, whom Perseus
destroys. One version of the myth associated Perseus with the fabulous
winged horse Pegasus, born of the body of Medusa, and described him
as having winged feet. In Christian iconography Perseus fuses with St.
Michael slaying the monstrous Satan, or with St. George and Angelica.
The male spirit delivers, protects and redeems; an amusing sub-section
portrays the women of Alexandria clamouring for the phallus (2, 358
"Es lebe der Phallus!") and receiving chastisement and reprimand, for
the Saviour can never be identified with primitive paganism (2, 359).
Female sexuality beguiles (the naked Andromeda) or beseeches (the
defenceless Angelica), but the glory of woman is the pure Virgin in
whose womb the Saviour quickens (2, 347).

The next, short, section "Roland" is bewildering, but it becomes
clear that the medieval story is inserted to show the battle against Islam
and, by inference, the triumph of Christianity. The legend of the
French epic hero Roland derives from the account of Charlemagne's
retreat from France through the defiles of the Pyrenees, where part of
his army was cut off from the main body by the Basques; later versions
talk of depredations by a vast army of Saracens. It was in Italy that the
legend of Roland (Orlando) had its greatest resonance; Charlemagne
and Roland appeared in Dante's *Paradiso* (canto xviii), and Däubler
may well have seen the statues of Roland and Oliver on the doorway of
the Cathedral at Verona. Roland and the Pyrenees — the associative
power of Däubler's imagination now invokes another setting in Northern Spain, Montsalvat (2, 436) and the knight Parzival (2, 439). The
story of Parzival lies at the centre of a vast group of texts devoted to the
quest for the Grail: here Parzival is portrayed as one who overcomes —
as Wagner portrays it — the temptation of Kundry. And the temptress

serves to deepen a sense of Christian compassion, a compassion devoid of carnal contact: Parzival becomes the chosen one who consecrates the new covenant between earth and heaven. The tone is, however, not sacerdotal. Däubler presents a lightness of tone also found in the next section, "Drei Ereignisse" with its portrayal of the "Northern shadow," a gnome which haunts us but which is shortest at midday. This shadow or "devil" is "at home in Germany!" (2, 453). This German heaviness, or brooding introspection, has something Mephistophelian about it, but the ghosts are dispelled by the lovely hymn to the Virgin Mary: "O Virgin, the dew of the corn is thy veil, / The golden fields are thy golden hair" (2, 459).

The work now moves towards its completion: "Die Auferstehung des Fleisches" preceded, in the Florentine edition, by an "Apocalypse," insists on the grave as a volcano (2, 487) from which light bursts, on apocalyptic figures ("Syphilis," "Greed," "Uproar"), on a vision of Tartarus, on resurrection. "Das Ararat speit!" consists of a series of sonnets and quietly insists that "I am the belief in the power of the sun" (2, 517); the section in terza rima has as its climax a vision of Dante (2, 535). But one closer to Däubler than Dante is the tutelary spirit of the work's culmination: Goethe, and specifically the Goethe of *Faust*, the ending of the second part of which inspired the passionate grandeur of Mahler's Eighth symphony and without which the ending of *Das Nordlicht* would be unthinkable. Mahler's symphony was first performed, under Mahler's direction, in Munich on September 12, 1910; Däubler had finished most of *Sahara* by then, even though some pieces were not completed until that year. The "Lieder im Seelen-schein" echo, unmistakably (2, 539), the song of Pater Ecstaticus in Goethe's *Faust II*, (lines 11858–11861); the penultimate section, "The flaming stream of lava" more closely resembles the "Walpurgnisnachts-traum" of *Faust I*, a cosmic ballet of stars, suns and comets. The "Songs in the Soul's Illumination" again explores the cluster of images moon/water/ woman; the moon is the "God of Death," dragged as a corpse through space by the earth (2, 541). "Der flammende Lavabruch" magnifies the spirit, glowing in crimson effulgence (2, 551); the sub-section "Das Sternenkind" (The stellar child) praises flight in an ecstatic frenzy: "Man must fly! Man must fly!" (2, 561), and this vast work moves through jubilant proclamations ("O Sun, Sun, I conceive my thoughts in bliss," 2, 569) through the "Golden ghosts, thundering through the North" (2, 571) towards the incontro-vertible statement: "Before that God who lost His son as world and word / The spirit lives and dwells, chosen by God himself" (2, 579). The "patient one at the well" is the Samaritan woman of *Faust II*

(12045–12052); spirits and eidola now move before us ("The Man on the Sea," "The Somnambulist," "A listening one on a blue meadow," "The Soothsayer") as an astral song resounds, a comet flares, an army of stars arises, a sun sets and returns. A "Nordlichtengel" (an "Angel of the Northern Light") rises; "the Man" speaks of his desire to return to the sun (2, 603); "the woman" offers her body, a gift of the moon, heavy with milk. "The Saviour of the Stars" was warmed at a woman's breast (2, 604), this the "White Angel" tells us: the divine passed through flesh in this incarnation, but moved toward Ascension. Goethe, at the very end of *Faust II*, extolled the "Eternally Feminine"; for Däubler sexuality is transcended, and it is "der Mensch" who speaks, welcoming the Pentecostal mystery and "praising stars no longer" since Christ held him and the sun together (2, 604). The ultimate section, "Der Geist" greets the "wondrous flower of light" which ignites the pole; the earth, consumed by fire, welcomes the dead moon, collapsing in conflagration — and this unique work ends with the exultant knowledge that "Die Welt versöhnt und übertönt der Geist!" (2, 622): the world is reconciled by that spirit which resounds in triumph.

What is the reader's reaction to this enormous work? One is stunned, perplexed, overwhelmed by its sheer bulk, the exuberance of the images, the wild and whirling tumult, the oceanic inundation. Yet the basic idea is not an alien one — the longing of the earth for illumination and of man for spiritual redemption, for a radiance which transfigures materiality and darkness.[15] The work is a vast variation on the message of Ernst Barlach's play *Der tote Tag* (The Day of Death, 1912) described by the playwright thus: "My play is a fantasy concerning an immaculate conception, that is, the spiritual derivation of man, in contrast to the physical which can be as sullied as you wish."[16] Some ultimate excarnation is posited in Däubler and Barlach, and the ultimate triumph of light; a heliotheistic vision fuses with the alchemical doctrine of "the sun which shines in the middle of the night" and assumes a crypto-Christian dimension. Haeckel may have welcomed solarism as being the best of all forms of theism and one which may most easily be reconciled with Monism, extolling sun-worship as superior to Christianity and condemning the latter's rejection of pantheism; Däubler's vast opus ends with a triumphant proclamation of the unity of sun and spirit, a solar Christology. Yet Däubler also insisted, in his *Selbstdeutung*, that "The earth must become radiant once more, yet it is the peoples themselves who are responsible for making this star, which is a dark one, into the brightest of all [. . .] We find in earnest souls the desire to fashion the primeval light in man, for in us is witness of the light" (1, 12). It is man who is the guardian of the flame, man who must ensure that the highest vision is preserved — Zarathustra, the "golden star" makes this the centre of his doctrine. Rudolf Steiner however, (and Däubler was acquainted with his writing) insisted in his meditations on St. John's Gospel that the light came from without, and that is was only Christ's sacrifice that made the earth into a radiant sun. "It was then [at Golgotha] that the earth began to glow, first as an astral body [. . .] But in the future the astral light will assume physical manifestation, and the earth will become a solar body, a glowing body."[17]

Däubler eschewed philosophical speculation, but there is much of the Hegelian world-spirit in his vision of "Geist," an affirmation of the totality of life and the need to overcome contradictions, the final goal being the spirit's triumphant progress throughout the world history and its final identification with secular facticity whose truth would now become "the Bacchic frenzy in which no member remains sober."[18] In the works which follow *Das Nordlicht* Däubler returns obsessively to images of light, of crystal, of Northern Light as Pentecostal fire: the essay *Das Eigentum Ägpytens* (The Property of Egypt, 1930), with its Nietzsche quotation from *Die fröhliche Wissenschaft*, insists that "We do not have an extrahuman, personal God such as the Hebrews do, and also the Muslims: God is our deepest idea, and Jesus Christ is His incarnation on earth" (*DuS* 735). Christ is a god of light and, the essay *Delos* (1925), contends, increasingly associated with Apollo. Däubler's love for Greece — he left Germany after the First World War and travelled to Ithaca, Skyros, Nauplia and Athens, where he was able to reside in the Germanic Institute — consolidated the desire to see Christ alongside the Greek deities; an eccentric syncretism is found in *Der Fischzug* (The Draught of Fishes) in 1930. There is a remarkable similarity between his work and that of Angelos Sikelianos (1884–1951) who sought to embrace the Greek tradition in its entirety and to fuse images and symbols derived from Orphism with Christianity to find a mystical unity that would embrace mankind and nature; a highly successful Delphic festival was organized by Sikelianos in 1927.

Däubler died in 1934; on his tomb, a simple stone sarcophagous, were inscribed the following two lines from *Das Nordlicht*: "I am the belief in the power of the sun" and that final utterance which has already been quoted: "The world is reconciled by the spirit which resounds in triumph." Sun, sea and the South, this had been Däubler's inspiration, a halcyon world of limpid radiance, the blue and silver of the glittering Mediterranean — this, finally, is the world of Nietzsche's *Zarathustra*, from which this quotation may not be inappropriate:

For she comes again, the glowing one — *her* love for the earth is coming! Innocence and creative power is the love of all suns! See, look as she rises, hastening over the sea! Dost thou not feel the thirst and the hot breath of her love? [. . .] Truly, it is as the sun that I love life and all deep oceans! (4, 158–9)

Notes

[1] Theodor Däubler. *Dichtungen und Schriften* (Munich: Kösel, 1956), 867. Hereafter *DuS*.

[2] Elisabeth Magee, *Richard Wagner and the Nibelungs* (Oxford: Oxford UP, 1990), 143.

[3] Ernst Barlach: "Ein selbsterzähltes Leben" in *Das dichterische Werk* (Munich: Piper, 1958), vol. 2, 56. See also *Seespeck* in the same volume, a fragmentary novel written between 1913 and 1916, where much is made (in chapters five and six) of Däubler's bulk, charisma, and prophecies. It may not be too far-fetched to see in certain of Barlach's sculptures the weight of Däubler's presence, for example *Die Vision* of 1912. (Barlach's bronze *Ruhender Däubler* is reproduced in "Theodor Däubler 1876–1934," *Marbacher Magazin* 30 (1984), 94.

[4] Theodor Däubler, *Das Nordlicht* (Leipzig: Insel, 1921–1922), vol. 1, 11. All references to *Das Nordlicht* will be taken from this two-volume "Genfer Ausgabe."

[5] Karl Heinz Bohrer, *Der Mythos vom Norden. Studien zur romantischen Geschichtsprophetie* (Cologne dissertation, 1961), 17. See also Richard Noll, *The Jung Cult. Origins of a Charismatic Movement* (Princeton: Princeton UP, 1994), 91 for Ernst Haeckel's belief that the earth was a fragment detached from the sun, also the alchemical notion that the sun is a symbol for the divine light within, and that the fiery magma at the earth's core is akin to a burning light within the human psyche (101). Carl Schmitt's *Theodor Däublers Nordlicht. Drei Studien* (reprinted Duncker and Humblot, Berlin 1991) traces the origins of these ideas from earliest sources. Däubler's grandfather corresponded with Haeckel: see Dieter Werner's essay in Dieter Werner (ed.), *Theodor Däubler–Biographie und Werk* (Mainz: Gardez! Verlag, 1996), 60.

[6] *Frühling der Seele. Pariser Trakl Symposion*. (ed. by Rémy Colombar and Gerald Stieg (Innsbruck: Haymon Verlag, 1995), 101.

[7] Martin Vogel, *Apollinisch und Dionysisch. Geschichte eines genialen Irrtums* (Regensburg: Gustav Bosse Verlag, 1966), 219.

[8] Fritz Martini, *Deutsche Literaturgeschichte. Von den Anfängen bis zur Gegenwart* (Stuttgart: Kröner, 1951), 463 makes the following comment: "Däubler was an impressive linguistic innovator, but he had no interest in se-

lectiveness and restraint. His work remained a torso where the magnificent is juxtaposed with the banal and the confused."

[9] Overt references to Nietzsche are sparse in Däubler's writing. In his Parisian journals he does, however, call himself a "Nietzschean spirit" and expresses gratitude to the Italian art historian and critic Ricciotto Canudo for mentioning Nietzsche's name ("we were friends from the very first moment you mentioned Nietzsche to me" — see Dieter Werner, *Däubler Biographie*, 146). A propos the "Hymn to Nietzsche" — Thomas Mann will later lampoon the earth-life-woman-breasts cult by mischievously putting (in *The Magic Mountain*) the following comment into the mouth of Mijnheer Peeperkorn (Gerhart Hauptmann): "Life, young man, is a woman spread before us, legs apart, with firm, swelling breasts. . ." For more on the Dionysian element in *Das Nordlicht* see Ludwig Pesch, *Die romantische Rebellion in der modernen Literatur und Kunst* (Munich: Beck, 1962), 133 and 139.

[10] The poems which come to mind are "At the Danube's Source" with the praise of the valleys of the Caucasus again; "Patmos" with its longing for Asia, landscape "growing quickly with the steps of the sun"; "Memory" and the journey to India, and the late fragment "The Eagle" which portrays this bird as "my father," floating above the Gotthard but whose ancestors came from "the forests of the Indus."

[11] There is much in the "Ra Drama" which anticipates Thomas Mann's immersion in Egyptian studies during the writing of the *Joseph* novels (1933–1943) — the solar myth itself, the androgynous hero, the association of male with light and female with darkness.

[12] See the "Höllenfahrt" section of *Joseph und seine Brüder*, Thomas Mann, *Gesammelte Werke in 13 Bänden*, vol. 4, 9.

[13] Was Däubler aware of "Mazdaznan," that eccentric Zoroastrianism introduced into Europe by Otto Hanisch? Hanisch and his disciple David Ammann published the journal *Mazdaznan* (the word means "Master Thought") in 1908; it dealt with philosophy, physical education and diet. The main centre for Mazdaznan in Europe was the cloistered *Lebensschule* at Herrliberg near Zurich. Johann Itten, teacher in the Bauhaus, was a disciple of Mazdaznan, insisting on shaven heads, purple dress and colonic irrigation. See Lothar Schreyer: *Erinnerungen an Sturm und Bauhaus* (Munich, Paul List, 1966), also Noll op.cit for information on Mithraism, the "Deus Leontocephalus" and "Aion" as derivations from Zoroastrianism.

[14] See Jürgen Schröder, *Gottfried Benn. Poesie und Sozialisation* (Stuttgart, Kohlhammer, 1978), 135.

[15] Moeller van den Bruck, "Theodor Däubler und die Idee des Nordlichts," *Deutsche Rundschau* 186 (1921) 20–34.

[16] Ernst Barlach, "Ein selbsterzähltes Leben, in *Das dichterische Werk*, vol. 2, 328.

[17] Dieter Werner, ed., *Theodor Däubler — Biographie und Werk* (Mainz: Gardez! Verlag, 1996), 75–76.
[18] G. W. F. Hegel, *Werke* (Frankfurt a. M.: Suhrkamp Taschenbuch Wissenschaft), vol. 3, 46.

Christian Morgenstern.
Courtesy of Schiller Nationalmuseum
and Deutsches Literaturarchiv, Marbach.

7 : Christian Morgenstern

> In the future there will be only one question to put to
> intelligent men — "What does Nietzsche mean to you?"
> For the degenerate he represents a supreme danger, and
> quite rightly so. For "we should push that which is already
> collapsing. . ."
>
> — Morgenstern, 1896

> The air is cleansed of 'God' —
> The Universe is free —
> Up, archers! Draw your bows!
> Aim at the furthest stars!
>
> — Morgenstern, 1898

O N MAY 6TH, 1895, his twenty-fourth birthday, Christian Morgenstern wrote the following letter to Nietzsche's mother, enclosing a
copy of his first anthology *In Phantas Schloß* (In Phanta's Castle):

> The moment in which I write these lines is the most solemn and
> moving of my whole life. I, a young man of twenty-four, dare to place
> my first poetic offering into the hands of *the* mother, the venerable
> mother who has given such a great son to the world, and to me espe-
> cially a liberator, as example of a man who inspires me to the loftiest
> struggles of life. That spirit of proud, victorious transfiguration of life,
> the feeling of sovereign domination over all things of which that be-
> loved, lonely man has so often spoken also pervades, I believe these
> poems submitted to you, the greater part of which I dare to call hu-
> morous in the most subtle sense of the word. My book is dedicated to
> the spirit of your noble, your unhappy son, in deepest gratitude and
> affection.[1]

Some five years later it would be to Elisabeth Förster-Nietzsche that
Morgenstern would write in condolence, replying to the announcement of Nietzsche's death, a woman who now, he explains, will be
"sacrosanct" to him and whose edition of the *Der Wille zur Macht*
(The Will to Power) would represent "one of the most powerful mani-

festations of the human spirit known to me" (*WB* 6, 805). An early poem "Mother and Son" (1893) had portrayed a son (Nietzsche) predeceasing a mother, dying in transfiguration after a thunderstorm, the sunlight "kissing his countenance" as a new world was about to emerge, a world which his spirit had conceived (*WB* 1, 559). And the grave in Röcken will become the place "where Germany lies buried," a place of future resurrection from which Germany's spirit would rise to "move across the earth" (*WB* 2, 439).

It may come as a surprise to many readers to find Christian Morgenstern in the company of those mystagogues and visionaries which this book is describing. Morgenstern is known above all as the creator of von Korf, Palmström, Palma Kunkel, the Nasobem, the Great Lalula, the Gingganz and other droll oddities, a kind of German Edward Lear who, after falling under the influence of Rudolf Steiner lost "the poetic graces which are so abundantly at his command in the humorous poems."[2] The "serious" Morgenstern is either ignored or treated in a cavalier fashion: Leonard Forster is typical in rejecting him as the writer of mystic kitsch whose fervent sentimentality was akin to that of Hedwig Courths-Maler.[3] It has only recently been possible, thanks to the Stuttgart edition of Morgenstern's writings, to gain an insight into this complex and interesting figure whose reception of Nietzsche, of Paul de Lagarde and of Ibsen will have to be looked at anew. This chapter will show Morgenstern's indebtedness to Nietzsche above all, for "there is scarcely a greater danger for a man like myself than to read Nietzsche [. . .]. It is like boring into the pain of my own inadequacy" (*WB* 5, 128). There is an enthrallment on Morgenstern's part which, certainly, will yield to a more critical stance and a final decision in favour of Rudolf Steiner, but the writer who called himself "Zarathustra's lark" (*WB* 5, 15) in 1893 was still able, some nineteen years later, to praise Nietzsche's unique greatness even though he, Morgenstern, cannot follow him into the darkness. "Nietzsche was the one who formed me and who was my passionate love for many a long year" and Martin Kiessig is surely correct in stressing that, although Morgenstern was to follow another teacher at the end, he never "overcame Nietzsche, and was never able to dismiss him entirely" (*WB* 1, 705).

It was in the winter of 1893–94, in Breslau, that Morgenstern first read Nietzsche, and the twenty-two year old was ravished by the force of Nietzsche's imagery and the iconoclasm of his thought. The picture of the lark dates from this time, as we know: "When the sun rises the larks awaken. The sun arises and I awake— Zarathustra's lark!" This is an entry from one of Morgenstern's diaries, a collection of aphorisms with the title *In me ipsum* and the Nietzschean motto "Nur wer sich wandelt, bleibt mit mir verwandt" (Only he who transforms himself remains akin to me). Not only the published collection of poetry but also the diary entries and the critical essays which Morgenstern wrote when he was struggling to support himself in Berlin give evidence of a deep involvement which Nietzsche; the young poet who lamented the fact that "neither parents nor teachers nor anyone else had really taken hold of me and educated me in the highest sense" and that he, "originally a person of brilliant talents have by and large remained an amateur," putting the blame on "the enormous mass of dilettantism, half-heartedness and lack of culture that I encounter" (*WB* 5, 38–9) implies, surely, that there was at least one mentor who could provide what other educators had signally failed to do.

In me ipsum contains many a telling, even startling utterance; a youthful *hauteur* emerges where life affirmation is awkwardly interfused with hardness. A crowd of people is seen whose thoughts, "like a black cloud above them," seethe with "tears and lightning" (*WB* 5, 16). Disgust is experienced and there is only one salvation — laughter. Honesty is preached and also cruelty — toward oneself. The young poet "burns in his own high expectations" yet seeks to devote himself to a "Dienst des Lebens," to serve life, in all its joy and darkness (*WB* 5, 22). In an unmistakable Zarathustra tone he announces the following: "You wish to love the possible? I only love that which is impossible." "Do you wish to know where I stand? In all places where war is raging [. . .]. My task is to *unsettle* each individual" (*WB* 5, 42). His aim is "to seek the goad to drive into my own lethargic flesh" (*WB* 5. 45) — the imagery, and the goal, is familiar. He castigates European civilization, lamenting its superficiality and its ignorant and banal trust in technology. An entry of 1907 explains that "I am extremely susceptible to two things — disgust and horror" (*WB* 5, 48). He seeks the path of hermits, of eccentrics, and longs for eternity, "to strike into eternity, changing, developing, higher and higher, flying from star to star, living and moving in ever more perfect manifestations [. . .] to highest joy and deepest pain — a never-waning life affirmation, an ideal in the highest sense!" (*WB* 5, 57). And it comes as no surprise that the power of the Will is extolled, a force which even bursts through the mechanical repetition of the eternal recurrence and demands a "Vorwärts," a thrusting breakthrough, "I demand a Forward — therefore there is, for me, a Forward. . ." (*WB* 5, 58). The hubris here is undeniable, and the young writer cannot withstand (and neither could Frederick Delius in his *Mass of Life*) Zarathustra's magisterial diapason:

O thou my Will, thou that canst shatter my misfortune, preserve me
from all trivial mysteries! O thou predestined guardian of my soul,
whom I call Fate! Thou who art in me and above me! Preserve me for
one great and final triumph [. . .] that at the great Noon-tide I may be
ready, like a glowing ore and a lightning-heavy cloud, to answer the
call of myself and my most secret Will! A bow yearning for its arrow,
an arrow yearning for its star, a star, ready and ripe in its Midday,
glowing and transfixed [. . .] O thou my Will!" (4, 268/9)

Morgenstern wrote an astonishing amount in his diaries and the
entries betray a highly intellectual and emotional reaction to nature, the
world of art and literature, politics, ethics, education, and psychology.
His father had been a landscape painter and Morgenstern extols the
natural world, greeting the sun above all as a remote and splendid deity
"O sun, sun, to wander as you, glowing, self-willed, careless, and yet
the joy of millions. Are you not the highest symbol of the Master?"
(WB 5, 66). Of great interest are Morgenstern's comments on art and
creativity. "None of you knows what creativity means. To paint a picture, to write a poem? No! To recast one's whole age, to impose upon
it the stamp of one's will, to fill it with beauty, to overwhelm it, to
overpower it with one's spirit" (WB 5, 87); an aphorism of 1891 rejects
the Christian denial of sensuality, a denial which must needs bring
about the death of art, and insists upon the unity of body and soul (WB
5, 88). In 1902, in Italy, Morgenstern remarks that "Art is the creation
of order — this word of Nietzsche's fills me with every step I take."[4] A
"great spirit" is envisaged in whom the creative urge, slumbering for
centuries, bursts forth into radiant blossom. A new energy is needed, a
new clarity and a new mythology. "I regard the task of future generations of poets to be the creation of new myths — and we shall prepare
the way" (WB 5, 101). The attack on "Literaturprofessoren" for their
pedantic sterility comes as no surprise, indeed, the word "Bildungsphilister" (educated philistine), Nietzsche's neologism, is also in evidence, metamorphosing into a "Bildungschamäleon" (WB 5, 110).
One striking apophthegm, dating from 1895, is the following — "To
save Christ from the hands of the Christians" (WB 5, 108): the sooty
palimpsest of Victorian institutionalized Christianity must be removed
so that the original radiance should shine forth more clearly. Some five
years later we hear Nietzsche's voice again in the following: "Tragedy is
the deepest song of the ecstasy of the world, and our eternal task is to
listen to it from time to time in the deafening hubbub of daily life"
(WB 5, 107); fitting, also, that it should be Hölderlin's fragmentary
Empedokles which is hailed as pointing the way that German drama
should have taken.

In the year 1896 Morgenstern wrote in a diary certain scattered thoughts on Nietzsche and Ibsen. The first statement we know already: "There is scarcely a greater danger for a man like myself than to read Nietzsche [. . .] It is like boring into the pain of my own inadequacy." Nietzsche's character is "herrlich," splendid — the character of a man who was, initially, modest and pious: "his whole life dissolves in thought, becomes visible to the world and streams before our eyes, pouring forth from mysterious depths and losing itself in impenetrable darkness [. . .] One gazes into Nietzsche's eyes and knows where mankind's goal may be found" (*WB* 5, 128). Some eight years later Morgenstern comments on the contradictions in Nietzsche's thought: "He who objects to these 'contradictions' has never thought with him (nor, what is more, *felt* with him), has never flown with him" (*WB* 5, 129). Morgenstern is aware that Nietzsche is not a philosopher with a system: "To understand a philosophical system simply requires a measure of intellect — no more. But to understand a passionate seeker like Nietzsche one needs more than a clever brain — one must also to a certain extent, be part of him." Was Nietzsche a paragon? Certainly not, but "I have not yet sufficiently acknowledged the depths of sorrow in which his spirit was submerged, and how he collapsed under the weight of his thoughts, his loneliness and his sickness — a frightful and yet grandiose human sacrifice" (*WB* 5, 129). Nietzsche was "a fighter, a wise man from the warrior-caste, not from the priesthood. Perhaps, in a second half of his life, he would have radiated a mildness of wisdom, and sent kindness as well as lightning-flashes amongst men." And what of *Thus Spake Zarathustra*? Morgenstern's evaluation varies. In 1905 he praised the prologue enthusiastically:

> Where is there a greater, more profound prologue to any destiny? Where is there a parable, an exhortation that could equal this setting and this prayer, that could equal it in earnestness, serenity and depth? There is a forest-idyll here, full of mild, evening sunshine, a path which leads to the turning-point of all human culture [. . .], a mountain which one will never, perhaps, climb and from which Zarathustra gazes at the waters flowing both East and West. (*WB* 5, 129)

In the following year, 1906, the response is less enthusiastic:

> *Zarathustra* is, despite the incontestable greatness of certain details, one of the worst books ever written. It is neither a book for the people, nor a book for the pampered and the lonely, but a mixture of the grandiose and the banal, in both content and execution. There is a pushing and straining here, a forcing of personal moods, a categorical

execution of things whose "categorical execution" only remain a "niaiserie" or foolishness, a game with poetic images and parables which is frequently great or tragic, but more often uncontrolled and garrulous. It is a book which could only be admitted to the ranks of the classics if its speeches were reduced to something between twelve and twenty. (*WB* 5, 130)

And the following sentence blames the time in which Nietzsche lived — "Wretched, petty time, you also oppressed him, your Greatest." *Thus Spake Zarathustra*, Morgenstern implies, was marred by the tendencies of the time in which it was written, conditioning it to become a neoromantic, pseudo-oriental farrago of sublimity and pretentious bathos. And yet — and there is always an "and yet" — Nietzsche was "a great artist, a great stylist" (*WB* 5, 131), a man of towering rank, both leader and creator. For Morgenstern Nietzsche was, as poet-musician, at one with the greatest mystics —it is not as Anti-Christ, but Ante-Christ that Morgenstern sees him, "the last great German philosopher ante Christum natum. To speak in his own language, he was the last Ante Christ" (*WB* 5, 132). Even the overwhelming experience of St John's gospel, dating from the winter of 1905–6 at the sanatorium of Birkenwerder, and the initiation into anthroposophy in 1909 will fail to expunge Nietzsche's imprint. The famous "Bild meines Lebens," or "Emblem of my Life" of 1910 (*WB* 5, 62) seeks to convey Nietzsche's supersession by St John, the stem (or "worldly period" — Nietzsche — terminated by illness) supporting the bowl filled with the "blood of fulfilment" and representing the experience of the Johannine. There is something of *Parsifal* in this image, but Zarathustra's animals are also present;[5] Hans Wildermann's drawing (*WB* 5, 449), based on Morgenstern's sketch, has both eagle and snake, Christian images indeed, but here in apparent repose. And Zarathustra likewise greeted the chalice, the sun chalice, glorious in its gleaming magnificence.

It is fascinating to read the fifty or so diaries and trace Morgenstern's intellectual development which owed much to copious reading, to translations from Scandinavian literature (not only Ibsen, but Bjørnson, Strindberg and Hamsun) and to a deep awareness of the social and political scene in the Berlin of his time. The thirty-five year old fears the triumph of Socialism, sensing that "blood would flow"; culture is the prerequisite of "a happy fear," a spiritual élite (*WB* 5, 169). Judaism is "predominantly destructive," with Jesus, "the greatest Jew" as the greatest "destroyer of the 'world'" (*WB* 5, 175); Spinoza and Fritz Mauthner follow. Nietzsche is their opponent, for he is the greatest contrast, for whom energy is creative, constructive, commanding and ordering. "Nietzsche wishes to ennoble the horror of human existence by the Will, he wishes to form, to create. Everything in Nietzsche is discipline and breeding ['Zuchtgedanke']." The Jews "are the opponents of creativity, they are its bad conscience" (*WB* 5, 175). These statements have a disagreeable ring about them: we remember that Morgenstern was an avid reader and admirer of Paul de Lagarde who will be referred to later. "Because the Jew always considers himself to be spiritually superior he will never reach a superior spirituality." But would the Christian fare any better? The younger Morgenstern had "looked upon the men of our times, they have flat feet, and were lame — this was their (Christian) religion — they limp throughout the age" (*WB* 5, 186). Churches were mere "Cages of God" where unhealthy emotionalism was concocted; Nietzsche's "letzte Menschen," these blinkered, sterile caricatures of humanity are personified by the figure of a professor who was working on the history of the word "and," and the modern age is deplored as one without a spiritual leader, and in which the herd mentality prevails (*WB* 5, 189). Men are simply painted dolls, and "Geist" or "spirit" has been debased to a market commodity, with German culture nothing more than a "gigantic bric-à-brac" (*WB* 5, 192).

Morgenstern's highly critical castigation of the materialism of the Wilhelminian era is worthy of his mentor: Nietzsche feared the extirpation of German culture at the expense of the German *Reich*, had exposed the pretensions of the "Bildungsphilister" and sought, through striking and provocative imagery, to preach the destruction of the moribund and the creation of a new cultural health. Morgenstern follows him closely. There can be "no success without striving, no conflagration without fire" he writes (*WB* 5, 204); vision is needed, and pride, the lack of which is regarded as an unforgivable sin (*WB* 5, 205). The concepts of mere existence, mere living is meaningless — "millions upon millions of beings exist without any significance at all." It is only when life "wishes to justify itself," when there are men "who wish to achieve something, for whom a goal is far more important than their own private concerns," only then does human existence have some value, some purpose (*WB* 5, 206). Contempt is need, for "only he who [. . .] despises the world will be of use to it." Is it Zarathustra or Morgenstern who is speaking here? "Happiness? Do you require happiness? Would I wish you a trace of happiness if it did not increase your worth? It is *value* that I wish for you" (*WB* 5, 209). "The great criminal cannot be a small, petty man. One could argue that the one in whom a devil is great is also the one in whom a god is great [. . .]" "Only he who is consumed by fire can be a wandering flame to mankind" (*WB* 5,

220). One can almost speak of a self-identification here, an obsession on Morgenstern's part with Nietzsche's heady pronouncements, pronouncements that seemed to him the most powerful revelation of the human spirit to him. "We feel a silent reverence," he wrote in 1902, "that Nietzsche wrote down this last legacy on the eve of his spiritual death with such vigour and clarity." He is referring to *Der Wille zur Macht* (The Will to Power), a dubious compilation by Elisabeth Förster-Nietzsche but one which convinced Morgenstern utterly of Nietzsche's prophetic genius. These diaries, of course, deal with other figures — Lagarde, Dostoevski, Tolstoy, Max Klinger — there is also a flirtation with the mysticism of Meister Eckhart — yet the Nietzschean presence is the ground bass which supports the basic structure. "The great seek out the storm when it is at its most violent — the weak bemoan it. . ." (*WB* 5, 229). "If you take away the harsh tragedy of life [. . .] then you have taken away its beauty"; "He who does not conquer the world daily will lose it from day to day" — the tone is earnest, exhortative and verges upon the ecstatic. "Seize life as a work of art . . . the creative man alone is the human being . . . Visual love! Creative love!" (*WB* 5, 248): a life affirmation is proclaimed which embraces and transforms tragedy and sickness, a world of fire, lightning and storm where dross is burned away and the highest vision triumphs.

And Rudolf Steiner? Aged twenty-nine, Steiner had moved to Weimar in 1890 to edit Goethe's scientific manuscripts for the famous Sophien-Ausgabe; there he met Elisabeth Förster-Nietzsche who visited the Goethe and Schiller Archive where he worked to ask about founding a similar venture for her brother. Steiner visited the home of Elisabeth and her mother in Naumburg, and was permitted to see the stricken man: his description is a telling one.

> He was lying on a couch. His exceptionally beautiful forehead was that of a thinker and an artist. It was early afternoon. His eyes, though dying, still reflected his soul; they took in his physical surroundings, but this no longer reached his mind. One stood there, but Nietzsche was not aware of one's presence. Observing his intelligent features one could believe they belonged to someone who had spent all morning engaged in thought and now wished to rest awhile [. . .] The inner shock I experienced led to what I can only describe as an insight into the genius of Nietzsche whose gaze, though directed towards me, did not meet mine. The very passivity of this gaze, resting upon me for a long time, released my inner comprehension [. . .] In inner perception I saw Nietzsche's soul as if hovering over his head, infinitely beautiful in its spirit-light, surrendered to the spirit worlds it had longed for so much but had been unable to find before illness had clouded his mind

[. . .] Previously I had *read* Nietzsche. Now I saw the actual bearer of ideals from the highest spirit realms, ideas that even here shone in their beauty despite having lost their original radiance on the way. A soul who had brought from former lives on earth golden riches of great spirituality but was unable to let it shine fully in the present life. I admired what Nietzsche had written, now I saw his radiant spirit behind what I so greatly admired.[6]

Morgenstern did not know of this description as it appeared in print some eleven years after his death, but Steiner's anthroposophical writings became increasingly familiar to him after his conversion in 1909; conversations with Steiner may also have touched upon Nietzsche's madness. Steiner saw in Nietzsche a profound thinker, a fierce opponent of triviality and utilitarianism and a man who sought to attain self-transcendence; the doctrine of the eternal recurrence could also be modified in an attempt to preach reincarnation. Morgenstern's somewhat abject praise of Steiner in the diaries and the published work, in *Wir fanden einen Pfad* (We Found a Path, 1914) leaves no doubts about the sincerity of his conversion to anthroposophy, for Steiner's cosmology provided him with a comprehensive view of all reality, both material and spiritual; the youthful (and, indeed, mature) intoxication by Nietzsche is found again, strangely transmuted, in Steiner who fuses Zarathustra's ecstasies and solemn praise of eternity with his own idiosyncratic Christology.

Before looking at Morgenstern's poetry two of his articles should be mentioned, "Nietzsche als Erzieher" (Nietzsche as Educator), with its echoes of Nietzsche and Julius Langbehn, which appeared in the *Neue deutsche Rundschau* in July 1896 and the unpublished "Versuch einer Fastenrede" (Attempt at a Sermon), a sketch dating from 1908. "Nietzsche als Erzieher," written during the night of the summer solstice, was meant to be a discussion of volumes nine and ten of Nietzsche's works, the *Schriften und Entwürfe aus den Jahren 1869–1872* but became instead a paean of praise for the creator of *Thus Spake Zarathustra*: Zarathustra is "the most beautiful man who walked on earth" and teaches the doctrine of "a still more beautiful man!" (*WB 6*, 90). The motto with which we are familiar is found here: the only question for the future of all thinking men is their attitude to Nietzsche. The moribund will be swept away, and this with justification — they should be helped on their way towards extinction. Nietzsche is there for the strong, for those with "the future in their blood": he is the great master and martinet, the lord and tamer of his instincts, the leader, not seducer ("Führer, nicht der Verführer"), the bringer of culture who determines the course of history — the tragic philosopher. Nietzsche can only be experienced, not simply read ("Man muß ihn erleben, nicht erlesen wollen"). The young must fight, Morgenstern writes, and they fight better "beneath the Nietzschean exclamation marks," for Nietzsche is an educator, a mentor whose divine epiphany will make the souls of the young glow and shudder. The rest of the review consists of extended quotations from the young Nietzsche and concentrates on education, on the need to educate the educators and to produce genius; as the sun streams into his room the reviewer greets the dawn in an ecstatic fashion and broods on a "Sonnenkult" such as the primitive Germans experienced. It was written at Friedrichshagen, the artist colony on the Müggelsee area of Berlin where Morgenstern — and later Steiner — were to reside.

The "Versuch einer Fastenrede (1908) was written in response to a survey sent to various writers to canvass their opinion on the writing of the journalist Maximilian Harden; Morgenstern says little about Harden but writes a "Bußpredigt" or "sermon calling to repentance," an admonition to the Germans to look at their culture and seek a higher goal. Bismarck's *Reich*, Morgenstern writes, brings forth awe and veneration from many quarters, but it is not an age of cultural splendour. Morgenstern refers to Ibsen, Lagarde and Nietzsche in his attack (*WB* 6, 334): Ibsen sought "beauty of the soul," Lagarde denounced shallowness and vulgarity, and Nietzsche coined the phrase "Europas Flachland" to castigate the lack of ideals amongst his fellow Germans. Technological and scientific achievements are acknowledged, but the ultimate aim, the emergence of the *Übermensch* is far from being realised. Morgenstern quotes Zarathustra with passion: "Ye have taken the path from worm to man, and there is much of the worm in thee. Once wert thou apes, and now there is still much more of the ape in man than in the ape itself. Behold, I preach unto thee the Superman! The Superman is the meaning of the earth. Let thy will speak: The Superman shall be the meaning of the earth!" (*WB* 6, 339/40). The Superman, Morgenstern concedes, is an Antichrist. But "that which has, after twenty centuries, become Christianity, and that which is publicly proclaimed as Christianity cannot help us win anything new, cannot help us reach beyond ourselves. And so away with it. Modern man, however, only hears that 'God is dead.' But he has very little idea that God awoke that same minute, awoke as a new 'Word.' And yet it is so. The will to the Superman is the new religion, as is every gigantic Will that wills beyond itself." And, Morgenstern continues, "Nobody has called out with such burning fervour 'Away, away from this wretched time!' as this spirit-and-antispirit of our age made flesh — unless it be its other hero, Paul de Lagarde" (*WB* 6, 341). It is under the tutelage of these two figures that the second German cultural epoch will begin — or else it will never begin. Nietzsche and Lagarde — a curious coupling, for Lagarde is remembered chiefly for his fervid nationalism and ferocious anti-Semitism, both of which were anathema to Nietzsche. But Morgenstern greatly esteemed Lagarde's *Deutsche Schriften* (1878–1881) with their call for a religious renewal of the German nation. A new culture, he asseverated, could only emerge with a new experience of Christianity, a Christianity cleansed of Semitic elements and exemplifying a heroic idealism. Morgenstern's poem "Zu Nieblum will ich begraben sein" (I Wish to Be Buried at Nieblum), which Steiner read out in his memorial address on April 14, 1914 in Vienna, praises the Frisian Islands, the grey North Sea and his own lonely grave, upon which "Read Lagarde" would be chiselled.

Let us now turn to the collections of poetry themselves. *In Phantas Schloß* (In Phanta's Castle) is dedicated to the "spirit of Friedrich Nietzsche"; the motto recommends "Unschuld" or innocence, the innocence of enjoyment. "Phanta" is best understood as imaginative play, free and amoral, a delight in the sparkling radiance of fantasy. The poet rejects the conventional and demands new stars, a new daring; most of the poems are written in a free rhythm reminiscent of Heine's *Nordsee* collection, but Morgenstern denied having read Heine at this time. The note of whimsy in certain poems ("Moonrise") seems remote from Nietzsche (the rising moon is a glistening soap bubble which Pan, lying in the bushes besides a pond, has blown into the air from a reed), but Zarathustra likewise knew that "butterflies and soap bubbles, and suchlike things among men, know most what happiness is. To see these light, dainty, volatile souls fluttering past — this moves Zarathustra to tears and songs. I could only believe in a god who knows how to dance [. . .]' (3.49). And dance is extolled on the first page (*WB* 1, 11) — "Arise, my heart! Upwards to the aether, dressed for the dance!" The unorthodox capitalization in "Homo Imperator" (Me, Myself, I — in German the first person singular is not capitalized) emphasizes the Promethean act of defiance: "I, Man, am thy soul / thy lord and Master / the soul and divinity / of everything" (*WB* 1, 30–31): it is interesting to remember that Morgenstern had met John Henry Mackay (who would later be a witness at Rudolf Steiner's wedding) in Friedrichshagen during the time that Mackay was working on the biography of Max Stirner, that uncompromising exponent of individualism and forerunner of Nietzsche. "Kosmogonie" greets the cosmos in the manner of Klopstock, but a "god of darkness" is portrayed who, tearing his bleeding eyeballs from his head, hurls them into the revolving spheres: this god is Lucifer. Less drastic is "Sunrise" where lofty emotions are expressed as the poet witnesses the dawn in the mountains and tells of his desire to "vibrate consciously with the ethereal waves of the universe, at one with the universe, oblivious, timeless, sensing the undulating chords of eternity within" (*WB* 1, 20–21). There is a passivity here, in contrast to the imperious stance of "Homo Triumphator," and a Jugendstil element is also detectable in the image of the soul standing with outstretched arms to greet the rising sun à la Fidus. The "sun and life" cult of certain of the Friedrichshagen circle is also evident here, a "Heliotellurik" with pagan overtones. The reference to "the gleaming of blood" (in "In a Dream") necessarily brings to mind Alfred Schuler's concept of "Blutleuchte," an ecstasy of the blood found in youthful male initiates similar to the ethereal liquid (ichor) traditionally found in the veins of the gods. "Das Hohelied," the "Song of Songs" is a paean of praise to love and the cosmos whose refrain is not far removed from the opening of Däubler's *Das Nordlicht*: the mutilated god of "Kosmogonie" is nowhere to be found.

There is nothing pretentious in these poems; mythology, cosmos and the banal (washing day) are juxtaposed in a lively and frequently droll manner. The imaginative power of the poet reigns supreme, "for with Phanta / nothing is impossible" (*WB* 1, 33). Pan, Phoebus and Lucifer are recreated in a jocose manner, and an all too earnest interpretation is precluded. The poem "The Cross" may lend itself to a Christian interpretation: the poet, lost in the mountains in the mist, stretches out his arms on the edge of an abyss, sees, as a Brocken spectre, the shape of the cross projected in front of him, and the wraiths of mist, the "angels of death," recede (*WB* 1, 44). In the following poem, however, "The Temptation," the Lord, a venerable but frail gentleman, cheerfully greets the poet and explains that it was His idea to save him by suggesting the cross-like shape; the poet is grateful but rejects the Lord's offer of the gift of the world's abundance and remains the "poor one," knowing that, through Phanta, the poet can control the world at will. The Lord is led from the mountain where He meets Pan; the two disappear and leave the poet to climb, a free, happy man, singing into "his splendid, clear, lonely heights" (*WB* 1, 46).

Morgenstern was fascinated by Nietzsche's restless spirit, his questioning and his seeking for new, ruthless vistas, and Zarathustra's conquest of the "Geist der Schwere," (the spirit of heaviness) was his exemplar and paradigm. Various plans date from this time, cyclical, cosmological, symphonic — *Kosmiade vom Weltkobold* (The Cosmic Song of the World-Goblin), *Sonnenaufgänge* (Sunrises), *Symphonie*, and *Poseidon und Selene*, a sea mythology in the manner of Böcklin. "The sun arises — ecstatic sun-choruses" (*WB* 1, 713) — this fragment recalls that line from *Faust II*, where "a monstrous uproar greets the approach of the sun," and is suffused with Nietzschean solar affirmation. The lyrical-epic fragment *Symphonie* claims that "I am in *all* that is / my laughter makes the furthest stars to shudder" (*WB* 1, 719). A monistic sense of oneness with all is the basic tenor, with dithyrambic *élan* alternating with solemnity, elemental rapture and a dash of ironic self-awareness. A "pan-cosmic religion without transcendence"[7] is adumbrated, a yearning for some religious awareness of life untrammelled by any Christian dogma. And Nietzsche is "the crystal bath, the fountain of youth, a *purgatorium*, the antimony of the Nona" (*WB* 2, 439) — this cryptic remark tell us that Nietzsche's cult of life stands forever opposed to the experience of the "ninth hour," the hour at which Christ cried out in anguish (Matthew 27, 40). Nietzsche may have moved "into the house of madness" (*WB* 2, 440), but he should not be lamented — "shuddering with ecstasy" he accepted this dark affliction and supersedes Christ as the greater prophet.

The later collections of poetry which are of interest to us in this chapter (*Auf vielen Wegen* [On many Paths] *Ich und die Welt* [The World and I], *Melancholie*) are less dithyrambic than *In Phantas Schloss*, but the Nietzschean imprint is no less prevalent. The poem "Legende" (*Auf vielen Wegen*) was inspired ostensibly by a Chopin prelude played by Morgenstern's friend Woldemar Runge; it tells of a Christ who, smiling, takes a young girl's hand and dances with her when on the way to the Mount of Olives (*WB* 1, 160–161). Zarathustra also appeared to his dancing girls and, not wishing to disturb their revels, commended them and praised the felicity of rapid motion: "I learned to walk, since then I ran, I learned to fly, since then nothing impedes me [. . .] Now I am light, now I am flying, I see myself beneath me — and now a god is dancing through me. . ." (*WB* 3, 49–50). Gods should dance, and men with them, without crutches and forms of restraint: "O raison d'esclave" (*Ich und die Welt*) rejects supports, tinted glasses which only permit a limited moral vision, and apron-strings, while Baal is worshipped as the new deity. The tone is obviously flippant here with its proliferation of exclamation marks; "Prometheus" and the "Hymn of Hatred" (*WB* 1, 234–35) are powerful expressions, however, of Morgenstern's refusal to accept Christian ideas of humility and submission. The former necessarily brings Goethe's *Sturm und Drang* ode to mind — it is, we notice, the "vulture madness" which feeds upon Prometheus who is dismissed in derogatory terms by two wanderers as "a sick spirit" creating "a world of sickness." The manuscript contains the original title together with the following dedication "To Nietzsche, whose life's work is constantly stigmatised as that of a madman" (*WB*

1, 847). The "Hymn to Hatred" praises the violence of raw emotion which is compared to a lightning flash which scars the face of the world, a burning acid that cauterizes and illuminates, a destructive "sun of the future," burning and terrifying. Similar ideas are expressed in "Übermut" (High Spirits) and "Bahn frei!" (Make Way!) where pride, energy and a dynamic forcefulness are portrayed. "An Friedrich Nietzsche" has a quieter tone: upon hearing the band in the park play *Lohengrin* the poet is overwhelmed by emotion — "You [Nietzsche} loved this music once, trembling, drinking it in greedily"; amongst a crowd of self-satisfied philistines the poet weeps uncontrollably (*WB* 1, 239).

An important poem is "Botschaft des Kaisers Julian an sein Volk" (The Emperor Julian's Message to his People). Julian the Apostate preaches the destruction of Christian temples, the annihilation of priests and the shattering of crucifixes: trumpets should blaze forth and the people exult in an abundance of roses. "The time is passed / When the cross stood firm. / The New Man now / Raises his hand" (*WB* 1, 246). This dates from 1898, the year in which Morgenstern had met Ibsen, and memories of the latter's *Emperor and Galilean* may have played a part. Morgenstern had been invited by Samuel Fischer to join the official translators of Ibsen's plays and had travelled to Norway in 1891 to acquire a knowledge of language and landscape (he had already met the deadline for the translation of the *Festival at Solhaug*). Friendly relationships were established between playwright and his translator, Ibsen having high praise for the German versions of *Brand*, *Peer Gynt* and the *Comedy of Love*; he would later express the wish that Morgenstern, even before Ibsen had finished it, should translate *When We Dead Awaken*, and after his death his widow sent a silver medallion and flowers from Ibsen's coffin to six personalities who had been most helpful in promoting her late husband's work (Morgenstern was one). He was not involved in the translation of *Emperor and Galilean* but certainly knew the play and sympathised with Ibsen's attempt to praise a religion shot through with the joy of life, that *livsglaede* which, in Michael Meyer's words, he felt badly lacking in contemporary Christian teaching.[8] When Ibsen commented that *Emperor and Galilean* contained more of his own personal experience than he would care to admit he was doubtless referring to the emotional straight jacket in which he found himself confined and from which, as from his childhood Christianity, he could never escape. The playwright who "was preternaturally shy about exposing his sexual organs even during medical examination" (Meyer, *Ibsen*, 400) had surely been stunted by bleak, Scandinavian Protestantism much as Nietzsche had suffered in Naumburg and the confines of the vicarage: both sought the south and its blandishments. On Nietzsche's birthday, 15 October, certain "Evening rêveries" commemorated his memory: one is particularly violent, calling for the removal of the body, the mummy, the dead Christ — "What is the dead amongst the living gods!" (*WB* 1, 252). "Concert by the Sea" describes that other giant, Richard Wagner, and the elemental force of his music. It was inspired by a concert given on the beach at Sylt (*WB* 1, 278). It is also from this anthology, *Ich und die Welt* that the second motto is found that was used at the beginning of this chapter — the air is cleansed of "God," and the universe is free ("Up, archers! Draw your bows! / Point at the furthest stars!") It is only when institutionalized religion is removed that man will be able to experience the true force of the numinous — "God" is removed in order that a new religion should prevail.

The collection *Melancholie* appeared in 1906, and a restless uncertainty is apparent in many of the poems. "Before the Frescoes of the Appartamenti Borgia" is a memory of a visit to Rome where Morgenstern saw the two frescoes and a Madonna by Pinturicchio in the Borgia apartments in the Vatican. It is believed that the Virgin and child is a representation of Pope Alexander the Sixth's mistress and first-born son; his daughter Lucrezia is the model for St. Catherine in a painting of the Disputation and in the painting of the Resurrection Alexander himself is kneeling in prayer whilst his son Cesare is recognisable as one of the two warriors before the empty tomb. The poet is dazzled by the monster, Borgia, by the excesses of the Italian Renaissance and the triumph of beauty and violence over morality; there are plans dating from this time for three Renaissance dramas, *Savonarola*, *Julius II* and *Cesare Borgia*. "Cesare Borgia as Pope" — Nietzsche's impious speculation inspired, as we know many a prurient artistic exploration, but Morgenstern realised that he did not have the talent for historical drama. Memories of Rome are also found in "Piazza Barberini," a poem referring to Nietzsche's stay in Rome (May and June 1883), in this square, close to the Bernini fountain whose splashing waters inspired the famous "Nachtlied" from *Thus Spake Zarathustra*, that "song, the loneliest song that has ever been created" (6, 341). Morgenstern had sought out the address (Piazza Barberini 56, ultimo piano) and gazed in awe at the place where Nietzsche had conceived the lines: "It is night: now all the fountains gush aloud, and my soul is also a gushing fountain. It is night: now all the songs of love arise, and my soul is also a song of love." Two other utterances relate to the Roman experience — one seeking to be "reinlich," clean, in this papal city, the other referring to the doctrine of the Immaculate Conception of Mary and the need to remember the last sections of Nietzsche's *Der Antichrist* when confronted by such a dogma. The need to elevate Mary as a symbol of purity untainted by sexuality Nietzsche found abhorrent. "I am ashamed to bring to mind what the church has made of such symbolism [. . .] And the doctrine of 'The Immaculate Conception'? But — by such a doctrine the church has maculated conception" (6, 207). Dürer's *Melancholia* gazes with disenchanted eyes at the futility of human achievement and history, but Nietzsche's forbidding legacy guides the poet through the Vanity Fair of existence with fire and a steely humour.

"There is in *Melancholie* the inexorable seriousness of his (Morgenstern's) longing and the awareness of participation in a spiritual realm not yet clearly perceived."[9] The collection appeared in 1906 and Morgenstern sensed (although tuberculosis proved him tragically wrong) that he was in the midday of his life and that a clearly defined path had yet to be discovered. As an associate of Wilhelm Bölsche in the Friedrichshagen Circle he may well have come across the latter's novel *Die Mittagsgöttin* (The Noonday Goddess, 1891) with its haunting portrayal of that figure from Wendish mythology, Pschiolnitza, who appears at midday to demand of men what they had done with their lives; death by strangulation was the punishment for failure to having lived to the full. Nietzsche's "Great Midday" is in contrast a time of ecstatic epiphany when Zarathustra, "glowing and powerful," leaves his cave "as the morning sun rising from dark mountains" (4, 408): it is a time of benediction. The monism of Bölsche and other thinkers at Friedrichshagen appealed greatly — monism being the doctrine which claims that only one being exists and denies any form of duality — particularly when fused with a rapturous pantheism. Bölsche's enormously popular *Das Liebesleben in der Natur. Eine Entwicklungsgeschichte der Liebe* (The Love Life of Nature: the Evolution of Love, 1898–1902) argued that man's task is to listen to the voice of nature and to vibrate in sympathy with that voice, where love becomes the driving force behind religious elevation. Later, in more mystical vein, Bölsche would argue, in *Von Sonnen-und Sonnenstäubchen. Kosmische Wanderungen* (Of Suns and Sun-specks, 1903) that all men are children of the Great Sun, their thoughts containing millions of suns.[10] What appealed to Morgenstern above all at this time was the insistence of the Circle on the rejection of crude naturalism and the cultivation of more mystical exploration. Bruno Wille's lyrical novel *Offenbarungen des Wacholderbaums* (The Revelations of the Juniper Tree: the Novel of One Who Sees All, 1901) had also spoken of a universal soul or "monon"; Julius Hart, in his collection of verse entitled *Triumph des Lebens* (The Triumph of Life, 1898), had similarly exulted in the unity of all things, the involvement of all in a cosmic unity; *Der Neue Gott* (The New God—A Vision of the Coming Century) published the same year, went beyond monism to the portrayal of a god-man who is the hub of the universe, the centre of the sun and the core of matter. The debilitating duality of the world is overcome, for Hart, by the fusion of unity and multiplicity, as the god-man rejoices in the infinite fluidity of life.

In much of the writing of this time a diffuse but intense religiosity is detectable which rejects conventional Christianity but insists on some quasi-divine experience of the world, a Nietzschean Mass of Life or hymn to eternity where, in an epic of initiation, the birth of God in man is celebrated. Rudolf Steiner, as has been noted, was also a close observer of the Friedrichshagen sodality; he had moved to Berlin in 1897 after disagreement with Elisabeth Förster-Nietzsche made further work in Weimar impossible. His book *Grundlinien einer Erkenntnis-theorie der Goetheschen Weltanschauung* (On the Theory of Knowledge Implicit in Goethe's World Conception) had appeared in 1886: in it Steiner argues that man is the centre of the world order and that things have existence only in so far as they are illuminated by him. Man possesses within himself the central essence of his own existence, and Steiner argues that man is far stronger than he realises, his mind transforming reality as the sun touches the world as it rises in the morning. He who has a rich mental life sees a thousand things that are as nothing to the mentally impoverished — man does not merely behold, he *creates*. This has an unmistakably Nietzschean ring about it; the later book, *Friedrich Nietzsche, ein Kämpfer gegen seine Zeit* (Friedrich Nietzsche, A Warrior Against His Age, 1895) extols Nietzsche's fearlessness, his rejection of shallowness and mendacity, seeing him both as critic and visionary, a man who created his own realities and had foreseen the future of human existence devoid of comforting illusions. In Berlin Steiner became a close associate of the poet Ludwig Jacobowski and also as we know of John Henry Mackay whose *Die Anarchisten* (1891) preached an untrammelled individualism. Steiner's involvement with, and rejection of, the German branch of the Theosophical Society, his impatience with the occult musings of Wilhelm Hübbe-Schleiden, editor of the journal *Sphinx*, and the formation of the Anthroposophical Society in 1913 can play no part in this chapter: suffice it to say that for Steiner the supersensible, spiritual world behind the material world became as real *as* the world, and that the faculties which made possible the spiritual investigations could be developed by all human beings who were allowed to pursue the proper course of spiritual training. And Morgenstern's yearning for some cosmology which would provide a comprehensive view of all reality, both spiritual and material, would find in Steiner its fulfilment.

And Nietzsche? In his autobiography, published in instalments in the Dornach journal *Das Goetheanum* (1923–1925) Steiner makes the following comment on Nietzsche:

> I felt that he was a personality who was compelled by disposition and education to live intensively in the cultural and spiritual life around him but who also felt "what has all this to do with me? So much of this repels me — there must be a different world, a world where I can live." This made him a fiery [geistbefeuert] critic of his time, but a man made ill by his own critique.[11]

Goethean health and energy is increasingly extolled by Steiner who sensed that there was something pathological in Nietzsche's attack, something forbidding and hardly exemplary. It was Goethe's *Märchen* which inspired Steiner's first play *Die Pforte der Einweihung* (1910); Morgenstern would be present at a later play *Der Seele Erwachen* in 1913 at the Volkstheater, Munich. There is much that is derived from *Parsifal* here, much grail-seeking, liturgy and initiation, an aetherial theatre of pallid eidola, which will later attempt to emulate the Festspielhaus on its green hill, that temple of art from which Nietzsche fled, appalled by the specious spirituality and pretentious hagiography. The place where the Redeemer was redeemed by Wagnerian art was, he knew, no place for him.

We are attempting to argue that the self-styled Antichrist appealed to those disaffected souls who sought to recapture "the redemptive impulse outside of traditional supernaturalism and the familiar modes of monotheistic religion."[12] Morgenstern, we remember, sought a "universe cleansed of 'God'" — the inverted commas highlighting a debased, institutionalized idol, devoid of the aura of the numinous, which God had become. Nietzsche's arrows of desire, like Blake's, are aimed at goals inaccessible to those trapped in stultifying, sanctimonious mediocrity, and Morgenstern could not but thrill to this imagery. The dancing Zarathustra, the Zarathustra of height, fire, laughter and affirmation — the one who praised "das Kind im Manne" (the child in man) — this is the Zarathustra who could also stand as godfather to some of Morgenstern's humorous poetry. The *Galgenlieder* (Gallow's Songs, 1905) are dedicated to "The Child in Man" and quotes Zarathustra: "In every true man there is a child who wishes to play": the opening quatrain shouts from the page "Let molecules rave / whatever they concoct! / Leave the fiddling, leave the fussing! / Sanctify all thing ecstatic!" (*WB* 3, 59). A ponderous interpretation however, which seeks Nietzsche everywhere, is mischievously debunked by Morgenstern; in "Das Gebet" (The Prayer) the fawns may pray in a manner which brings to the educated reader echoes of Zarathustra's "Midnight Song" ("halb acht! halb neun!") but, the poet insists, godfather to this poem was *not* Nietzsche — "o you profound interpreters!" (*WB 3*, 630). Punning and play, an "Umwortung aller Worte,"[13] may be derived from Morgenstern's reading of the journalist and satirist Fritz Mauthner, but it is difficult not to hear the Nietzschean presence in "Palmas Mutter" (*WB 3*, 277) who, "still and plainly" utters the following: "Nahst du Frauen, vergiß die Geißel nicht" (If you approach women, do not forget the scourge); it is, she explains, spoken by a philosopher who was "tormented by women," a reference, presumably, to Nietzsche's relationship with Lou Andreas-Salomé. Oblique and entertaining references are also made to Kant and Schopenhauer, also to Stefan George's *l'art pour l'art*, particularly interesting is the reference to Max Klinger in the "*Ordens-Epos*" of 1894 (*WB 3*, 346). Morgenstern was a keen admirer of Klinger's work, frequently linking him with Böcklin, and felt a great affinity to Klinger, even contemplating dedicating his second volume of poetry to him. In Leipzig he had seen Klinger's famous painting "Christus im Olymp" and was deeply moved — "That was a red-letter day. . . I can as easily describe the Alps as I can this painting!" (in a letter of 12.9.1897). Christ and the Greeks — the juxtaposition is startling and thought-provoking. Christ and Apollo? Christ and Dionysus? Nietzsche as the last disciple of Dionysus, Dionysus, who appeared in emerald lightning to Ariadne on the very brink of Nietzsche's mental collapse, Dionysus as an exemplification of the will to power, of life-affirmation, of "Ja-sagen"? Morgenstern's reaction to Klinger's painting is predictable, moved as he was as though before a vast manifestation of nature.[14] But there is also a reluctance to indulge in earnest metaphysical speculation — humour intercedes at this stage, a humour not incompatible with mystical insights. "I define humour as a way of looking at the finite from the point of view of the infinite" (*WB 3*, 891), humour being the antidote to self-satisfaction and self-importance.[15] Nietzsche, at the end of his mental life, announced that he would rather be a "Hanswurst," or buffoon, than a saint (6, 365). Zarathustra's laughter and his conquest of the spirit of gravity, informs many of Morgenstern's humorous poems — an all-too-earnest interpretation is forbidden.

> Humour saved him [Morgenstern] from Nietzsche's nihilism, from Ibsen's icy, hopeless critique of society [. . .] it became the spiritual therapeutic of a mystic who can now face — and heal — an

unbalanced experience of suffering, a self-centred anchoretism and an arrogant denial of the world.[16]

The anthroposophist Friedrich Hiebel sees in humour Morgenstern's way of overcoming solipsism and a bridge towards the salvation offered by Steiner. It is doubtful from what has been argued in this chapter that the experience of Nietzsche was a nihilistic one — both Morgenstern and Steiner had seen in Nietzsche a thinker who strove to overcome baseness and self deception and to realise the highest potential in man; the doctrine of eternal recurrence, although rejected by both would be seen by both as Zarathustra's vision of eternity whose acceptance brings highest joy. Steiner would substitute the concept of reincarnation and develop a fantastic cosmology of aeons, Saturn, spiritual energies, of sun, moon and earth as one entity, of Elohim and spirits of light, of physical, aetherial and astral bodies, of cosmic hierarchies, sunseparation, logos and irradiation by solar light, of *Karma* and reincarnation. It is to this world that Morgenstern would turn to in the end, although, as late as 1913. Nietzsche is listed (with Steiner) as one of "the most important events of my life."[17] The last anthology, *Wir fanden einen Pfad* (1914) is dedicated to Steiner whose "Sonnengeist" illuminates the earth (*WB 2. 204*); Morgenstern's mystical pilgrimage ends with a glimpse of a temple in high mountains with a steep path leading up to it (*WB 2, 211*). In *his* high mountains Nietzsche celebrated the feast of festivals, the marriage of light and darkness, the rending of the "horrid veil" and Zarathustra's epiphany. There is no other communicant.

Notes

[1] Quotations from Morgenstern will be taken from the definitive edition *Werke und Briefe* (Stuttgart: Urachhaus) which supersedes all others. The edition has so far appeared in five volumes, volume one (*Lyrik* 1887–1905, ed. by Martin Kießig, 1988) and volume two (*Lyrik* 1906–1914, by the same editor, 1992); volume three (*Humoristische Lyrik*, ed. by Maurice Cureau, 1990); volume five (*Aphorismen*, ed. by Reinhardt Habel, 1987) and volume six (*Kritische Schriften*, ed. Helmut Gumtau, 1987). This edition will be referred to in the text as *WB* plus volume and page number. The *Briefe* have not yet appeared and will consequently be quoted from another source: here *Gesammelte Briefe*, Munich, 1962.

[2] William Witte, "Humour and Mysticism in Christian Morgenstern's Poetry," *German Life and Letters* 1 (1947–48), 124–130.

[3] Christian Morgenstern, *Sämtliche Galgenlieder* (Zurich: Manesse, 1985), 505.

[4] In a letter to Efraim Frisch (18 December 1902), quoted in R. Mazur, *The Late Lyric Poetry of Christian Morgenstern* (Ann Arbor: University of Michigan, 1974), 26.

[5] For a discussion of eagle and snake in *Thus spake Zarathustra* see David Thatcher, "Eagle and Serpent in *Zarathustra*," *Nietzsche Studien* 6 (1977), 240–260.

[6] Rudolf Steiner, *Mein Lebensgang. Ausgewählte Werke* (Frankfurt a. M.: Fischer, 1985), vol. 7, 252–254. Such descriptions of the insane Nietzsche were not uncommon at the time: Stanislaus Przybyszewski compared the sick man (whom Przybyszewski saw on a veranda in Weimar) to "a gigantic ruin, as though a mighty, holy Gothic cathedral had collapsed, filling the observer with the shuddering thrill of something monstrous!" (in Sander Gilman and Ingeborg Reichenbach [eds.], *Begegnungen mit Nietzsche* [Bonn: Bouvier, 1981], 773).

[7] Steven Aschheim, *The Nietzsche Legacy in Germany 1890–1900* (Berkeley, Los Angeles, London: U of California P, 1992), 215.

[8] Michael Meyer, *Ibsen*, 400.

[9] R. Mazur, *Late Lyric Poetry*, 43.

[10] For a comparison with Gerhart Hauptmann's *Sonnen Meditationen* see Philip Mellen, "A Syncretistic Odyssey," *Germanic Review* 70 (Winter 1995), 1.

[11] Rudolf Steiner, *Lebensgang*, 250.

[12] Aschheim, 213.

[13] Jethro Bithell, *Modern German Literature 1880–1950* (London: Methuen, 3. ed., 1959), 66.

[14] Richard Dehmel was less reverential in his "Jesus und Psyche. Phantasie bei Klinger," where Christ removes the crown of thorns and prepares for a wedding night with Psyche to the accompaniment of Beethoven's Ninth Symphony. In Richard Dehmel, *Gesammelte Werke in 3 Bänden* (Berlin: Fischer, 1918), vol. 1, 190.

[15] Witte, *Humour and Mysticism*, 125.

[16] Friedrich Hiebel, *Christian Morgenstern. Wende und Aufbruch unseres Jahrhunderts* (Bern: Francke, 1957), 9.

[17] Ernst Kretschmer, *Christian Morgenstern* (Stuttgart: Metzler, 1985), 1.

Epilogue

"WITH THE DITHYRAMBS OF THE LAST PART of Book Three of *Zarathustra*, the 'Die Sieben Siegel', I soared a thousand miles above what was hitherto called poetry" (6, 305): this claim of Nietzsche's is remarkable indeed. This book has sought to explore the subjection of a group of largely unfamiliar writers to Nietzsche's forbidding stature, his hyperbolic claims and powerful imagery. The prophet whose cave symbolised the dark, Dionysian powers of the earth greets the sun, Apollo's glowing emblem — Dionysian ecstasies and flickering solar energies have occupied us here, as have a cosmogenetic Eros, a celestial reveller, blood-radiance, life-worship and a cult of harsh heroic Christianity, together with archers who are exhorted to aim at the furthest stars and to seek the cosmic light. There is no neoromantic velleity here but an exhortation and a yearning for high places, for Roman ruthlessness, for Life unencumbered with ratiocination, for *Kosmos Atheos* and a stringent, religious absolutism. And Zarathustra, the one who preached the need for chaos from which a dancing star could be born (4, 19), and for a will so strong that the stars would revolve around it (4, 80) would not have despised these mythopoeic and life-adoring visionaries with whom we have concerned ourselves. Nietzsche may, mischievously, have suggested to his sister that his "son" Zarathustra was "one of my preparations, my intermezzos" and warn her not to assume that father and son were identical:[1] *this* work was the one which "contained, in the sharpest delineation, an image of my essential being [. . .] having within it so much of what I have suffered and personally experienced."[2] The euphoric claims of *Ecce Homo* need not be repeated here, but the description of the work as a deep well into which no pail descends without bringing back "gold and goodness" (6, 259) is one with which we may concur.

Writing of Wagner's tetralogy *Der Ring des Nibelungen* Nietzsche explains that "the *poetic* element in Wagner is seen in the fact that, in both the visual and the perceptible, Wagner does not think in concepts, but mythically [. . .] Myth is not erected upon a foundation of rational thought (as the children of an artificial culture have suspected): myth is itself a form of thinking" (1, 485). The same has been claimed for

Nietzsche himself: using the above quotation O'Flaherty argues that "in his prose writing Nietzsche is a Greek, in *Zarathustra* he has become a Jew. However much or little the Hebraic mode of thought requires a historical element, it is essentially mythic."[3] I have written elsewhere that the mythic underpinning of so many works written in the twentieth century owes an incalculable debt to Wagner's art, where mythical archetypes are brought to the surface, instinct with symbolic resonance. Wagner's symbolism is, of course, enhanced by music of unparalleled force of suggestion; in Nietzsche's case it is the striking use of metaphorical or analogical imagery, in *Zarathustra* above all, which encouraged an esoteric mythology.[4] Wagner drew on ancient legends: Nietzsche drew on the figure of Zarathustra but moulded this image in a highly idiosyncratic manner and endowed it with potent attributes and accoutrements. The excesses of the "Martyr and Prophet" cult notwithstanding (and the Kitsch of a Paul Friedrich, with his silver and gold Zarathustra, beribboned and girt with a leopard skin)[5] — *this* Zarathustra image struck with the force of lightning, and a life-enhancing myth was created.

For Thomas Mann, Nietzsche, Wagner, and Schopenhauer were "a triple star of spirits, eternally conjoined";[6] writing of Wagner's music Mann tells in passionate terms of his reaction to it, the hours of deep and single bliss in the midst of the theatre throngs, the hours of nervous and intellectual rapture, the perceptions of great and moving import, such as only Wagner's art vouchsafes. Like Wagner, Nietzsche spoke to those disenchanted with platitudes and tepid conformity, to those who sought loneliness and self-transcendence; images of height, as we have noted, of stellar radiance, sunrise, fire and struggle ousted the world of domestic drabness and vulgar superficiality. Man is now seen against a cosmic dimension, or on a high mountain peak, bathed in sunlight. Life is extolled beyond normal categories and transformed into a rhapsodic corybantic dance. Struggle and self-overcoming, *amor fati*, the aesthetics of health and joy are the watchwords, a denial of decadence, of life-denying creeds; the vision of the world is one of godlessness if God is equated with morbid life denial. And Nietzsche-Zarathustra is passionate in his love for eternity, a love which is sanctified by blessing. Mombert saw eternity in a crystal's flash, Däubler in the Northern Light which guaranteed mystical illumination; Pannwitz sought the eternal recurrence in the footsteps of his "only friend." For Klages it was Life which was to be worshipped, suffused by a cosmogenetic eroticism; for Schuler "open life" (exemplified by Imperial Rome and certain post-classical figures such as Ludwig II) and rapturous dance expressed an ultimate affirmation. For Derleth a stark and violent

Christianity was fused with a will to power and a hierarchical structure; for Morgenstern the grave at Röcken radiated powerful energies. Nietzsche's writing was experienced as a cleansing fire, burning away the dross and igniting the tinder to a glowing incandescence.

A variation of the "Song of Seven Seals," Zarathustra's impassioned expression of his love for eternity, tells of his desire "to press his hand upon the wax of millennia . . . to melt the stars in the goblet of joy" (14, 325); a "golden-eyed eternity" gleams on dark waters as the boat, a golden vessel, floats amongst the "icy peaks" of life, greeting life's "innocence" and "a monstrous redemption" (14, 326). Rarely has eternity been greeted in such a sensuous fashion, and the nuptial "ring of rings" celebrates an ecstatic affirmation. The poem "Fame and Eternity" from the *Dionysos-Dithyramben* hails the "shield of necessity, the highest constellation of being!" together with that "table of eternal imagery" which inflames the love of the poet and confirms his love for eternal existence (6, 404–405). And such a mentor spoke immediately to those who moved easily in cosmic realms or who sought to praise life as a talismanic presence, a "continuous, deeply moving shudder [. . .], a wild, woeful exultation!"[7] Small wonder that our lost generation are in his thrall.

Wolfskehl will have the last word here, as he did in chapter 3. His threnody "Zarathustra" (included as one of the *Nänien*) speaks of the sage who had sat enthroned by the gateway whilst the turmoil of life, its "joy, pain and tumult," passed year after year;[8] it was at that gateway that Zarathustra encountered the dwarf and faced the momentous meaning of the eternal recurrence. The "highest form of life" (Zarathustra) accepts the consequences of the doctrine and, in ever-increasing loneliness and ecstatic intoxication, is enveloped in the crepuscular radiance of sunset. The radiance now becomes a glowing flame which engulfs him, the one who, as on a funeral pyre, is transfigured by Heraclitean fire. The physical body is incinerated whilst the spirit, a powerful tongue of flame, lives and consumes. A fulsome tribute, perhaps, but one which rightly speaks of an awesome brilliance. It is the illumination of unfamiliar corners which this book has tried to describe in the hope that future scholars will probe more deeply under Nietzsche's tutelage.

Notes

[1] *Briefe*, vol. 7, 48.

[2] *Briefe*, vol. 3, 1, 326.

[3] O'Flaherty, *The Quarrel of Reason with Itself. Essays on Hamann, Michaelis, Lessing and Nietzsche* (Columbia, SC: Camden House, 1988), 239.

[4] For a convincing comparison between Wagner's *Ring* and *Thus spake Zarathustra* see Roger Hollinrake, *Nietzsche, Wagner and the Philosophy of Pessimism* (London: Allen and Unwin, 1982).

[5] Aschheim, *The Nietzsche Legacy in Germany 1890–1900* (Berkeley, Los Angeles, London: U of California P, 1992), 36.

[6] Thomas Mann, *Gesammelte Werke in 13 Bänden*, vol. 12, 79.

[7] Ludwig Klages, *Rhythmen und Runen. Nachlaß herausgegeben von ihm selbst* (Leipzig: Johann Ambrosius Barth, 1944), 270.

[8] Karl Wolfskehl, "Zarathustra," *Blätter für die Kunst* 5, vol. 1 (1901), 7.

Works Consulted

I LIST HERE ONLY THE WRITINGS that have been of use in the making of this book. This bibliography is by no means a complete record of all the works and sources I have consulted; in the case of Nietzsche it is highly selective. But it indicates the substance and range of reading upon which I have formed my ideas, and I arrange it to serve as a help for those who wish to pursue the study further.

General Surveys

Abrams, M. H. *The Mirror and the Lamp. Romantic Theory and Critical Tradition.* New York: Oxford UP, 1953.

——. *Natural Supernaturalism. Tradition and Revolution in Romantic Literature.* New York: Oxford UP, 1971.

Ahearn, Edward J. *Visionary Fictions. Apocalyptic Writing from Blake to the Modern Age.* Newhaven: Yale UP, 1996.

Bachofen, J. J. *Das Mutterrecht.* (2d ed.) Basel: Benno Schwabe, 1897.

Baeumler, Alfred. *Das mystische Weltalter. Bachofens romantische Deutung des Altertums.* Munich: Beck, 1965.

Bloom, Harold. *The Anxiety of Influence. A Theory of Poetry.* New York: Oxford UP, 1973.

Bohrer, Karl-Heinz. *Mythos und Moderne.* Frankfurt a. M.: Suhrkamp, 1983.

Borchmeyer, Dieter, ed. *Wege des Mythos in der Moderne. Richard Wagners "Der Ring des Nibelungen."* Munich: DTV, 1987.

Bowen, Robert. *Universal Ice. Science and Ideology in the Nazi State.* London: Belhaven Press, 1993.

Breuer, Stefan. *Ästhetischer Fundamentalismus. Stefan George und der deutsche Antimodernismus.* Darmstadt: Wissenschaftliche Buchgesellschaft, 1993.

Cantwell, R. W. "The Friedrichshagener Dichterkreis. A Study of Change and Continuity in the German Literature of the Jahrhundertwende." U. of Michigan, diss., 1967.

Darge, Elisabeth. *Lebensbejahung in der deutschen Literatur um 1900.* Breslau: Deutschkundliche Arbeiten, 1934.

Faber, Richard and Renate Schlesier, eds. *Die Restauration der Götter. Antike Religion und Neopaganismus.* Würzburg: Königshausen und Neumann, 1986.

Frank, Manfred. *Der kommende Gott.* Frankfurt a. M.: Suhrkamp, 1982.

———. *Gott im Exil.* Frankfurt a. M.: Suhrkamp, 1988.

Frecot, J., J. F. Geist and D. Kerbs. *Fidus 1868–1948. Zur aesthetischen Praxis bürgerlicher Fluchtbewegungen.* Munich: Rogner und Bernhard, 1972.

Godwin, Joscelyn. *Arktos. The Polar Myth in Science, Symbolism and Nazi Survival.* London: Thames and Hudson, 1993.

Green, Martin. *Mountain of Truth. The Counterculture Begins. Ascona 1900–1920.* Hanover, NH and London: UP of New England, 1986.

Gruber, Bettina. ed. *Erfahrung und System. Mystik und Esoterik in der Literatur der Moderne.* Opladen: 1977.

Hamburger, Michael. *From Prophecy to Exorcism. The Premisses of Modern German Literature.* London: Longmans, 1965.

———. *A Proliferation of Prophets. Essays on German Writers from Nietzsche to Brecht.* Manchester: Carcanet, 1983.

Hein, Peter Ulrich. *Die Brücke ins Geisterreich. Künstlerische Avantgarde zwischen Kulturkritik und Faschimus.* Reinbek bei Hamburg: Rowohlt, 1992.

Heller, Erich. *The Disinherited. Mind. Essays in Modern German Literature and Thought.* Cambridge: Bowes and Bowes, 1952.

Hermand, Jost. *Der Schein des schönen Lebens. Studien zur Jahrhundertwende.* Frankfurt a. M.: Athenäum, 1972.

Kemper, Peter. ed. *Macht des Mythos—Ohnmacht der Vernunft?* Frankfurt a. M.: Fischer, 1989.

Kern, Hans. *Von Paracelsus bis Klages. Studien zur Philosophie des Lebens.* Berlin: Widukind Verlag, 1942.

Krause, Jürgen. *"Märtyrer" und "Prophet". Studien zum Nietzsche-Kult in der bildenden Kunst der Jahrhundertwende.* Berlin: de Gruyter, 1984.

Lessing, Theodor. *Einmal und nie wieder.* Gütersloh: Bertelsmann, 1969.

Linse, Ulrich. *Barfüssige Propheten. Erlöser der zwanziger Jahre.* Berlin: Siedler, 1983.

Löwith, Karl. *Von Hegel zu Nietzsche. Der revolutionäre Bruch im Denken des 19. Jahrhunderts.* Zurich: Europa, 1941.

Lukács, Georg. *Die Zerstörung der Vernunft. Der Weg des Irrationalismus von Schelling zu Hitler.* Berlin: Aufbau, 1955.

Mosse, George L. "The Mystical Origins of National Socialism." *Journal of the History of Ideas* 22, 1961.

Noll, Richard. *The Jung Cult. Origins of a Charismatic Movement.* Princeton: Princeton UP, 1994.

Nordau, Max. *Degeneration*, translated from the second edition of the work, with an introduction by George L. Mosse. Lincoln: U of Nebraska P, 1993.

O'Flaherty, James C. *The Quarrel of Reason with Itself. Essays on Hamann, Michaelis, Lessing and Nietzsche.* Columbia, SC: Camden House, 1988.

Pascal, Roy. *From Naturalism to Expressionism. German Literature and Society 1880–1918.* London: Weidenfeld and Nicolson, 1973.

Quinn, Malcolm. *The Swastika. Constructing the Symbol.* London: Routledge, 1994.

Reventlow, Franziska. *Herrn Dames Aufzeichnungen, oder Begebenheiten aus einem merkwürdigen Stadtteil.* Berlin: Buchverlag der Morgen, 1990.

——. *Tagebücher 1895–1910*, ed. Else Reventlow. Frankfurt a. M.: Fischer, 1976.

Rickert, Heinrich. *Die Philosophie des Lebens: Darstellung und Kritik der philosophischen Modeströmungen unserer Zeit.* (2d ed.) Tübingen: J. C. B. Mohr Verlag, 1922.

Rosenberg, Alfred. *Der Mythus des 20. Jahrhunderts. Eine Wertung der seelisch-geistigen Gestaltenkämpfe unserer Zeit.* Munich: Hoheneichen Verlag, 1936.

Rosteutscher, J. H. W. *Die Wiederkunft des Dionysos. Der naturmystische Irrationalismus in Deutschland.* Bern: Francke, 1947.

Sokel, Walter. *The Writer in Extremis. Expressionism in Twentieth Century German Literature.* Stanford: Stanford UP, 1959.

Sprengel, Peter. *Die Wirklichkeit der Mythen. Untersuchungen zum Werk Gerhart Hauptmanns.* Berlin: Erich Schmidt Verlag, 1982.

Taylor, Seth. *Left-wing Nietzscheans.* Berlin: de Gruyter, 1990.

Vogel, Martin. *Apollinisch und Dionysisch. Geschichte eines genialen Irrtums.* Regensburg: Gustav Bosse Verlag, 1966.

Wagner-Egelhaaf, Martina. *Mystik und Moderne. Die visionäre Ästhetik der deutschen Literatur im 20. Jahrhundert.* Stuttgart: Metzler, 1989.

Wesel, Uwe. *Der Mythos vom Matriarchat.* Frankfurt a. M.: Suhrkamp, 1980.

Wiedmann, August. *The German Quest for Primal Origins in Art, Culture and Politics.* Lewiston/Queenston/Lampeter: Edwin Mellen Press, 1995.

Wilson, Colin. *Rudolf Steiner. The Man and his Vision.* Wellingborough: Aquarian Press, 1985.

Friedrich Nietzsche

Ackermann, Robert J. *Nietzsche: A Frenzied Look.* Amherst: U of Massachusetts, 1990.

Aschheim, Steven. *The Nietzsche Legacy in Germany 1890–1900.* Berkeley, Los Angeles, London: U of California P, 1992.

Bennholdt-Thomsen, Anke. *Nietzsches "Also sprach Zarathustra" als literarisches Phänomen. Eine Revision.* Frankfurt a. M.: Athenäum, 1974.

Bindschedler, Marie. *Nietzsche und die poetische Lüge.* Berlin: de Gruyter, 1966.

Brinton, Crane. *Nietzsche.* New York: Harper and Rowe, 1965.

de Bleeckert, S. *"Also sprach Zarathustra* : Die Neugestaltung der *Geburt der Tragödie."* Nietzsche-Studien 3, 1979.

Cauchi, Francesca. *Zarathustra contra Zarathustra. The Tragic Buffoon.* Aldershot/Brookfield, VT: Ashgate, 1998.

Cosineau, Robert J. *Zarathustra and the Ethical Ideal.* Amsterdam: J. Benjamins, 1991.

Del Caro, Adrian. "The Immolation of Zarathustra. A Look at *The Fire Beacon."* Colloquia Germanica 3–4 (1984), 251–256.

Deleuze, Gilles. *Nietzsche and Philosophy.* New York: Columbia UP, 1983.

de Man, Paul. *Allegories of Reading. Figural Language in Rousseau, Nietzsche, Rilke and Proust.* New Haven: Yale UP, 1979.

Derrida, Jaques. *Spurs. Nietzsche's Styles.* Chicago: Chicago UP, 1978.

Duhamel, Roland. *Nietzsches Zarathustra: Mystiker des Nihilismus. Eine Interpretation.* Würzburg: Königshausen und Neumann, 1991.

Foster, John B. *Heirs to Dionysus. A Nietzschean Current in Literary Modernism.* Princeton, NJ: Princeton UP, 1981.

Gadamer, H. G. "Das Drama Zarathustras." *Nietzsche Studien* 15, 1986.

Gilman, Sander. *Nietzschean Parody. An Introduction to Reading Nietzsche.* Bonn: Bouvier, 1976.

Goicoechea, D. (ed.). *The Great Year of Zarathustra 1881–1981.* New York: Lanham, 1983.

Haase, Marie-Luise. "Der Übermensch in *Also Sprach Zarathustra* und im Zarathustra-Nachlaß 1882–1885." *Nietzsche Studien* 13, 1984.

Happ, Winfried. *Nietzsches Zarathustra als moderne Tragödie.* Frankfurt a. M.: Peter Lang, 1987.

Hawes, James. *Nietzsche and the End of Freedom. The Neo-Romantic Dilemma in Kafka, the Brothers Mann, Rilke and Musil 1904–1914.* Frankfurt a. M.: Peter Lang, 1993.

Hayman, Ronald. *Nietzsche. A Critical Life.* New York: Oxford UP, 1980.

Heidegger, Martin. *Nietzsche* (2 vols.). Pfullingen: Neske, 1961.

Heller, Erich. *The Importance of Nietzsche. Ten Essays.* Chicago: U of Chicago P, 1988.

Higgins, Kathleen. *Nietzsche's Zarathustra.* Philadelphia: Temple UP, 1987.

Hollingdale, R. J. *Nietzsche, The Man and his Philosophy.* London: Routledge and Kegan Paul, 1965.

Hollinrake, Roger. *Nietzsche, Wagner and the Philosophy of Pessimism.* London: Allen and Unwin, 1982.

Jaspers, Karl. *Nietzsche. An Introduction to the Understanding of his Philosophical Activity.* Chicago: Regnery, 1965.

Kaufmann, Walter. *Nietzsche. Philosopher, Psychologist, Antichrist.* (4th ed.), Princeton, NJ: Princeton UP, 1974.

Klages, Ludwig. *Die psychologischen Errungenschaften Nietzsches.* Leipzig: Karl Ambrosius Barth, 1926.

Krummel, Richard Frank. *Nietzsche und der deutsche Geist.* Berlin and New York: de Gruyter, 2 vols., 1974 and 1983.

Lampert, Lawrence. *Nietzsche's Teaching. An Interpretation of Thus Spake Zarathustra.* New Haven: Yale UP, 1986.

Löwith, Karl. *Nietzsches Philosophie der Ewigen Wiederkehr des Gleichen.* Stuttgart: Kohlhammer, 1986.

Luke, F. D. "Nietzsche and the Imagery of Height" in *Nietzsche. Imagery and Thought. A Collection of Essays,* ed. by Malcolm Pasley. London: Methuen, 1978.

Magnus, Bernd. "Eternal Recurrence." *Nietzsche Studien* 8, 1979.

Miller, C. A. "Nietzsche's 'Daughters of the Desert'. A Reconsideration." *Nietzsche Studien* 2, 1973.

Montinari, Mazzino. *Nietzsche Lesen.* Berlin: de Gruyter, 1980.

Nehamas, Alexander. *Nietzsche. Life as Literature.* Cambridge, MA: Harvard UP, 1985.

Nelson, Donald F. "Nietzsche, Zarathustra and Jesus Redivivus: the Unholy Trinity." *Germanic Review* 47, no. 1 (Jan.) 1973.

O'Flaherty, J. C. "The Intuitive Mode of Reasoning in *Zarathustra.*" *International Studies in Philosophy* 15, no. 2, 1983.

Parkes, Graham. *Composing the Soul. Reaches of Nietzsche's Psychology.* Chicago: Chicago UP, 1994.

Paronis, Margot. *"Also sprach Zarathustra". Die Ironie Nietzsches als Gestaltungsprinzip.* Bonn: Grundmann, 1976.

Pasley, Malcolm (ed.). *Nietzsche. Imagery and Thought. A Collection of Essays.* London: Methuen, 1978.

Pütz, Peter. *Friedrich Nietzsche.* Stuttgart: Metzler, 1967.

Pieper, Anna-Marie. *"Ein Seil geknüpft zwischen Tier und Übermensch". Philosophische Erläuterungen zu Nietzsches erstem Zarathustra.* Stuttgart: Klett-Cotta, 1990.

Rolleston, James. "Nietzsche, Expressionism and Modern Poetics." *Nietzsche Studien* 9, 1980.

Reichert, Herbert. *Friedrich Nietzsche's Impact on Modern German Literature, Five Essays.* Chapel Hill: U of North Carolina P, 1975.

Schacht, Richard, *Nietzsche.* London: Routledge and Kegan Paul, 1983.

Schlechta, Karl. *Nietzsches Großer Mittag.* Frankfurt a. M.: Klostermann, 1954.

Shapiro, Gary. *Nietzschean Narratives.* Bloomington: Indiana UP, 1989.

Silk, M. S. and J. P. Stern. *Nietzsche on Tragedy.* Cambridge: Cambridge UP, 1981.

Stern, J. P. *A Study of Nietzsche.* Cambridge: Cambridge UP, 1979.

Thatcher, David. "Eagle and Serpent in *Zarathustra.*" *Nietzsche Studien* 6, 1977.

Thumfort, Stefan. *Der Leib in Nietzsches "Zarathustra."* Frankfurt a. M.: Peter Lang, 1990.

Whitlock, G. *Returning to Sils Maria. A Commentary to Nietzsche's Also sprach Zarathustra.* Frankfurt a. M.: Peter Lang, 1990.

Rudolf Pannwitz

Guth, Alfred. *Rudolf Pannwitz. Un européen, penseur et poète allemand en quête de totalité.* Paris: Librairie Klincksieck, 1973.

Jaeckle, Erwin. "Rudolf Pannwitz. Eine Einführung." In *Hugo von Hofmannsthal — Rudolph Pannwitz Briefwechsel 1907–1926.* Ed. Gerhard Schuster. Frankfurt a. M.: Fischer, 1993.

——. *Verlorene und Vergessene. Rudolf Pannwitz. Eine Auswahl aus seinem Werk.* Wiesbaden: Steiner Verlag, 1983.

Koch, Hans-Joachim. "Die Nietzsche-Rezeption durch Rudolf Pannwitz. Eine kritische Kosmologie." *Nietzsche Studien* 26, 1997.

Rukser, Udo. *Über den Denker Rudolf Pannwitz.* Meisenheim am Glan: Verlag Anton Hain, 1970.

Samuel, R. and Thomas S. Hinton. *Expressionism in German Life, Literature and the Theatre 1910–1924.* Cambridge: Heffer, 1939.

Schuster, Gerhard. ed. *Hugo von Hofmannsthal — Rudolf Pannwitz Briefwechsel 1907–1926*. Frankfurt a. M.: Fischer, 1993.

Weeks, Charles A. "Hofmannsthal, Pannwitz und *Der Turm* von Hugo von Hofmannsthal." *Jahrbuch des Freien Deutschen Hochstifts*, 1987.

Weltmann, Lutz. "Eminent European. An approach to the work of Rudolf Pannwitz." *German Life and Letters* 9, 1955–56.

Alfred Mombert

Adorno, Th. W. "Lieder nach Hebbel und Mombert" in *Berg. Der Meister des kleinsten Übergangs*. Vienna: Lafite, 1968.

Barker, Christine. "Alfred Mombert's Cosmology. The Aeon Trilogy." *German Life and Letters* 29, 1975–76.

Behrmann, A. "Das Werk Alfred Momberts im Spiegel seiner Deuter und Kritiker." Diss., F. U. Berlin, 1956.

Benndorf, Friedrich Kurt. *Alfred Mombert. Der Dichter und Mystiker*. Leipzig: Xenien, 1910.

Büchler, Frank. *Alfred Mombert: siderische Sicht. Wasserscheide zweier Zeitalter*. Heidelberg: Lothar Stiehm, 1970.

Benz, Richard. *Der Dichter Alfred Mombert*. Heidelberg: Pfeffer, 1947.

Carossa, Hans. "Lebensbericht" in *Ungleiche Welten*. Stuttgart: Insel, 1951.

——. "Bekenntnis zu Mombert" in *Das Inselschiff* 13, no. 2, 1932.

Fischer, Max. "Alfred Mombert. 1872–1942." *Monatshefte* 44, 1952.

Haenicke, Hans. "Alfred Mombert" in *Dichtung und Dasein. Gesammelte Essays*. Berlin: Henssel, 1950.

——. *Alfred Mombert. Eine Einführung in sein Werk und eine Auswahl*. Wiesbaden: Akademie der Wissenschaften und der Literatur, 1952.

Herberg, Elisabeth. *Die Sprache Alfred Momberts. Die Prinzipien ihrer Gestaltung und ihrer Zusammenhänge*. Diss., Hamburg, 1959.

Hermand, Jost. "Die Urfrühe. Zum Prozeß des mystischen 'Bilderns' bei Mombert." *Monatshefte* 53, no. 3, 1961.

Heselhaus, Clemens. "Alfred Momberts Bildersprache" in *Deutsche Lyrik der Moderne von Nietzsche bis Yvan Goll*. Düsseldorf: Bagel, 1962.

Mombert, Alfred. *Ausstellung zum 25. Todestag. Badische Landesbibliothek, Ausstellungskatalog*. Karlsruhe: F. A. Schmidt, 1967.

Morse, B. J. ed. *Alfred Mombert, Briefe 1893–1942*. Heidelberg/Darmstadt: Verlag Lambert-Schneider, 1961.

Pannwitz, Rudolf. "Momberts Aeon Drama." *Die Flöte* 2, nos. 8–9, 1919

Rang, Bernhard. "Vorläufer des Expressionismus," in *Expressionismus. Gestalten einer literarischen Bewegung*, ed. H. Friedemann and O. Mann. Heidelberg: W. Rothe, 1956.

Scott-James, Marilyn. "Constellar Imagery as the structural basis for 'Der himmlische Zecher.'" Diss., University of Oregon, 1975.

Usinger, Fritz. "Der Dichter des Weltalls." *Neue literarische Welt*, Jg. 3. Darmstadt: 1952.

Alfred Schuler

Huch, Roderich. *Alfred Schuler, Ludwig Klages, Stefan George. Erinnerungen an Kreise und Krisen der Jahrhundertwende in München-Schwabing.* Amsterdam: Castrum Peregreni, 1973.

Pauen, Michael. *Alfred Schuler: Heidentum und Heilsgeschichte.* Amsterdam: Castrum Peregrini, 1993.

Müller, Baal. "'Mein Abgrund neben mir.' Alfred Schuler zwischen Esoterik und emphatischer Moderne" in Bettina Gruber (ed.) *Erfahrung und System. Mystik und Esoterik in der Literatur der Moderne.* Opladen: 1997, 157–181.

Plumpe, Gerhard. *Alfred Schuler. Chaos und Neubeginn. Zur Funktion des Mythos in der Moderne.* Berlin: Agora Verlag, 1978.

——. "Alfred Schuler und die 'Kosmische Runde'" in Manfred Frank. *Gott im Exil. Vorlesungen über die neue Mythologie.* Frankfurt a. M.: Suhrkamp, 1988.

Ludwig Klages

Alksnis, Gunnar. "Ludwig Klages and His Attack on Rationalism." Diss., Kansas State University, 1970.

Balmer, Heinrich, ed. *Martin Heidegger und Ludwig Klages. Daseinsanalytik und Metaphysik.* Munich: Kindler, 1976.

Fuld, Werner. "Walther Benjamins Beziehung zu Ludwig Klages." *Akzente,* 28, 1981.

Hinton Thomas, Richard. "Nietzsche in Weimar Germany and the Case of Ludwig Klages" in *The Weimar Dilemma. Intellectuals in the Weimar Republic*, ed. Anthony Phelan. Manchester: Manchester UP, 1985.

Kasdorff, Hans. *Ludwig Klages: Werk und Wirkung. Einführung und kommentierte Bibliographie.* 2 vols. Bonn: Bouvier, 1969 and 1974.

Kuckartz, Wilfried. *Ludwig Klages als Erzieher.* Bonn: Bouvier, 1978.

Schröder, Hans Eggert. *Ludwig Klages. Die Geschichte seines Lebens. Teil 1: Die Jugend*, Bonn: Bouvier, 1966. *Teil 2: Das Werk. 1. Halbband*, Bonn: Bouvier, 1972; *Teil 2: Das Werk. 2. Halbband* ed. Franz Tenigl, Bonn: Bouvier, 1992.

Wiedmann, August. *The German Quest for Primal Origins in Art, Culture and Politics 1900–1933*. Lewiston/Queenston/Lampeter: Edwin Mellen, 1995.

Ludwig Derleth

Aler, Jan. "Ludwig Derleth. 1870–1948. Ein katholischer Mystiker, der auch auf Nietzsche und Kierkegaard hörte." *Duitse Kroniek* 33, 1983.

Aler, Jan, ed. *Gestalten um Stefan George*. Amsterdam: Rodopi, 1984.

Balthasar, Hans Urs von. *Apokalypse der deutschen Seele*. Vol. 3. Salzburg: Verlag Anton Pustet, 1939.

Derleth, Christine, *Das Fleischlich-Geistige. Meine Erinnerungen an Ludwig Derleth*. Gladenbach/Hessen: Hinder and Deelmann, 1973.

Furness, Raymond. "Ludwig Derleth and the *Proklamationen*." *Forum for Modern Language Studies* 15:1, 1979.

Jost, Dominik. *Ludwig Derleth. Gestalt und Leistung*. Stuttgart: Kohlhammer, 1965.

———. *Die Dichtung Ludwig Derleths. Einführung in das Werk*. Gladenbach/Hessen: Hinder and Deelmann, 1974.

———. *Ludwig Derleth Gedenkbuch*. Amsterdam: Castrum Peregrini, 1958.

Ratzki, Anne. *Die Elitevorstellungen im Werke Ludwig Derleths und ihre Grundlage in seinem Bilde vom Menschen*. Cologne: Druck Walter Kleikamp, 1968.

Theodor Däubler

Eppelsheimer, Rudolf. *Mimesis und Imitatio Christi bei Loerke, Däubler, Morgenstern und Hölderlin*. Bern and Munich: Francke, 1968.

Huder, Walter. "Else Lasker-Schüler und Theodor Däubler. Zwei tragische Monster des poetischen Expressionismus." *Neue deutsche Hefte* 31, 1984.

Huellen, Werner. "Die Sonne als Kristall. Mitteilungen aus dem Nachlaß Theodor Däublers." *Euphorion* 47, 1953.

Kemp, Friedhelm and Friedrich Pfäfflin. "Theodor Däubler 1876–1934." *Marbacher Magazin* 30, 1984.

Nienhaus, Stefan. "Theodor Däublers *Nordlicht* und die Kunst der Renaissance." *Wirkendes Wort* 42, 1992.

Rang, Bernhard. "Vorläufer des Expressionismus." In *Expressionismus. Gestalten einer literarischen Bewegung*, ed. H. Friedemann and O. Mann. Heidelberg: W. Rothe, 1956.

Rietzschel, Thomas. *Theodor Däubler. Eine Collage.* Leipzig: Reclam, 1988.

——. "Dichtung des Mythos, Mythos der Dichtung." *Sinn und Form* 41, 1989.

Schmitt, Carl. *Theodor Däublers "Nordlicht". Drei Studien über die Elemente, den Geist und die Aktualität des Werkes.* Reprinted Berlin: Duncker and Humblot, 1991.

Werner, Dieter (ed.). *Theodor Däubler—Biographie und Werk.* Mainz: Gardez! Verlag, 1996.

Christian Morgenstern

Bauer, Michael. *Christian Morgenstern. Wende und Aufbruch unseres Jahrhunderts.* Frankfurt a. M.: Fischer, 1984.

Beheim-Schwarzbach, Martin. *Christian Morgenstern in Selbstzeugnissen und Bilddokumenten.* Reinbek: Rowohlt, 1980.

Eppelsheimer, Rudolf. *Mimesis und Imitatio Christi.* . . . (See Däubler)

Forster, Leonard. *Christian Morgenstern* in *German Men of Letters*, vol. 2, ed. by Alex Natan. London: Oswald Wolff, 1963.

Hiebel, Friedrich. *Christian Morgenstern. Wende und Aufbruch unseres Jahrhunderts.* Frankfurt a. M.: Peter Lang, 1992.

Gumtau, Helmut. *Christian Morgenstern.* Berlin: Colloquium, 1971.

Giffei, Herbert. "Christian Morgenstern als Mystiker." Diss.: Bern, 1931.

Hofacker, Erich. *Christian Morgenstern.* TWAS 508, 1978.

Kretschmer, Ernst. *Christian Morgenstern.* Stuttgart: Metzler, 1985.

Mazur, Ronald. *The Late Lyric Poetry of Christian Morgenstern.* Diss.: University of Michigan, 1974.

Platritis, Christos. *Christian Morgenstern. Dichtung und Weltanschauung.* Frankfurt a. M.: Peter Lang, 1992.

Steffen, Albert. *Vom Geistesweg Christian Morgensterns.* Dornach, 1971.

Witte, William. "Humour and Mysticism in Christian Morgenstern's Poetry." *German Life and Letters* 1, 1947–48.

Index